The Art of Understanding Your Mate

The Art of Understanding Your Mate

by
CECIL G. OSBORNE

With Leader's Guide
by Nancy Becker

ZONDERVAN
PUBLISHING HOUSE OF THE ZONDERVAN CORPORATION
GRAND RAPIDS, MICHIGAN 49506

THE ART OF UNDERSTANDING YOUR MATE
© 1970 by Zondervan Publishing House
Grand Rapids, Michigan

Leader's Guide copyright © 1977 by the Board of Evangelism and
Christian Education of Mennonite Brethren Churches, Fresno, Cali-
fornia. Used by permission.

Leader's Guide edition 1979
Fifth Printing December, 1981
ISBN 0-310-30602-7

Library of Congress Catalog Card Number: 74-95047

Grateful acknowledgment is made to Harcourt, Brace and World for
permission to quote from *The Cocktail Party* by T. S. Eliot, copyright
© 1950.

Unless otherwise specified, all Scripture quotations are from the Re-
vised Standard Version of the Bible.

All names used throughout the book are fictitious.

Printed in the United States of America

7   8   9   10   11   12   13   14

Contents

MARRIAGE

1 CAN BE WONDERFUL —
AND FRUSTRATING!

> Matrimony—the high seas for which no compass
> has yet been invented.   —*Heine*

Marriage is the most rewarding, and the most difficult, relationship known to man. It began when "the
Lord God said, 'It is not good that the man should
be alone; I will make a helper fit for him'" (Gen.
2:18). Margaret Mead calls the home "the toughest
institution we have." Sociologist Ralph Linton says:
"In the Gotterdammerung which overwise science and
overfoolish statesmanship are preparing for us, the
last man will spend his last hours searching for his
wife and child."

Alarmists point to the fact that our divorce rate is
the highest of any nation in the Western world,
with one marriage out of four ending in divorce, and
it is predicted that the number will reach one in three
within the next few years.

Yet ninety percent of Americans marry, and the
divorce rate is less disturbing when we remember
that only a small fraction are repeat divorces, that
two out of three divorced persons remarry, and nine-
tenths of those remain married. A far higher percentage of business ventures fail than marriages. The
statistics are less alarming if we allow a fourth of
those venturing into matrimonial waters one mistake.

The statistical evidence is still less disturbing when we remind ourselves that no other human relationship is fraught with so many possibilities of failure. There are no perfect marriages for the simple reason that there are no perfect people, and no one person can satisfy *all* of one's needs. The difficulty of achieving a workable marriage is compounded enormously by genetic differences between any two persons. Their environmental backgrounds are different, as are their personalities, needs, goals, drives, and emotional responses.

If we add to the environmental, genetic, and personal differences of any two individuals the great emotional differences existing between men and women, we are rather surprised that there are so many successful marriages!

A young woman may know intellectually that it is impossible for two imperfect people to achieve a perfect marriage, yet at a deep feeling level she entertains a romantic dream of perfect fulfillment with a husband who is gentle and considerate, yet strong and wise—a man who will meet all her needs. At this point no one man can fulfill all of her varying, limitless needs. She wants to be protected, cherished, loved, yet she desires complete freedom and autonomy. She will often push and test the limits just to make sure they are there, and to test her husband's strength. She receives a sense of security from knowing that he is strong enough to resist, but wise enough to know when to give in! She needs to know what is expected of her, but without limiting her freedom of choice. She wants to be appreciated and to have her self-identity reinforced by oft-repeated signs of recognition, approval, and affection.

She wants, basically, to be a helper, not the boss, but she will seem to seek dominance as she pushes and tests. She desires to control within her own sphere, which involves the home and children, yet she needs a husband's concern and strength. She wants her "sphere of influence" to be reasonably flexible, depending upon her fluctuating emotional needs; she wants to have affection expressed in many ways, both great and small. These needs may vary enormously in degree from day to day, and she expects her husband to come equipped with a degree of extra-sensory perception so that he can be aware of her variable emotional states.

Little expressions of affection and approval mean more to her than a man imagines. She wants to be remembered, adored, cherished, complimented, listened to; she wants to have her feelings validated even when they seem childish or unreasonable to her husband. She needs to be made to feel feminine by being protected, cared for, looked after, to have affection often without sex, to be accepted especially when she feels unacceptable to herself.

She needs the security of the male and may prod, nag, fight, or provoke him in order to get this sense of security. This is usually an unconscious effort to make sure she is loved and especially to make certain that he is strong enough to stand against her, yet sufficiently wise to let her have her own way often enough to preserve her own identity. She frequently wants to dominate, yet needs to feel that he is in charge. She wants to be "taken care of."

She wants him to be strong enough, wise enough, competent enough, to satisfy her needs for emotional security, which she gets from a control that does not dominate or rob her of freedom. His control of the situation must not give her the feeling that she is being manipulated, and his strength must be expressed with something other than pure male logic. She subconsciously seeks a father who is indulgent of her whims, yet firm, tactful, and wise; a lover who is gentle and who will subdue her when she feels aggressive, yet be understanding when she needs to express hostility; a husband who is concerned about the nest whether he feels like it or not; a handyman eager to keep the nest intact. In short, she desires a father, lover, handyman, and playmate—a kind of composite of John the Beloved, a movie star lover, a businessman with a brief case in one hand and a box of tools in the other, and an all-wise father. This paragon of male virtue must share his life with her, but without boring her with too many details or personal worries which would create insecurity in her. He should be able to meet these needs without neglecting his work.

She may provoke an argument by blowing up some insignificant trifle out of all proportion, and then get it all tangled up with non-essentials such as relatives or something that happened two or twenty years ago. She may leap to what he feels are wild and unsupported conclusions, relying upon feminine intuition rather than upon male logic. She wants to have her feelings validated, whether they are "reasonable" or not. She often wants understanding more than an argument, but may resent him when he refuses to play the game of "uproar." She will want to have the last word, but as often as not she will feel disappointed if she wins the argument, which reduces him to something less than a man in her eyes. More than she actually wants to win the argument, she feels a need to express her feelings. She can be both triumphant and disappointed from having gained her point in an argument.

She wants adult conversation and may seek it when he is tired and uncommunicative. She takes his lack of interest in her world as a personal affront and feels rejected. She wants him to feel that her interests are important, too. He meets her need by listening, without arguing each point and showing her where she is wrong, even when she may suspect that she is. When she is worn out with playing the mother-wife role, she may temporarily regress to the little girl stage and desperately need him to play the role of the strong, wise, understanding, indulgent father.

The male sees this womanly personality as a mixture of conflicting, unrealistic, illogical needs which no man could completely satisfy. But he has a surprising variety of needs, too. He wants to be made to feel competent, worthwhile, believed in. He may have inner doubts about whether he is going to "make it," but cannot admit this even to himself, much less to his wife. He needs to be encouraged without being lectured to, argued with, or criticized. His ego strength needs to be built up to enable him to function in a highly competitive society. He wants his self-image reinforced, not torn down by being shown where he is wrong, even when he is.

He wants his self-identity restored subtly with sincerity and much affection, but in such a way as will not remind him of his mother, lest he be made to feel like a little boy, especially when he acts like one. He needs a wife-mother who will not dominate, yet who will minister to his needs; a mistress who can seduce and be seduced, whether she feels like it or not; who will appear as attractive to him as the women he meets during the day; a housekeeper who will take care of the home and children without making him feel guilty when he doesn't do his part. As the home is an extension of her personality, his work is an extension of his. He cannot be as much interested in the home as she, any more than she can be as interested in his work as he is. He needs to be allowed to have his male pursuits and hobbies without being made to feel guilty. As she has her female friends and pursuits, he needs his male interests.

Whining, self-pity, complaining—in an effort to win attention from him—only succeed in driving him to the basement, the garage, the bar, or into the cold gray castle of his own loneliness. He normally hates an argument, feeling that she won't stay on the subject and that he can't win. He wants to be left alone when he is pulling the tattered edges of his ego together and is tired or preoccupied—to rest without being harried with small talk, which he feels could come at a more appropriate time or not at all. He wants her to listen to his problems and interests and takes it as a personal affront when her attention wanders, but he often has little interest in the minutiae of her daily experiences. The passive side of his nature, which he rejects, may cause him to retreat into silence or erupt in an angry outburst when he feels threatened. Such outbursts, during an argument, are the result of having his male authority challenged, a feeling of exasperation at being unable to make himself understood; or he has been made to feel like a little boy by some motherly-type rebuke.

He needs to be made to feel that he is in charge, even when he isn't, without being manipulated. Incessant demands that he take more interest in the home may cause him to balk entirely, for he may be reminded of his mother and the feeling of continual harrassment of his boyhood years.

The need to maintain his male identity may cause him to feel threatened if his wife turns out to be right after all, and a reminder of this later can provoke some form of retaliation. He responds better to gentle persuasion, a seductive approach, than to demands and ultimatums. The "now look here" stance is reminiscent of mother and again he is reduced to childhood. Direct criticism, especially in public, or any form of humiliation, may provoke either an angry outburst or silent withdrawal. He does not want his wife to be in competition with him in any area.

As she is seeking a mature, understanding, strong, gentle husband, he is also seeking the impossible: an all-forgiving, ever-loving, understanding, wife-mother-mistress; a combination of a mother giving unconditional love, a movie star who is a good housekeeper, a sounding board, an ego builder, an obedient, adoring daughter who thinks his utterances are either profound or quite witty.

This picture would seem ridiculously overdrawn to a young couple about to embark upon the matrimonial seas. I long ago abandoned as futile the effort to instruct young couples in these matters before marriage. They tended to look at me through star dust, with amused tolerance. Yes, they had had their disagreements and realized their life would not be one hundred percent bliss, but they had pretty well worked these matters out and had come to an understanding of each other. Finally I have come to the point where I ask only one thing of them: a solemn agreement that they will seek a competent marriage counselor or minister at the first sign that they are not communicating well. I tell them that the husband will normally reject any such proposal until the marriage is almost hopeless. My sole requirement is for both to be willing to seek professional assistance before arguments have turned to bitterness.

In one group session, which consisted chiefly of married persons, a perceptive executive said one evening, "I've been married for twenty years, but I have learned more about women in these few brief sessions than during the entire twenty years of our marriage." He paused, and then made a profound statement. "As I see it, women are insatiable, and men are obtuse." He was expressing his personal feelings about his own marriage. "I guess I've never really heard what my wife has been saying all these years," he said. "I grew up in a boys' school, with no mother to relate to. I've never really bothered to try to understand women's needs. But by the same token, I cannot help feeling that women are insatiable in their demands and expectations; that is, if my wife and the women of this group are typical."

In a sense he was right. A woman often appears to her husband to be insatiable in her drive to make a better marriage, to try to make her husband understand her and meet her emotional needs. With her the feminine need is essentially built in to create the best possible home and marriage and to push until she gets it. If the woman is seemingly insatiable (whether she be gentle, concealed, and tactful, or angry and demanding), the husband may appear obtuse, lacking in perception, and often dully uncomprehending when his wife is experiencing some emotional need.

All married couples are, to some degree, incompatible. To give incompatibility as a cause for divorce would seem rather ridiculous. Any two persons are somewhat incompatible, and this fact is intensified in the unique, close, day to day relationship of husband and wife. A husband and wife are incompatible from the beginning because they have radically different goals, drives, emotional needs, and environmental conditioning. She wants to be the most important interest in his life, but she wants him to be successful, too, which means that his work will have to become the most important aspect of his life. Unless he can balance these two in such a way as to meet her need to be his chief interest and still succeed in his life work, she can come to resent his work virtually as much as she might resent a mistress or any other competitor.

This truth was illustrated by a young husband who reported to me that he and his wife were having trouble with their children. I said, "Such a problem usually results from a dominant or controlling mother." I learned later, somewhat to my chagrin, that he had reported our conversation verbatim to his wife, quoting me as the author of the statement. I knew and liked his wife and expected her to turn her wrath upon me.

On the contrary, she turned the full force of her indignation onto her husband: "Maybe I am a dominating, controlling mother; but when you come home at night, if you'd stay vertical long enough to be a father to these kids, instead of flopping on the sofa, maybe I could stop being a dominant wife." She went on to tell him that the main image she and the children had of him was that of a worn-out young husband-father lying prone on the sofa.

He said, recalling her shattering observation, "I decided then and there to try to present a somewhat different image to my children. My wife was right."

Of course he was tired after a hard day's work and felt that he deserved some rest, but the greater demands of the home now took precedence over his need to rest. His personal needs, in this case, were incompatible with those of his family. Instead of allowing their home to break up over "incompatibility," he resolved the conflict by deciding what was most important to him. Not only are husband and wife incompatible, but we each have within ourselves conflicting needs and drives which must somehow be resolved.

Some marriages are doomed to failure at the outset by the neurotic needs of one or both of the parties. I was once asked by the aunt of a young woman if anything could be done for her niece, who was in deep depression and undergoing psychiatric care. She had been married only a few months and her depression was becoming progressively worse. In my initial counseling session with the young woman I found that she had experienced a traumatic childhood. Her father had been rejecting and brutal, and her older brothers had made life a living hell for her. She had left home at the first opportunity and had been on her own for some time.

Eventually she married a young man who came from a culture in which the husband was the dominant force in the home. He proceeded to act in the only manner with which he was familiar. She considered him domineering and much like her father and brothers. Unconsciously, of course, she had chosen a male who would recreate the only kind of emotional climate with which she was familiar. After a number of counseling sessions and participation in a group, she lost much of her pathological fear of people and became able to express herself with much more freedom. At home she began for the first time to defend herself. As she began to express some of her hostile feelings, her depression began to lessen. She gained so much release that she began to explode at her husband with increasing frequency and often with great violence. In following sessions I explained to her that we need to learn how to accept our emotions of rage, as well as love, and to be able to express them, but that in the interests of preserving her marriage it would be necessary for her to learn how to control some of her feelings without denying them. Having learned from her husband of her violent explosions, and sensing that she was at the breaking point, I urged her to mix some love and consideration with her new-found freedom of expression. She tried for a few days, but phoned subsequently to report that she was going into depression again and feared that she would be hospitalized if she could not release her feelings. At this point she was caught between the need to explode at her husband and the need to preserve her marriage, which meant controlling some of her rage. If she exercised any control, she became terribly depressed. If she did not show some restraint, her husband told her, he would leave her. This possibility posed a real threat to her, for she could not endure the prospect of being abandoned.

She said to me, "He will just have to learn to meet my needs. He doesn't understand me. He will have to, that's all. I don't really love him, but I cannot stand it if he leaves me. I don't want to be all alone in the world."

This young wife was unconsciously trying to get back at her father and brothers by punishing her husband vicariously. She had so much hostility toward all men that it appeared utterly impossible for her to work out a satisfactory marriage relationship with any man until she had undergone a great deal of counseling. She had an enormous fear of her emotions, hostility toward men, uncertainty about her own identity as a woman, and a deep fear of living alone.

As the result of participating in a Yokefellow group, together with occasional counseling, she became able to resolve her deep hatred of men. Although there is still need for additional growth, she is now relating to men in a much more relaxed manner and has established a satisfactory relationship with her husband. Her future looks bright.

The neurotic personality seeks—and needs—absolute, unconditional love. No one can give unconditional love constantly. A workable marriage is built upon something more stable than the fulfillment of deep, neurotic needs. Just as there are marriages which never should have been undertaken, so there are marital situations for which divorce is seemingly the only possible solution. The question is not whether one "believes in divorce." A union not blessed of God cannot be expected to endure.

We often find marriages which seem so hopeless that there appears no way out but separation or divorce, the only answer to an intolerable situation which should never have existed. However, often seemingly insoluble conflicts do yield to an intelligent and persistent course of action. Becky and Tom, married about eight years, provide a case in point. They were typical sophisticated young suburbanites with plenty of money and an active social life. Becky would have said that theirs was a perfectly happy marriage until the blowup came. She began hearing rumors that Tom had been seeing a great deal of a woman with a dubious reputation. She secured the services of a detective, who turned up evidence upon which she based her divorce claims. Divorce papers were filed, and there had been considerable wrangling over the divorce settlement when a relative urged them to see me.

At our first meeting he was indifferent and glum. She was tense and hostile. I began by asking her if she was at all interested in working toward a reconciliation.

She said, "Yes, I think I'd like to give it a try." I asked him the same question. He shrugged.

I said, "Would you say there is one chance in ten, one in fifty, or one chance in a hundred of a reconciliation?"

He answered, "Maybe one in a hundred. I'm not much interested as you can see."

I described a type of group which dealt with marital and other personal problems, and said, "Even if you don't solve this marital problem, you will find out who you are, and you will have a better chance the next time. Would you care to try?"

"I'd give it a chance on that basis," Tom replied, "because I really don't know who I am, and I'd like to find out." He and Becky agreed to attend the group meeting scheduled for the next week.

At the first meeting Becky opened up with a frightful barrage. "Do you know why I have joined this group?" she asked, looking around the circle. "I want to get vengeance on that man! His unfaithfulness and lies have put me in the hands of a psychiatrist, and I've only barely managed to preserve my sanity. All I want is to make him suffer!" She continued her tirade for some minutes. Tom listened with complete disinterest. At subsequent sessions she berated him mercilessly, while he appeared alternately bored or mildly intrigued by the ferocity of her attack. In a private session with her I asked if she felt that her approach could conceivably help create an atmosphere in which we could effect a reconciliation. She then unleashed some of her anger on me.

During the next twelve months her hostile outbursts

diminished somewhat, until one night she revealed to the group that she had discovered that Tom had been supporting and living with another woman for several years. Now her anger knew no bounds. Tom listened and finally, for the first time, became personal.

"All right," he said, "I'll get down to brass tacks. I've been living a pack of lies for so long I'm glad to get it all off my chest. I've told five lies to cover one, ten to cover the five, and hundreds to cover the whole sorry mess."

With complete candor he told the story of his duplicity. It had caught up with him at last. The story was out, and he came clean. In addition he indicated, with obvious sincerity, that he was glad he could break off the other relationship. He now felt that he wanted to work out a relationship with Becky based upon complete honesty and trust. After the session, when Tom had finished the lengthy story of his unfaithfulness and expressed deep regret for the pain he had caused his wife, one of the wives present went to him and put her arms around him.

"Tom," she said, "I want you to know that I love you. You've been honest, and honesty is beautiful, even if what it reveals is ugly." She hugged him, and in her warm, friendly embrace there was something redemptive and healing.

One of the men touched him on the arm and said, "Great, Tom. I think you will make it now." Another gripped his hand in a silent, heartfelt expression of understanding and Christian love.

That was only the start. It was another year before open lines of communication had been firmly established and before Becky's understandable suspicions could be laid to rest. Within a year and a half from the time they had made their inauspicious beginning, they were back together and experiencing a better than average marriage. They continue to report improvement in every area.

In the light of many experiences like that of Tom and Becky, I am loath to abandon hope no matter how much hostility has been generated. However, there seemed little hope for a solution to the problem of Ben and Ginger. In this instance Ben took the initiative, for Ginger had no interest whatever in continuing the marriage. They were young and had several children. In their initial conference with me they revealed that both of them had had extramarital affairs. Ben's had been a single misadventure with Ginger's best friend. Ginger had fallen in love with a much older married man.

She was hostile and indifferent during our first conference and later confessed, "I agreed to the conference only because I thought it would look better if I did. I didn't love Ben and wanted no part of him. All I wanted was my neurotic, impossible love affair."

In addition to their marriage tangle, their finances were in a hopeless mess, Ben's job was insecure, and the children were reacting badly to the tension in the home. I encouraged them to see me as often as they felt might be necessary, but explained that they could get a great deal of help from a group experience where marriage relationships and other personal problems were being worked out. Ginger did not want to undertake this seemingly hopeless gesture, but agreed with some reluctance. The group to which they were assigned, consisting of about eight persons, accepted them with open arms. The atmosphere was such that before long Ben was sharing his own fears, doubts, and insecurities. He did not lay any blame on Ginger, but almost masochistically shared his own deficiencies.

Ginger said, sneeringly, "He's winning Brownie points by all this, but it doesn't fool me one bit. I know what he's really like inside."

The details of how they gradually worked out their problems are unimportant, but the group members will long remember the "cliff hanger" type of story that was unfolded week by week as new developments in their tangled lives were revealed. Ben and Ginger and the others knew that in the loving intimacy of the group their stories were safe. No one would have related outside the circle anything that was shared, any more than they would have revealed their own family secrets, for it was a genuine, loving family group.

It was three months before Ginger's hostile exterior cracked, or rather was melted away with tears. She became another person, gentle and receptive. Ben gave up some of his self-punishing attitude, and both of them learned the art of communication. There was nothing, now, that they could not reveal to one another. The honesty within the group was carried home, and the communication went on day by day between weekly group meetings. Within six months they had a good marriage. All was forgiven, love had replaced hostility, and both were maturing emotionally and spiritually. A year or so from the time of their entry into the group they not only had a remarkably fine marriage, but Ben's finances had been straightened out and he had achieved the greatest goal of his life in terms of a new type of job. The marriage relationship had been worked out, not because they had learned new techniques, but because both were growing spiritually and emotionally.

In the course of their year in the group each of the members took one of the spiritual growth inventories which are often used as a help in self-understanding. Ben found, to his dismay, that he scored four out of a possible one hundred on self mastery. This and some other revealing scores gave him a starting point for his own personal growth. From the test Ginger discovered areas of her personality in need of attention. As they each worked on the islands of immaturity in their own lives, they found that they were automatically achieving a better relationship within the home. Instead of criticism, recrimination, charges and countercharges, there was now only an effort to change themselves. The children began to respond to the improved atmosphere.

Ben and Ginger, and others in the group, came to understand early in the group experience that there is a universal law of mind and spirit, in three parts. They memorized it:

1. I can change no other person by direct action.
2. I can change only myself.
3. When I change, others tend to change in reaction to me.

Many who hear this for the first time agree to apply it, but often use it simply as a form of manipulation.

One wife said, "I made some radical changes in the way I acted for two whole weeks, and not once did I see any change in my husband!" The group helped her to see that she had to effect the changes within her own personality, not as a bribe to her husband, but *because the changes needed to be made*, whether he ever changed or not. Her husband had responded to her charge with the dry comment. "She's made a lot of ten-day or two-week changes before, but I'm not going to believe she means business until I see that the changes are permanent."

There are three basic kinds of marital situations: the impossible, the personal, and the situational. In dealing with couples who come to me for counseling I find it necessary to discover as soon as possible into which category their marriage falls.

I would define the "impossible" situation as one in which the two should never have married in the first place, and in which there appears to be little or no willingness on the part of one or both to make any significant change in their personalities or procedures. I have dealt with many such persons, among them people either too young chronologically or too immature emotionally to grasp even the most fundamental principles of mutuality. I think of a young husband so sadistic and brutal that no woman in her right mind would have remained under the same roof with him; a young wife so neurotically attached to her father that no man could ever have measured up to her fantastic demands and expectations; a passive husband so deeply attached to his mother that he was incapable of forming any kind of a mature relationship with any other woman; and an emotionally dependent young woman whose jealousy bordered on the pathological, and who made life a continuous torture for her husband. Perhaps after years of psychotherapy, each of these could have become mature enough to have succeeded in marriage, but in each case these egocentric and immature personalities rejected any suggestion that they needed counseling. They all wanted someone to compel their marriage partners to conform to their neurotic demands.

The second category of marital difficulties involves the "personal," that is, those individuals with personality problems who are sufficiently realistic to work toward the goal of greater emotional growth. When such individuals are willing to undertake counseling or group therapy, their problems as individuals can usually be worked out. When they are mature enough to go to work on their own "islands of immaturity," their marriages can be made to function more smoothly. They can have, if not an ideal marriage, at least a satisfying and workable relationship. Tom and Becky and Ben and Ginger, whose problems seemed monumental, fall into this category. Though they had experienced grave difficulties in their marriages, they were open enough to undertake a creative course of action. The results were excellent in both instances.

The third category involves the "situational," where a husband and wife are basically mature, reasonably well suited to each other by temperament and background, but have not learned some of the important techniques by which daily issues are resolved.

In an all-male group the discussion turned to marriage. Men are much more reluctant to discuss their marriages and their mates than are women. It was with some reluctance that they responded to my suggestion that we might share some of our marital problems. Finally one young man said that he and his wife had been having some difficulties. She had become increasingly moody and depressed and snapped at him at the slightest provocation. She had begun to yell at the children, something she had never done before.

"I don't know what's come over her," he said. "She used to be sweet and even tempered, but lately she's been terrible to live with. I'm about at the end of my rope. I find myself spending more and more time at the office on one pretext or another. I just hate to go home."

I asked, "What was the last big argument about?"

"Well, I guess it was when we decided to redecorate the house. It just so happens that I am rather artistic, and my sense of color is much better than my wife's, and we had a real battle over the colors for the various rooms. The big blow-up was over the bedroom. I wanted it one color and she wanted it another. I refused to give in, partly because her judgment in these matters is not too good, and partly because, though I am slightly passive, I refuse to be dominated. I don't want to lose my identity."

The group discussed this impasse for a time, and finally I asked him how he would feel if his wife went to his office, rearranged the office furniture, countermanded his instructions to his secretary, and showed him where he was wrong on many of his decisions.

"I'd not put up with that for a minute," he said.

I explained to him that, as his job and office are an extension of his personality, the home and all that pertains to it are an extension of his wife's personality. "For instance," I said, "if you went home and rearranged everything in 'her' kitchen on the grounds that your system was much more efficient, she would feel very much the same as if you had tried to alter her personality." Someone in the group asked why these decisions concerning the house couldn't be decided by mutual agreement.

I said, "Fine, if you can agree, but the wife should have the veto power, the final say-so. She wants her husband's interest and his approval if possible; but she must have the final word."

The young husband looked amazed. "Why has no one ever told me this before?" he asked. Then in a slightly defensive manner, "But what if her taste in decoration is inferior to mine?"

I said, "If she wants to paint the bedroom black, let it be black, and you will discover that you'll have a changed wife."

He said, "I'm going home and tell her that she can do anything she wants with the house, that it is her domain, and she can have a free hand."

A member of the group added a final warning. "But if you do, make sure that even if you don't like her decisions, you're to make no complaints. Accept it good-naturedly."

The next week as the meeting began, the young husband said, "I'd like to make a report. I went home and told my wife that from now on the house is her domain and that she can do anything she wants to with it, and that I'll keep hands off. She looked shocked, almost unbelieving, then said, 'Did those men in your Yokefellow group tell you to do this?' I told her they had convinced me I was one hundred percent wrong; and she said, 'I'm going over and kiss every one of those men!' And you know, fellows, she has been a changed woman ever since!"

Someone asked, "By the way, Gary, what color had you wanted to paint the bedroom?"

"Bright red," he said.

MALE AND
2 FEMALE
DIFFERENCES

> In our civilization men are afraid they will not be
> man enough, and women are afraid that they might
> be considered only women.   —*Theodor Reik*

There is an ancient Greek myth to the effect that
the earth was once populated by beings who were
half-man, half-woman. They were each complete in
themselves, and deemed themselves perfect. In their
pride they rebelled against the gods, whereupon the
irate Zeus split each of them in half, scattering the
halves over the earth. Ever since, the myth has it, each
half has been searching for its other half. This yearn-
ing for completion and fulfillment through finding
one's "other self" is what we call love.

There are so many emotional, mental, and physical
differences between the male and the female of the
species that it seems surprising that the institution
of marriage has been able to survive as the basis of
our civilization, unless we assume that there is some
subtle fragment of truth to the Greek myth.

One of the basic emotional differences between the
sexes is that men are basically "do-ers," while women
are "be-ers." Obviously those traits would vary from
person to person but evidence of this fundamental
difference is found in the fact that men are essentially
the achievers, while women generally prefer the less

activistic role of homemaker. Even in professions and interests normally thought of as feminine, such as cooking, dress designing, musical composition, and a score of other areas, men predominate as leaders in the field. This fact can be attributed to the greater aggressiveness of the man, the tendency to be an achiever rather than a "be-er." Women generally do not possess the aggressive drive to motivate them to reach the top in many pursuits, except in fairly rare instances. They do not lack the ability, but the drive. The male is the experimenter, the explorer, the director, builder, creator in most areas of human endeavor, though there are individual women who equal or surpass them in many instances. That they do not do so more often does not imply a deficiency or inferiority in any sense. It is simply that other things seem more important to women than some of the highly competitive endeavors.

A woman finds her fulfillment more in "be-ing," and unless she deprecates true femininity, her essential femininity is expressed in being that for which God created her—to be a "helper." That she plays a secondary role is not implied in any sense. She finds her fulfillment as a woman when she is being a person, a mother, a wife, the keeper of spiritual and moral values. It has often been observed that women are more spiritually minded than men. More women than men attend church. Normally the wife first seeks help for a failing marriage, and then finds herself frustrated by her foot-dragging husband, who usually displays a wholly unrealistic attitude in the matter.

More than women, men tend to take chances and run risks, and assume responsibility. Women are not incapable of taking leadership, but when they do so to any great degree, it is either because they have had leadership thrust upon them by circumstances, or they have acquired some of the so-called masculine traits.

One wife said, "I don't see why any man would

be willing to undertake the responsibility of supporting a family. *I* would never want to take on such a responsibility!" Yet many women, widowed or divorced, have assumed the arduous responsibility of working, keeping house, and rearing their children, trying to function as both mother and father. When they do so, however, though their innate capacity to assume an enormous responsibility is demonstrated, they always have the feeling that something went wrong—as indeed it did.

There is a basic emotional as well as biological drive within the woman to bear children, rear them, and keep the home. Even when she is employed outside the home, from choice or necessity, her basic and primary interest is usually not in her work, but in her home. There are deeply rooted masculine and feminine biological and emotional drives which, varying from person to person, are still basic. One of the female goals is to bear and rear children and nurture the family. She produces the children; he produces the means of sustaining them. She finds fulfillment in her children, he in his work. Yet neither finds *total* fulfillment in these spheres, for they each have other needs and goals.

A woman may look with awe or admiration or even unconscious jealousy upon her husband's activities. He disappears daily into what must be an exciting world of challenge and infinite variety, while she is left with what, to many women, is a dull routine of repetitious housework, often with many interruptions from children.

A husband may look upon childbirth with awe and wonder. His wife has accomplished something beyond his power to achieve. But he may also return from an exhausting day at work, silently envying his wife who, when she is tired, can at least break the monotony with a television show. Neither may be fully aware of the psychic energy expended by the other in the daily routine.

Stella, married and with four children, disliked housework and as soon as her children were old enough, she secured a position. Her husband prepared the evening meal, an older daughter did most of the housework, and Stella assumed a minimum of household responsibilities, yet in counseling sessions which continued over a two-year period, she never referred to her activities at the office. Her interests centered upon her family, her husband, her children, and herself. The family was an extension of herself, and her primary concern.

A man, on the other hand, feels his work to be an extension of *his* personality; his job, his future, the relationships at work, usually are uppermost in his mind. This interest is quite normal and simply underscores the division of labor, which in turn is based upon the emotional differences of the sexes.

Stella's husband, a typical male, attended a small therapy group for a few months in an effort to work out some marital problems, but soon dropped out. He had no particular interest in "feelings" or in delving into the inner workings of the personality. He found fulfillment in his work, which occupied most of his time and attention. If his wife wanted to try to improve herself, well and good. He had no particular interest in change. In fact, it all seemed faintly ridiculous to him. But Stella stuck with the group, for she felt she could never be fulfilled until her marriage, and the home relationships, were improved. If she had to do it alone, then that was the way it would have to be.

The differences of the sexes are seen quite early in small boys and girls. Boys build, explore, play aggressive games, fight, dig, climb, and dare each other to try dangerous exploits. Girls may engage in the same activities and can feel rejected if not permitted to do so, but in general their activities are less aggressive. They begin quite early to play house and "have babies." The small boy's interests center primarily around activity, while the little girl's interests deal more with nurturing.

Many women feel somewhat ill at ease and uncertain of the feminine role in today's culture because ours is an activistic society. A frantic atmosphere of activity pervades nearly every aspect of life. In a sense it is a man's world, as women so frequently charge, and men are "do-ers." Because women are essentially "be-ers" and find their fulfillment most readily in being themselves, all of this emphasis upon frantic activity causes them to be uneasy. The woman's basic tendency to "be" may involve motherhood and homemaking, with countless activities, great and small, but throughout the whole process she is doing these chores because she is being herself. She may, in the role of wife and mother, be more active physically than her husband. But her *doing* springs out of her sense of *being*. Unless she has been rendered neurotically activistic by a masculinized mother, or through strong identification with her father, her highest moments are those when she is engaged in the art of living, of being herself.

There are two basic reasons for the feeling that women cannot be understood. One is that they do not operate on the same logical wave length as men, which makes them incomprehensible to a man who is determined to rely upon pure logic for understanding. The other is that a woman is at her best when she is engaged in the art of being—pure being. And to man, the activist, this is incomprehensible unless he happens to be an artist, poet, or mystic. There is nothing mysterious about women. They are just "different." To the male they are mysterious only because he does not understand how one can tap some spring of emotional or spiritual "beingness" which cannot be analyzed logically.

An interesting male-female difference is the tendency of men to "externalize," whereas women "internalize." Men deal, in general, with the exterior world—business, industry, earning a living, facts, figures, politics, general concepts.

Women are quite capable of functioning adequately in any of these areas, but by nature and preference they have a much stronger tendency to "internalize" —to get into things at a feeling level. Put simply, to be completely fulfilled a woman needs to get into a man's emotions, get married, get pregnant and become a mother, get her "nest" properly arranged, and make sure by testing that her husband will be strong enough to take care of her and her children.

These female tendencies usually operate on a totally unconscious level. They are instinctual drives, with their roots deep in the emotional structure.

Most men have, in varying degrees, a need to conquer and achieve. Whether a man is climbing the ladder of success in some chosen field, climbing a mountain, or winning a woman, the instinct is to conquer.

A woman, on the other hand, having less of the conquering instinct, wants to be conquered with gentleness and strength. She may do the initial selecting and even subtly manipulate a reluctant male into a situation where he finds himself proposing marriage; what she really wants, however, is to be swept off her feet, to be conquered. Exceptions, of course, are the overly dominant females and the overly passive males, who tend to reverse their roles.

There is a subtle difference between the sexes implied in the giving and receiving of gifts. When a man gives a woman a substantial gift, the implication to the woman is that he is willing to take on some form of responsibility. However, when a woman gives a man a substantial gift, she is implying that she would be happy to be his responsibility.

Gifts in general, whatever the value, mean something different for men and women. To a woman, gifts loom large and they are accepted, not primarily as ornamental or valuable, but as tributes to herself as a person. They constitute an expression of love or thoughtfulness. She may imagine that the male attaches as much importance to the gift as she does, and that it has the same meaning to him as it does to her, which is seldom true.

A husband's willingness to buy a gift for his wife which she has suggested or picked out has much less significance for her than if he had thought of it himself. The great need of a woman to be cherished is fulfilled if her husband is thoughtful enough to bring an unexpected gift or to suggest going out to dinner. If she is the one who must initiate such things, her enjoyment is diminished by that fact. "He should have thought of it himself," is her feeling.

If, however, she has—for reasons valid or otherwise —criticized, attacked, demeaned, or challenged him, he may have no interest in surprising her with a gift. His feeling as often as not will be, "I have no interest in going out of my way to surprise my wife with a lot' of goodies when she acts the way she does." In this case both are defeating themselves by their attitudes.

Women are, *in general*, more vulnerable to criticism, at some points, while in other areas they may be much less so than their husbands. If a man cooks and serves a steak to a male friend, and the friend asks, "Where did you get this steak?" the host will reply, "At the supermarket." If a husband asks his wife, "Where did you get this steak?" her reply will be, "Why, what's the matter with it?"

Men and women are vulnerable to criticism *at different points*. In general it can be said that a woman is especially vulnerable in areas pertaining to her feminine role—getting a husband, rearing her children, and maintaining her physical appearance. Her self-image can be damaged at any of these points. Women are often surprised to discover that their husbands seem abnormally sensitive. Because of a man's greater aggressiveness and capacity to face obstacles which many women would find threatening, women imagine that men should be less sensitive. But men are vulnerable, too, in such areas as their capacity to earn a living (hold a job, win success), in the area of sexual performance, and in any area which challenges their male image. Obviously such vulnerability varies from person to person, but in some degree any normal male feels sensitive to criticism when challenged or criticized at these points.

A wife can emasculate a man by holding him up to ridicule or berating, criticizing, or challenging him. He can be provoked into a towering rage or caused to retreat into the silence of his own loneliness by a remark which he perceives as an attack or a challenge. To her this is sheer childishness.

An attractive and intelligent married woman stopped me at a retreat and said, "I need to make an appointment with you. I think I'm heading for trouble." From the expression on her face I guessed the truth, and said, "You've fallen in love with someone?"

"Yes, but I don't want it to go any farther."

"You'd better make an appointment now, or you can get hurt, and hurt your husband."

"Well, I'll call you."

I sensed, however, that she intended walking as close to the brink as she could, and being fond of both her and her husband, I hoped that she would call for an appointment soon, but I doubted that she would. A month or so later she did call, and from the tone of her voice I knew that she had gone over the brink. She came to see me and displayed none of the remorse one would have expected, but rather a surprising reaction. "I don't really feel any guilt about it," she said. "It was beautiful. I am surprised that I feel no guilt, except toward my husband; none within myself."

She described the experience, and asked why it was that she felt none of the deep remorse that she had thought would engulf her. I said, "We are dealing here with a strange law I have run into often. It can be crudely expressed in this way: The flow of sex hormones shuts off the circulation of oxygen to the brain!" She laughed and asked if she would feel guilty later on. I said, "You *are* guilty, whether you feel it or not. You love your husband and have betrayed him and yourself. I am not judging you, just stating facts. All you can do now is to use whatever brain power is still functioning. Cut off the relationship or you will destroy your marriage. In addition, the guilt you do not feel consciously will take its toll in some other manner. You will become accident prone or develop physical or emotional symptoms; guilt demands punishment, and you will punish yourself." She thanked me.

"I know you are right," she said, "and I hoped you would tell me just that, because I don't have the strength to do it without such encouragement."

A husband can wound his wife by failure to comment on a meal which she has gone to great pains to prepare or by failure to notice her new dress or hat. One logical but rather obtuse husband said, "My wife doesn't make a big deal of my bringing home a pay check after I've knocked myself out to earn it; why should I be expected to jump up and down in ecstasy over some dish she spent twenty minutes preparing?" From a logical viewpoint he was quite right, but in marriage we are dealing with feelings as well as logic. And one of the main ingredients of a good marriage is to discover the emotional needs of the other and do everything possible to validate those feelings, whether they seem logical or not.

Women are commonly more sensitive to criticism from someone close to them—a husband, friend, or a relative. Many find extreme difficulty in admitting defeat in an argument; the greater their insecurity, the more difficulty they have. This trait is not in any sense limited to women, but the somewhat greater insecurity of the female makes it more difficult for her to accept criticism or admit defeat.

An elderly man said, "In fifty years of marriage I have never known my wife to admit that she was wrong. I learned in business early in life that everyone makes mistakes, and the only realistic approach is to admit the mistake and move on. My wife would rather die than admit that she was ever wrong." I said, "This is the measure of her insecurity, and you would do well at this point to accept it and live with it, just as she may be living with some of your attitudes which she finds difficult to understand."

A wife complained that her husband flew into a wild rage whenever she tried to point out some mistake he had made. "I am better educated than he," she said, "and if I try to correct his grammar, or make the slightest suggestion, he goes out of his mind with anger."

I said, "You remind him of his mother, and he is taking it out on you."

She said, "Yes, his mother was a domineering personality who ruled everyone with a firm hand."

"You are not going to eradicate his fear of dominant women," I replied. "But if you unconsciously assume the mother role, he will always react in this manner. When you remind him of his mother, all of the repressed rage of boyhood is directed at you. Don't try to change him, correct him, or make him over. Take him as he is. You have been winning all of the battles and losing the war. Give up the mother role and be a wife to him."

One commonly observed difference of the sexes is that women in general seem to require more frequent reassurance. A rather unimaginative husband complained, "My wife is always asking if I love her. I've told her a thousand times that I do, but she still keeps asking. I feel like hanging up a framed certificate in the kitchen, indicating that I love her and will continue to do so until the certificate is revoked!"

I said to him, "When a woman asks her husband if he loves her, she is not asking for information, but for reassurance. It is partly an effort to recreate something of the earlier feeling of youthful romance, which diminishes with time, and partly because she—being a woman—needs frequent reassurance."

Women, who have far greater emotional drives and needs than men, are more "fluid" emotionally; their ego states tend to vary more, and they can lose their sense of identity more rapidly. Frequent reassurance, in a number of different ways, helps them maintain their sense of identity.

A wife who had been constantly berated, condemned, and belittled by an alcoholic husband, said to me, "I've been told so often by him that I'm stupid that I don't really know whether I am or not." Far from being stupid, she was a highly intelligent woman, and emotionally quite mature, yet she had come to doubt herself because of her husband's constant criticism. I was able to reassure her, during subsequent counseling sessions, and she regained her normal self-assurance and self-identity without difficulty.

If women tend to lose their identity more rapidly, they can also regain it more quickly than men. The alcoholic husband had lost his self-respect and self-confidence, and in his case several years were required for him to regain it. When he did, he gave up his alcoholism and became a respected and successful individual. When he was no longer beset by guilt feelings and self-rejection, he did not feel any need to condemn and criticize his wife.

Freud maintained that it is essential to a successful marriage that a wife develop some maternal attitudes toward her husband. Many a woman will understandably react to his contention: "I don't want to be a mother to my husband." Yet there is a sense in which a man marries a "wife-mother," and a woman marries a "husband-father." Actually, it is much more complex than that. She marries a "husband-father-son," while he marries a "wife-mother-daughter." There are times when each of the marriage partners shifts from one ego state to the other. A typical instance might go something like this:

She serves him his breakfast and asks solicitously if his cold is better (mother role). He replies that it is a little better, but he'd like to gargle before leaving for work, and he can't find the bottle (child role). She finds the bottle for him, murmuring patronizingly, "Men never can find anything." Feeling somewhat better after breakfast, he prepares to leave for work. "Don't forget to pick up my suit at the cleaners" (husband role). "Yes, dear" (wife role).

He returns in the evening and finds her moody and depressed. "What's wrong?" (husband role). "Oh, nothing" (wife role). "Well, something is. You're all out of sorts, What is it?" She bursts into tears (daughter role). "For heaven's sake, what's wrong?" (father role). Tears subside. "I went to the PTA today, and one of the women said the most terrible things to me. I was making a report, and she challenged some of the things I said and virtually implied that I was a liar. I couldn't document my facts and I was never so embarrassed and angry in my life." More tears (daughter role).

"Take it easy, honey. Don't let some stupid woman's criticism ruin your life. It isn't all that bad. Give me the facts and we'll straighten it all out. You can go to the next meeting and calmly give them the straight dope" (father role). "Oh, but you don't understand. After the way I messed it up, and that woman challenging me, I'm so embarrassed I don't think I can ever go back" (daughter role).

"Look, let's talk it over after dinner. I'm beaten right down to my sox, and I can think better after I've had something to eat" (husband role). After dinner as they discuss the problem, they talk about it with less emotion on the wife's part and it becomes a husband-wife discussion on an adult-to-adult basis.

There are really three distinct ego states within each of us—the Parent (conscience, authority, the disciplinarian); the Child (spontaneous, primitive, demanding instant gratification, sometimes petulant); the Adult (the more mature self). It is the function of the Adult self to try to bring harmony between the other warring selves. The Adult can challenge the punitive Parent or rebuke the selfish Child. Each of the three ego states has a valid function. There are times when it is quite appropriate for each of the three selves to take over.

It is the inner Child who wants to go on a picnic, run on the beach, play games, who may also become unreasonably angry. It is the Parent, the conscience, who reminds one that he is already overweight and suggests that he skip dessert, or start a savings account, or make amends after a quarrel. It is the inner Adult who can call an overly strict Parent to account and who can decide in the final analysis which of the three is to be chairman of the committee of selves for the moment.

A husband confronted with a wife whose inner Child is in control may be baffled and become angry because he doesn't know how to deal with this ego state. A wife may be puzzled or angry when her husband's inner Child acts up in what appears to be an unreasonable manner.

If each can be aware of the rapidly changing ego states of the other, this awareness can help immeasurably in achieving a more harmonious relationship. Each of us is entitled to slip from one ego state to another, to play the Child, Parent, or Adult role from time to time. If we can discover which of the three selves is temporarily in charge in the other person, we can deal with the situation much more realistically. One cannot expect the marriage partner always to be mature, considerate, thoughtful, and reasonable.

This would be completely unrealistic. We are all entitled to our "down" periods, moments of depression or discouragement.

A husband revealed in a counseling session that he always felt vaguely hostile when his wife became ill. "It upsets me no end," he said. "I know I'm being unreasonable, but I can't give her any sympathy. I just want to get out of the house, and I'm depressed the entire time she is ill. It's almost as if I felt she were being ill to spite me, and of course, that's ridiculous. She feels hurt and rejected when I react in this manner."

We probed into his childhood and discovered that his mother had been a partial invalid, ill much of the time. He had been told often that his mother might not live long, though she actually lived to be ninety-three. He recalled being told that if he made an undue amount of noise he could be responsible for his mother's death. He lived in constant fear that if she died, he would be held responsible. This was a frightening responsibility for a small child, and now, in adult life, he was simply acting out one of the unresolved conflicts of childhood. As soon as he could bring these partially buried memories into consciousness he became able to react normally when his wife was ill. The change did not occur overnight, of course, for he had to remind himself when the old feeling of helplessness and depression settled over him that it was a childhood hold-over, and that he was now free to act in an adult manner. By discussing the problem with his wife he was able to discharge some of the anxiety and guilt he felt, and she was able to cope with his behavior.

There is a distinct and interesting difference between the way men watch women, and women observe men. Virtually all normal men are "girl watchers." In our culture "watching" is done somewhat more discreetly than in some European countries—Italy, for example. A man derives pleasure from looking at a pretty face or an attractive figure. His interest does not imply any disloyalty to his wife. He has not been struck blind simply because he is married! He might enjoy his own new car and appreciate its beauty, yet glance with wholehearted appreciation at another car on the road. His approving appraisal of the other car does not imply that he would prefer it to his own. He is simply appreciating something highly attractive to his male eye.

Women, however, are not "man watchers" to the same degree nor in the same manner. A married woman might be aware of an attractive man on the street and take mental note of his broad shoulders and general masculine build, and she may make some mental comparisons with her own husband, but in general her "man watching" is much more discreet and subtle. She would be embarrassed to be caught eyeing a man in the same direct manner which a man employs in looking at a woman.

In a social gathering a typical, loyal, loving wife may be engaged in animated conversation with someone and at the same time let her gaze light momentarily on some man—ever so briefly—and wonder what kind of husband he would make. If he seems poised and cultured she may recall in the back of her mind some of the clumsiness of her own husband. If the man appears gentle and considerate, she may—while still carrying on the conversation—remember the frightful quarrel she and her husband had over his lack of consideration, or the suffering she endured when he failed to remember some anniversary.

In general the difference in girl watching and man watching is that the male tends to see the woman as a female, and the woman tends to evaluate the man in terms of husband material. The man tends to be a short-term viewer, the woman a calculating window shopper, who may have no intention whatever of buying.

There is another subtle difference between the

sexes. When a woman walks into a room she glances instantly at the other women present. Even if there are men present, her attention is first devoted to the women. She compares herself with them. It is an impersonal, appraising, instantaneous inventory, which takes in clothes, face, figure, and personality of the other women. She may be possessed of charm, beauty, and poise, but still she must compare. This instinct is so universal and unconscious that some women are almost unaware that it is an automatic response. Most women, however, are quite well aware of it, and wonder why men would think it odd. If another woman is wearing an identical dress or hat, this is a devastating experience for a woman. I recall, as a young man, walking down the street with a young woman wearing a new dress. Approaching us was another young woman wearing an identical dress. The two girls eyed each other with the cool, appraising look women accept as normal, and the one approaching us said, with an attempt to be condescending, "I got mine first, dearie!"

I recall asking, in my youthful ignorance, "What difference does it make if two women are wearing identical dresses?"

The young lady said, "You wouldn't understand."

Shakespeare deals with this feminine tendency, intensified by jealousy in the case of Cleopatra, who bids Alexis:

> Report the features of Octavia, her years,
> Her inclination; let him not leave out
> The colour of her hair:—
>   bring me word quickly. . . .
> Bring me word how tall she is.

Later, in Cleopatra's palace:

> Didst thou behold Octavia?
> Is she as tall as me?
> Didst hear her speak? Is she shrill-tongued,
>   or low? . . .
> What majesty is in her gait? Remember,

> If e'er thou look'dst on majesty
> Guess at her years, I prithee,
> Bear'st thou her face in mind? Is't long or round?
> Told that her face is round:
> For the most part, too, they are foolish that are so.
> Her hair, what colour?

A man upon entering a room filled with people does not look at the other men first. He has no interest in what other men are wearing, whether they are handsomer or taller than he. He is looking at the women. He does not wonder what the other men think of him, but rather what kind of impression he will make upon any of the attractive women present. Men compete with men in business and industry. The rules are all laid down and are as fixed and rigid as in the jousting combats of knights of old. Women compete with women. It is only when women begin to compete with men that the male becomes uncomfortable. At this point men feel that women have stepped out of their roles as females. Male hostility on this point is based not on a fear that some woman might best them at their game, but because men do not know whether to treat such a woman as a female, with courtesy, deference, gentleness, or as they would a male competitor. They feel much like one who, playing tennis, has just discovered that the opponent has started to play badminton. They are confused and hostile over the change.

There are not only psychological, physiological, emotional, spiritual, and social differences between the sexes, but some so subtle that they have not yet been measured or named. No one knows, for instance, why it is that women live 7.9 years longer than men, or why they have thirty-eight percent fewer organic diseases. Their greater longevity is a hollow victory, as millions of widows can attest. Whether the greater stress occasioned by our highly competitive society can account for it, or whether there are numerous other factors at work, is unknown.

Differences are observed early in the behavior of boys and girls. Studies have shown that little boys start more fights, make more noise, take more risks, think more independently, and are harder to educate. Yet, they are the more fragile of the sexes. More males are conceived, and more miscarried fetuses are male. More males die in the first year of life, and in each subsequent decade thereafter. There are more boy than girl stutterers, and boys are more likely to have reading problems. Girls are more compliant, but boys tend to lag a year or more behind girls in physical development.

Little girls are more robust physically, yet more dependent, much more conforming and less adventurous. They show less interest in *things* and more interest in *people*. Their styles of learning are different. Girls excel in verbal ability, while boys do better in abstract thinking. Boys are more creative and independent. The female has a chromosomal composition which seems to lend her protection against disease and infection. Scientists at the National Institute of Mental Health have observed infants immediately after birth and in the weeks following, and have seen differences between male and female babies much too great to be caused by environment.

Studies have shown that girls are most conscientious, while boys are more argumentative and boastful. Paradoxically, more boys than girls tend to be introverted, and often appear sad and withdrawn. A teacher who had always preferred girls because they learned more readily and were more compliant was quoted by one psychologist: "I had spent years trying to keep boys from disturbing everyone. In the experiment, in which we taught classes of all boys or all girls, I found that boys can concentrate even when they are noisy. I always liked girls until I got a whole classful of them. It finally dawned on me that they were not doing their own thinking. Parrot-like, they repeated everything the teacher said. I wondered

45

what we are doing to these girls to make them so conforming?" Separated, the boys did better work, and the girls became more creative and independent in their thinking.

Further studies have shown that, as one scientist put it, "Females are 'social-emotional specialists,' while men are more task oriented. Females show greater social awareness than do males, even from an early age."

Some of these differences, both innate and acquired, show up later in life in the marriage relationship. Though boys seem better equipped to do abstract thinking and lean toward the venturesome, in marriage usually the wife is the one who takes the initiative in trying to effect a better relationship. Furthermore, she is often far more realistic in her approach, whether it has to do with marriage or other problems.

One wife came to see me about her husband, who had begun to drink rather heavily following a business failure. His male pride had been hurt badly and he found it difficult even to go out and look for work. He spent much time holed up at home or at insignificant tasks, rather than tackling the problem of finding a job. She could see that he was disintegrating emotionally. Through a mutual friend she arranged for a job offer to be made to him without her husband knowing that she was involved, but the job was not as good as his previous one, and he refused even to go for an interview. Sensing his growing depression and discouragement, she proposed that he join a therapy group, but he stoutly resisted. Here was a wife, with every reason to feel insecure over their financial picture reluctantly taking the initiative, but frustrated at every turn by the stubborn pride of a man too insecure to avail himself of opportunities offered him.

There are pressures in our culture which predispose the male toward the idea that he must never fail; that he must always be the super-strong individual, able to conquer all obstacles. There are numerous instances of men who refuse to see a physician when ill; millions of men who would rather face divorce than sit down with a marriage counselor or minister to work out a marital problem.

The number of neurotic men of this type is matched by an equal number of neurotic women who carry within their minds the concept of a teen-age romanticized marriage, who marry in the belief that "the pure love of a good woman can change any man," who refuse to grow up and assume adult responsibilities. It comes as something of a shock to most young couples to discover that marriages are not simply "consummated"; they are worked at, hammered out, prayed through, suffered through. Often the starry-eyed dreams of romance give way to the harsh realities of diapers, drudgery, debt, and despair; however, where there is a measure of maturity, a willingness to face facts, and the humility to recognize that both may be at fault, a good marriage can usually be worked out.

WOMEN'S

3 NEEDS AND

PROBLEMS

A woman must be a genius to create a good
husband.   —*Balzac*

Lucille was a charming woman when I first met
her and her husband. She was a perfect hostess and
entertained a great deal. Her husband, a quiet, friendly person, held a fine position with a national or-
ganization.

In the next few years that I knew them, he changed
jobs several times, and I began to detect signs of a
rift in the marriage. Lucille shared with me some of
her apprehension about his frequent job changes.
Eventually I sensed a change in him. He appeared
uncertain of himself, and there were indications that
he was drinking rather heavily. Lucille phoned me
one night to tell me that George was in jail on a
drunk driving charge. I bailed him out and subsequently became involved as an active listener in their
marital affairs.

They came in for a number of counseling sessions,
during which Lucille spent most of the time berating
him for his drinking, lack of purpose, and failure as
a husband. I listened for some time in one session,
and finally turned to George. He said, "She has told
me ten thousand times that the whole trouble is me.
She points her finger at me and begins every sen-

tence with 'The trouble with you is—' and I've listened to that phrase so many thousands of times that I'm sick of it."

Eventually I asked them to take a fairly simple psychological test which is frequently used with married couples to ascertain emotional needs and traits. At the next session I looked over the results with them. One item on the test results concerned self-reliance. She had scored ninety-two, and his score was twelve. I asked her if she felt that he had been lacking in self-reliance when she had married him.

"No," she said, "he was self-reliant and full of confidence. I don't know what's happened to him."

I said, "Lucille, someone appears to have whittled down his self-confidence through the years. I wonder who it was."

She looked startled. "I guess it was I," she said.

George erupted. "You're right for once! I used to believe in myself, but you've whittled away at my self-confidence with that forefinger of yours so many thousands of times that I don't know who I am anymore. If I hear any more of your criticism, I'm walking out."

She turned on him with flashing anger. "The trouble with you—" George got up quietly and walked out. Lucille sat stunned. I said as gently as I knew how, "Lucille, I don't know that you are any more to blame for the marital mess than George, but if you want your marriage to last, you'll have to find a way to help restore his self-confidence. Attacking him is not the answer. He needs reassurance, not condemnation."

We discussed this at some length, but I had the feeling that she had no intention of giving up her threatening, attacking methods.

They did not ask for another appointment, and I sensed that the possibility of any personality change was far too threatening for Lucille. Her excessive dominance and the need to change George and control him were so strong that she could not face the fact that she would have to change, too.

It was five years before there was any significant change in the situation, during which time they virtually withdrew from all relationships with their friends. Eventually George seemed to gain enough strength from some inner source to hold his own. Lucille became quieter and somewhat less dominant as George gained more self-confidence. He finally accepted a position which a relative secured for him in another city, and they moved away. I sensed that there had been some subtle but important changes taking place in their personalities and consequently in their relationship.

What is it that causes a wife to become overly dominant, while the husband remains passive? In their case the wife had apparently always been somewhat more dominant than her husband, and his frequent job changes created such anxiety in her that she became even more controlling and critical. As she complained, criticized, and threatened, he lost still more of his self-confidence until he began to drink as an escape from her shrill tongue, and to bolster his faltering ego.

The need for security is one of the strongest emotional needs a woman possesses. The term security does not mean merely financial security, though this is one aspect. Ideally she gains her security both from a husband whom she loves, trusts, and admires, and from faith in herself as a person. When the husband begins to falter, if she has considerable anxiety and doubts about herself, all manner of insecurity is triggered within her.

A woman's sense of security can be threatened when her husband fails in his work or begins to drink excessively. If, instead of panicking, she can become the helper and give loving emotional support, the husband will have a far better chance of succeeding.

The business world is highly competitive. A man can make only a given number of mistakes before the axe falls. The last thing a man needs in today's world is to come home to a barrage of criticism and fault-finding. His wife has a need for security and love, and if she doesn't receive it in proper amounts, she can easily fall into the trap of becoming her husband's worst enemy—the one who is doing him the most damage at a time when, of all things, he needs strong emotional support from his wife.

Freud once said, "After thirty years of studying them, I ask myself, 'What is it that women want?'" His bewilderment is echoed not only by men, but by women themselves, very few of whom could possibly agree on what it is that women want beyond such generalizations as "security," "love," or "understanding."

The difficulty of achieving a happy marriage is compounded by the fact that men and women are basically incompatible, in that they have goals, needs, emotions, and drives which are incompatible with those of the opposite sex.

Women, for instance, are more "personal" than men. Whereas men in general tend to deal more in terms of material things, values, and intellectual concepts, women have a deeper interest in persons and feelings. It is not that they lack a capacity for abstract thought, or have no interest in material things, but for them life consists more of people than of things. What men often label female gossip is simply the manifesting of interest in persons to a degree that is incomprehensible if not frustrating to a man.

This tendency to be deeply interested in persons and feelings results in women taking things very personally. A man looked up from his magazine and said to his wife. "It says here that the trouble with women is that they take everything personally." His wife said quickly, "I don't!"

Oswald Schwarz in *The Psychology of Sex* lists some of the commonly observed female traits as "passivity, emotionality, lack of abstract interests, greater intensity of personal relationships, receptivity, submissiveness, tact, practical realism, sexuality, vanity, inclination to envy and jealousy, weaker moral sense, timidity, shyness, prudishness, compassion, coquetry, playfulness, fondness for children, chastity, modesty, hypocrisy . . ."

With this list, as with any set of generalizations, there would naturally be exceptions and objections. One main characteristic which women possess is the innate tendency to be "at one" with people and things, rather than viewing life from the outside. Women have the capacity to feel a sense of oneness with nature, people, and events more than most men. This trait is possessed by children before they lose their sense of wonder and by primitive people living close to nature. The emotional nature of man evolved long before the higher brain centers, and women are essentially closer to the basic, elemental aspects of nature and to the core of humans. It is this sense of feeling "at one" with another person which gives rise to the belief in woman's intuition, a trait which often baffles men. However, as Birchall and Gerson point out, it is not so much intuition as an unconscious perception of minute things not normally observed by a male; since it is an unconscious process, the woman does not know how she arrived at the conclusion.

But to use the term intuition as it is usually applied, women often arrive at a conclusion by "knowing and being" simultaneously. A woman does not normally rely upon laborious analysis, reducing a situation to its component parts and deducing certain facts as a man does, but she "perceives" a person, thing, or circumstance by an entirely different process. She "feels with it," "becomes one with it," without being aware that she is doing so and comes up with a "feeling" which is not the result of a purely logical process.

A man, however, delights in trying to reduce something to a basic principle. He strives to understand a thing by breaking it down into its component parts, whereas a woman identifies herself with the person or situation, feels a part of it, and reacts on the basis of her emotional "findings." She may then feel a need to rationalize by giving any number of logical explanations, but the intuitive response is arrived at long before she has even begun to explain "why" she feels as she does.

A woman instinctively and intuitively wants to "help" her husband; because no man is without faults, she sets herself the task of helping him change. She may feel a need to correct or help him with his financial responsibility, religion, basic moral concepts, or any other area in which he seems to her to be deficient.

She wants to improve him, to make him a better person, a better husband. She may want him to be more outgoing or more restrained if he is uninhibited, less cautious with money if he is ultra-conservative. If he is careless in financial matters, she will try to make him more responsible. In whatever area he is deficient she will more or less automatically set out to make him over.

Many men need this substitute mother-wife and profit from her efforts; but if she seeks to help him too rapidly, or with direct criticism, or tactlessly, the marriage relationship can be damaged seriously.

What are the traits in a woman which men value most highly? In general, most men desire these characteristics:

1. *Warmth and affection.* One would suppose that men, being the wage earners, would rate security highest among their needs, but tests and surveys reveal that their strongest need is for warmth and affection. Studies have shown that many unmarried

women are either painfully shy or overly aggressive. Men tend to avoid both types in an unconscious need to find gentleness and warmth in a woman.

2. *Responsiveness.* This suggests the quality of genuine aliveness, or being in love with life. It implies a certain spontaneity as opposed to a fearful approach to life.

3. *A genuine, unselfconscious femininity.* Most women's magazines stress the external, superficial aspects of femininity: clothes, make-up, hair-do, style, entertaining. Any modern woman may well make use of all appropriate beauty aids, but true femininity is far deeper. Such a woman is not in competition with men, even unconsciously; the unfortunate thing about female competitiveness (the so-called masculine protest) is that when a woman has it she is nearly always unconscious of it. A truly feminine woman accepts herself as a woman and as a person. She is emotionally mature enough to have no need for either dominance or aggression, while possessing sufficient self-respect to be sure of herself. Such a woman is neither pushing herself or her femininity. She is neither shyly reticent nor aggressively feminine. As one man expressed it, "When you're with such a woman, you feel like a man."

4. *A strong capacity to love.* Love in this sense is not limited to romantic love, but embraces the whole spectrum of love: friendship, affection, Christian love, love of children, of nature, of life, and of God. It is not external appearances which make a woman feminine, but tenderness and a concern for others. In a dominant woman, the concern for others can become controlling, cloying, overwhelming. A truly feminine woman has a type of love and tenderness which respects the personality of others and allows them to be themselves *without trying to change them,* even when it is obvious that they need to change.

5. *Intelligence.* Contrary to the oft-expressed opin-

ion of many well-educated women, men do not resent intelligent women. It is the intelligent, *aggressive, competitive woman* whom men resent. Unfortunately, most women who are aggressively competitive with men are totally unaware of this unconscious trait. If a woman uses her intelligence to hold a man up to ridicule, show him where he is wrong, best him in an argument, he may well seek safer, more comforting companionship.

As a woman enjoys being around a man who makes her feel more like a woman, so men enjoy the presence of women who make them feel more like a man. If a man comes home to a steady barrage of criticism, nagging, and whining, the time may arrive when he will come home with more and more reluctance and devote more time to outside interests. In Genesis we read that God, having created Adam, "made a helper suitable for him." In her heart, a truly feminine woman wants to be a helper, not the boss—an equal in all things, yet aware of the areas in which her capacities are most needed and valued.

There are times in the life of every woman when she feels insecure and uncertain of herself. Assigned an inferior role for thousands of years, she suddenly became emancipated. In striving for equality, the more aggressive woman determined to prove herself the equal of any man. Usually at an unconscious level she had some feeling of competition and a need to prove that she was not inferior. In striving to prove her point, she often took on masculine traits and feeling tones. A masculinized woman is as ridiculous and unattractive as a feminized man. Often she did not know just *how* to fulfill her role as a woman.

To compound the situation, modern society placed upon her duties and responsibilities normally assumed by men. As mother, wife, housekeeper, den mother, chauffeur, church or club officer, she sought to find her identity and often discovered that she was neither finding satisfaction for herself nor satisfying her husband. If she took a job, she was thrown into a male world where masculine values and traits predominated. Small wonder she was often confused.

A normal woman can experience some occasional uncertainty about her ability to fulfill her role as a wife, homemaker, mother, manager of the budget, sex partner, and participant in community activities. She may wonder if she is as attractive as other women, especially those whom her husband meets during the day. She may doubt her femininity to such an extent that she may dress so as to over-emphasize her sexuality, or flirt in an attempt to prove to herself that she has not lost her appeal. Occasionally the flirtation gets out of hand, and she finds herself caught in an extramarital affair which can threaten her marriage.

In an earlier chapter reference was made to the perceptive comment of a husband who said he had discovered that "women are insatiable and men are obtuse." There are elements of truth in his observation. A woman usually enters marriage with lofty ideals and expectations. She desperately wants the marriage to succeed. If, however, her expectations are unrealistic, she will be frustrated and bitterly disappointed. As she wants gentleness and strength in her husband, he wants tenderness and warmth in her. If, expecting instant gratification of all her emotional needs, she does not find her husband to be as strong and gentle as she had anticipated, she is apt to be disappointed. It is unrealistic to expect any one man to fulfill all of her needs—at least immediately. Perhaps no one person can ever gratify all our needs, so there will always be some sense of disappointment.

Neither a wife nor a husband can concentrate on one person as an ideal, and expect another to meet all of one's expectations. It is a futile hope and will always end in disillusionment. If the wife is determined to achieve perpetual bliss and utter fulfillment, if she is insatiable in her demands that all of her needs be met, if she pushes, demands, threatens, the marriage will end in either bitterness, a stalemate, or divorce.

What can a wife do when her husband is obtuse, uncomprehending, unable or unwilling to meet her emotional needs for love and security? One alternative is to become demanding. Another is to withdraw, turning the hostility inward. Neither is a creative solution.

I recall two similar instances in which the wife turned her resentments inward and became emotionally ill. In one case the husband was an outgoing energetic carpenter who determined to build his own home, paying for it as he went along. When it was about three-fourths completed they moved in, and he worked on it weekends. He phoned me one morning to tell me that his wife needed help. I visited them and spent an hour or more with his wife. She was in a state of deep depression, sitting dully in a chair. She answered my questions slowly, without feeling or expression. She had no idea why she was so depressed. Her husband told me that she had been slowly losing interest in the home and children and finally spent the day just sitting, in deep despair.

The living room was completed, but through the open door I could look into the kitchen. It appeared to be unfinished, and I asked the husband if I might look through the house to see his handiwork. In the kitchen I found utter confusion. It was the one room in the house that remained unfinished. Cabinets had not been installed, and dishes and other kitchen equipment lay in a clutter on tables and chairs. The sink was only partially installed.

I asked the young husband how long it would take to complete the kitchen. He said that he had run out of money and had no intention of going into debt. It might be another six months before he would have enough money to buy the needed materials.

I said, "Joe, this is only an educated guess at this

point, but my feeling is that you should go to the bank and borrow enough money to complete this home. Your wife spends her entire life in this place; you just come home at the end of the day. No woman is going to be happy working in a kitchen like this. I think it highly probable that her depression is simply the result of what is termed 'inwardly directed hostility.' She is too kind and uncritical to complain, yet she feels frustrated and hostile over having to live in an uncompleted house. She has repressed these feelings, burying them deep within. Now they have erupted in the form of deep depression. You have a choice of borrowing money for psychiatric care, which can be long and expensive, or you can borrow it to complete the house."

Joe had an obsession about not going into debt, and he tried to convince himself that she would "snap out of it."

I said, "You can try, but I think you are being very foolish, and besides you are gambling with the sanity of your wife." He looked startled and reluctantly agreed to borrow the needed money.

Soon after Joe went to work on the kitchen, his wife showed considerable improvement. By the time he had completed it, she was completely well. Her deep depression was simply an inner protest against what, to a wife, amounted to an intolerable situation. A loving, earnest, but obtuse husband had simply been unaware of the importance of the home to a wife.

Another instance involved the wife of a corporation executive who consulted me about her extreme depression. She had been hospitalized and had been given electric shock therapy. Results had been negative, and she came home. For months she had lived in a state of depression so vast that she said, "I am simply in hell. There is a curtain pulled down between me and all of life."

I probed into her past life, her relationships, emotions, and present situation. We discussed her feelings toward her husband, whom she assured me was delightful and considerate. It was at this point that she threw me off the track.

The only dissatisfaction I could discover concerned the fact that her husband had selected their home before she moved to the state, and she had never liked the house. She described it as inconvenient and utterly frustrating to live in. However, she insisted that she felt no resentment toward her husband, since he had exercised his best judgment.

I suggested to her that she ask her husband if he would drop in for a visit. She did so and he angrily refused. At our next session I said, "We seem to have reached an impasse for the moment, but there are other resources available to us if we seek them. Can you follow some simple instructions?"

"I'll try!"

"Fine. Go home and focus on one thing—the perfect, glorious, wonderful will of God. He desires our happiness and well-being more than we do for ourselves. Do not seek for healing, or for your husband to change, or anything else except the perfect will of God for both of you. I'll pray for the same thing." She agreed.

A week or so later I received a phone call from the husband. He asked if he could see me. He left work early the next day and came to my office. He began to talk quietly.

"I'm totally responsible for my wife's illness. I've been proud, self-centered, and egotistical. This past week I've come to see myself in a new light. I'm stubborn and demanding, a perfectionist. My wife's illness, as I now see it, must be the result of her inability to reach me, to receive any warmth or genuine affection from me."

He went on at some length. He was not so much berating himself as seeing himself honestly for the first time. When he had finished I asked, "Would you be willing to share this with your wife?"

"Of course. She's out in the car."

"Would you bring her in?"

He did so, and seated on the arm of her chair, he told her in essence what he had shared with me. He spoke gently, tenderly, and with deep humility. So deep was her depression that she could not respond immediately. She scarcely heard him, but thanked him when he had finished.

He then said to me, "I used to go to church when I was a kid. I haven't attended church for years. Maybe there's a spiritual lack in our lives, particularly mine."

I then outlined a proposed course of action for them both—church attendance, participation in the life of the church, and some specific reading which dealt with the spiritual side of man's nature. They both agreed.

Hers was not an instantaneous cure. It was several weeks before she emerged from the depths of her hopeless depression and despair. When she did, I found her to be a delightful person, alive with laughter and capable of enjoying life to its fullest. Their church attendance and participation continued, as did their emotional and spiritual growth. He became a church officer in time and devoted long hours to active participation in the life of the church. Friends of the wife told her that she was much more of a person than she had been before she became emotionally ill.

The basic problem, in their case, was not the purchase by the husband of a home which she detested, though this was apparently a contributory factor. Basically their marriage had begun to founder. There was no communication or deep understanding. Unable to express her dissatisfaction, she had buried it and refused to face the fact that she felt hostility toward her husband. This was a denial of her true feelings, and when feelings are denied, they tend to go underground and erupt in the form of emotional or physical illness.

Shock therapy had not effected a cure, nor had any other form of psychotherapy, though she had been in the hands of a competent psychiatrist. The eventual solution came as the result of her willingness to apply the simple formula of Jesus: "Seek first his Kingdom and his righteousness, and all these things shall be yours as well" (Matt. 6:33). Instead of focusing upon the problems and becoming problem centered, she focused upon the goodness of God and affirmed His desire to heal her. The basic problem was not her emotional illness. That was only a symptom. The underlying difficulty lay in the husband's personality, in alienation from God and from the husband, and in the wife's refusal to face her true feelings and talk them out.

It is normal to experience resentment. All emotions have been given us by God for a specific reason. Anger is one of them. On more than one occasion the anger of Jesus is recorded. "He looked upon them with anger, grieved at their hardness of hearts" (Mark 3:5), is one instance. It is important that we become aware of the emotion of anger, for if we deny it, this is a lie to the self. Anger, or even mild resentment, must be admitted into awareness. We must then decide whether it is appropriate to express it or suppress it. To suppress does not mean to *repress*. The latter term means to deny and bury a feeling, which can produce symptoms. But it is often appropriate, even necessary, to suppress our anger. Sometimes it is more creative to deal with it openly, discussing it with the person or persons involved. One discovers through experience when it is creative and appropriate to do so.

The manner in which young couples are married and thrust into husband-wife roles, and into parenthood, resembles nothing so much as a nightmare in which one discovers he is being pushed onto the stage before a vast audience and told to play a violin solo without ever having studied music. The command to play anyway is given by some invisible source. The totally irrational belief that one can succeed in marriage and as a parent without any more preparation than the emotional experience of having fallen in love, borders upon the absurd. There is no more complex and difficult relationship than marriage, and to assume that we shall automatically be proficient at it without thorough training and preparation is something akin to the belief that one could become a chemical engineer without studying chemistry.

Unfortunately our society has not yet reached the place where intensive training in marriage and parenthood are deemed as important as courses in archery, philosophy, and foreign languages. Future generations will read with astonishment and unbelief of our insistence upon studying foreign languages while providing no courses in the art of communication and the basic elements of human relations. By the time a couple finds themselves at swords point, it is often too late to effect a reconciliation. Marriage counselors are a poor substitute for comprehensive courses in marriage.

One important discovery made by Freud concerned what he termed the Oedipus complex and the Electra complex. The Oedipus complex relates to the apparently universal need of the small boy to relate to and "possess" his mother, to make her the sole object of his affection and win her from the father. The Electra complex is the same tendency on the part of the little girl, who feels a strong need to win her father. She "fantasizes" growing up and marrying Daddy. Mother will "disappear" or get lost or die in her fantasy. Because of guilt feelings toward the mother, whom she dispossesses in fantasy, she later buries this memory in the unconscious.

In some subtle sense this act of winning the parent of the opposite sex seems to be an important factor in helping the small child to achieve a sense of maleness in the little boy, of femaleness in the girl. When a girl fails to "win" her father, either because he is not affectionate or because he rejects her, or for some other reason, she often grows into a woman who has doubts about her femininity. Her femaleness had not been "ratified" when she was young. Something is missing in the feeling tones of such women. This reaction is not necessarily inevitable or universal. Sometimes other factors are brought to bear which minimize this loss of feminine identity.

Occasionally, in an earnest attempt to win the father, the little girl identifies with him so strongly that she draws in from him certain masculine feeling tones which can cause her to become masculinized, either emotionally or physically or both.

For instance a woman who never married and felt no strong attraction to men, could recall wanting to be with her father constantly. He called her "my little boy." She had older brothers whom she felt were favored, and she unconsciously sought to compete with them for her father's affection and attention. As a child she wore boy's clothes most of the time. She seldom spoke of her mother, who receded into the background as a factor in her emotional development. As a consequence the little girl grew into a woman with a weak feminine identity, unsure of her femininity and not even sure that she wanted to marry. She was mechanically minded, and the thought of having to depend upon some male left her cold.

Another young woman sought to win her father's attention constantly, but failed. In her persistent attempt to win him, she imitated his mannerisms, his walk, and his speech. As a woman there was nothing feminine about her until she began to dig into the roots of her childhood and discovered the reason for having no sense of identity as a female. As a result, she began to make a conscious effort to dress and act in a more feminine manner. In time she began to feel more feminine, and for the first time began to feel somewhat at ease with men.

A variation in the Electra fixation is found in the case of the little girl who feels she has failed to win her father, and as an adult over-compensates by appearing excessively feminine. The extremes to which she goes to appear feminine often give a clue to her unconscious doubts about her femininity.

Sexually promiscuous women are not oversexed, but are seeking frantically to reassure themselves that they are attractive as women. The reassurance gained from such activities is short-lived. No woman can gain a permanent sense of being truly feminine from sexual promiscuity, or even from occasional extra-marital affairs.

A woman's emotional structure is much more fluid than that of a man, and consequently she can lose her sense of identity more readily than a man. If she has doubts concerning her femininity, she will desire and seek constant reassurance. Even a woman who has no serious doubts on this score can feel a strong need to be reassured, to have her selfhood as a woman reaffirmed.

In marriage we are seeking to fulfill the unfulfilled in ourselves—to find our counterpart, the other part of the self. Far below the level of consciousness a woman feels a need for that which she does not possess.

Love, and the attraction between the sexes, originates in an unconscious envy of what another possesses and a desire to have it. "If I do not have it," one feels, "I will find it in another. He will provide what I lack." Envy is then transformed into need, need into desire, desire into affection, affection into love.

It is an unfortunate trait of many women, who are unaware of this deep-seated envy of the male, to seek unconsciously to possess and then defeat the male. Totally unaware of what she is doing, a woman may both love a man as a person and hate him as a male. She wants the qualities he possesses as a male, but hates the fact that she does not have them in herself. In subtle ways she may then seek to confront, confound, and defeat him, all in the name of love.

An overly aggressive woman, married to a passive, intellectual male, made herself ridiculous and offensive by her challenging, dominant manner. When questions were addressed to him, she would answer for him, while he patiently smoked his pipe and waited for her to subside. She corrected and criticized him in public and appeared totally oblivious of the incongruity of the excessively dominant role she played.

Another such woman, married to a passive husband, sat in group sessions for four years and berated her husband for his passivity. She interrupted him constantly and demanded that he assume more of the masculine role, but when he tried to do so, she took over and found fault with him. Eventually I put them in separate groups where he felt less challenged and could express himself. He was, in this instance, as much at fault as she. They were unable to find their proper role, since neither had a strong identity as male or female. After more than four years the transformation took place, more or less simultaneously. As she relaxed her hostile, demanding stance, he was able to manifest more of the masculine traits. The relationship eventuated in a beautiful, happy marriage.

The prospect of spending four years, or even one year, working out a satisfactory marriage makes some persons feel discouraged. What they are seeking is a quick, easy answer to a difficult situation.

During the first five or six years of life, when the basis of personality is formed, thousands of incidents and emotions are recorded and filed away. More than ninety-nine percent of all that transpires in those earliest years is buried in the unconscious mind; but those feelings and reactions are all affecting each of us every moment of our lives. The way we react to a given situation at age thirty or forty was largely determined in the first five years of life. Heredity, upon which environment impinges, has predetermined our basic reactions and feeling tones. We can modify, change, correct, alter these reactions by a conscious effort, but the effect of what happened to us in the first few years of life can never be totally eradicated.

However, we are not helpless victims of genes, hormones, and environment. An enlightened conscience, plus insight and determination and the grace of God, can give one an altered destiny. A crash program may be required for some, a determined effort to change one's reactions to life. Essentially we can change no one but ourselves, yet when we change, others tend to change in reaction to us.

Women are far more idealistic, in general, than men. They are more responsive, more realistic, and more determined as a rule to achieve a good marriage. Since their emotional structures are more fluid and susceptible to change, the woman usually assumes the major responsibility for achieving a better marriage. Since marriage and the home are an extension of a woman's personality, she has more at stake. This does not relieve the husband of responsibility in this area, but men are taught from infancy to suppress their emotions. Hence they are usually more hesitant to embark upon a course of action which may involve a marriage counselor, a therapy group, an effort to learn the art of communication.

One husband, new to a group, stated that his wife had insisted that they see a psychiatrist. "I went faithfully for a year," he related. "At every session I gave him a 'snow job.' I was pretty resistant underneath. Then we went to a therapy group, at my wife's insistence. We sat through that without my gaining much from it. Finally when she suggested this Yoke-fellow group, I came with the same 'mind-set' as I had taken to the psychiatrist and the therapy group.

"However," he said, "I am beginning to see the light. I see where I have failed as a husband and as a person, due to early conditioning in my childhood. I am now making some progress, whether my wife agrees or not; and I am going to see it through."

In this instance the wife had taken the initiative in all three instances. The first two had produced negative results. She was still determined to work at the marriage, and finally they were seeing results.

Most women are much less afraid of their feelings than men. Henry and Alice provide an illustration of this. They had been recently married, and stresses and strains were beginning to show. He was quiet, passive, and uncommunicative. She was spontaneous. They were in separate groups, at their own request. Henry said one night to his group, "Something must be done about women. My wife is always pushing my red buttons, just to get a response. I don't think she cares much what kind of a response she gets, just so long as I react. She pushed so hard the other day that I finally yelled at her and told her to lay off. She grinned as though I had given her a bouquet of flowers. She said, 'Usually I get no feeling out of you. I'd rather you yelled at me than to have you just sit there.'"

Some of the women in the group enlightened him. One said, "A woman wants to be loved and to have her feelings validated. If she can't get a positive response, she'll settle for a negative one, just so long as she is not totally ignored. Your wife wants you to make her feel needed, to feel feminine, to be aware of her feelings, and when you're just sitting there like a lump of protoplasm she feels rejected. She'll keep on pushing your buttons until you meet her emotional needs."

Henry said, "Okay, I'm willing to learn, but it isn't going to be easy. I'm afraid of my feelings, especially feelings of hostility and tenderness. But already I'm beginning to be able to identify my feelings for the first time, and to some degree I am accepting them. Maybe in time I can meet her emotional needs. If that's involved in marriage, I'd better get on the ball and acquire some skills."

Henry and Alice began early in their marriage and consequently began to work out some of their problems the first year. Among other things they discovered that a good marriage does not come ready-made, just because two people are in love. It came to both of them as something of a shock to discover that a marriage has to be worked at. Before their first anniversary they had achieved a better relationship than many couples do in the first ten or twenty years, chiefly because they began working on their marriage before disaster threatened and scar tissue had formed.

A delightful and intelligent divorced woman with three marriages behind her joined a group, bringing with her a man whom she contemplated marrying. It developed that her three previous husbands had all been alcoholics. When she married them there was no evidence of alcoholism, but as tensions mounted, each became a problem drinker. She took one of the personality inventories with the group and was horrified to discover that she scored ninety-one on dominance. She was also quite high on aggression. Outwardly feminine, she was unaware of these traits within herself. She began to discover why she had married three men who became alcoholics. Problem drinkers are virtually all passive, dependent individuals. Some who have a capacity for hostility could be labeled passive-aggressive individuals. Because of her innate need to control, she had unconsciously chosen passive men; they, being passive and dependent, had unconsciously sought in her the strength which they lacked in themselves. Consciously she wanted a strong, gentle husband. Unconsciously she was seeking one who would be weak enough so that she could control him, and consequently each marriage ended in disaster.

Constance had experienced twenty years of marital uproar before she finally sought a divorce. In counseling sessions I came to discover that I was dealing with two women, in a sense, instead of one. Initially she displayed a quiet, passive, martyr-like personality. She manifested this "self" for months, during which time she was separated from her husband. When her husband returned and they made a new start, the passive, gentle personality began to disappear. In its place I began to discover a strong, intractable, unyielding, dominant personality.

She preferred to be person number one when she was not with her husband. But when they were together, because he was hostile and aggressive, she felt an unconscious need to summon another aspect of her personality in order to maintain her identity. She was trapped. He had married her for qualities I had first seen, but his hostile nature brought out an aspect of her nature that he could not endure. The marriage finally ended in divorce. Both had sought help in numerous ways and had worked diligently to achieve a workable marriage. The two simply could not live under the same roof. Whether either of them can ever effect a satisfactory marriage with anyone else still remains to be seen.

It cannot be overemphasized: women need to have their feelings validated and accepted. It is not primarily solutions they seek so much as understanding. Later on, perhaps, there will be a time to seek for solutions; but when a woman is upset, all she wants is to be listened to. If her husband listens with one eye on the television or the newspaper, or with an abstracted look, it will not suffice. In our culture, love is so exclusively identifed with romance or sex that we tend to forget the deeper meaning of the word.

Love in its deepest sense might involve a wife's being considerate enough not to begin unloading her frustrations on her husband the minute he enters the door. One husband said, "When I come home at night, about all I want to do for the first half hour is to pull myself together. When my wife meets me at the door with tales of what the children have done, and expects me to listen to all of the difficulties which she has faced during the day, it is almost more than I can endure. I am not only uninterested, I am hostile. I've spent all of my energy at work, then fight traffic on the way home. To be met with another batch of problems the minute I get home makes me want to stay longer at the office, just in order to postpone the strain of having to listen to her problems."

A woman's need for a close relationship is so great that if she cannot achieve it one way, she will instinctively try another. If her efforts at communication are balked by the husband's silence, she has all sorts of alternatives at her disposal: she may become angry over a trifle, or accusatory, or depressed. In an almost frantic attempt to force some kind of communication she will push any button on his control panel; if he finally erupts with anger, she will feel that at least she has gotten *some* response. Some women become ill in an unconscious effort to get attention. This illness is seldom imaginary, a form of malingering, but a cry of the entire organism: "Notice me! Pay me some attention!" Occasionally, in some types of women, it will take the form of being accident prone—another attention-getting device. At a totally unconscious level the wife is saying, "I'd like first class love. If I cannot have that, I'll settle for attention. If I fail to get your attention, I'll get your sympathy. If that fails, I'll get you where it hurts—I'll have an accident, or a symptom." And some women, those who are desperate for love, will say deep within themselves, "If I cannot have your attention, I'll get the attention of *some other* man." Then begins an affair, or at least a flirtation, out of a woman's need to prove to herself that she has not lost her appeal.

Since the home is her nest, a husband's neglect of the home is a rejection of her as a person. A leaky faucet or a bedroom that needs to be painted may represent, to the male, simply a job that needs to be done. Whether it is done today or next month may not seem of great importance. To his wife, however, to neglect the repair job is a rejection of her.

In a group discussion this issue came up. A practical-minded engineer said, "Why, it's very simple. If a wife wants things done, she should make out a list and give each item a priority number. We have a little blackboard in our kitchen where such things are always written down."

His wife said, "A lot of good that does! You never get more than half the things done, no matter what priority I assign them." He grinned and she reached over instinctively and took his hand. She smiled, too, and the group sensed that she had come to accept him as he was.

A basic principle is involved here. In a happy marriage, each tries to meet the needs of the other, but since it is rare to have all our needs completely fulfilled in any relationship, we can learn to accept this fact good-naturedly.

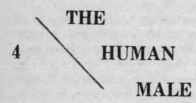

4 THE HUMAN MALE

> It destroys one's nerves to be amiable every day
> to the same human being.　　　—*Disraeli*

A cartoon depicts a grumpy husband reading the paper, with his aggrieved wife standing before him. He is saying, "Do we *have* to try to save our marriage while I'm reading the sports page?" His reaction points up one of the most common complaints of wives: "My husband doesn't talk to me."

An intelligent wife said, "My husband comes home from work, turns on the TV and watches it until dinner time. During the meal he doesn't appear to be listening when I talk. There is no response. After dinner he reads the sports page, then watches television until bedtime. We never go anyplace unless I plan it and prod him into action. I feel I am in charge of the home, the children, the budget, and all planning for the future. He brings home a paycheck, turns it over to me, and retires from life."

She happened to be an unusually even-tempered, uncomplaining wife. Her husband admitted that she did not nag. In his case, he was not retreating from a nagging wife; he was simply a non-communicative individual, virtually incapable of carrying on a conversation.

There is another family situation in which the husband retreats from his wife's barrage of words. One such wife was described as a one-woman grievance committee, always in session. Her husband's only alternatives were to listen sympathetically night after night, which was, for him, an impossible task; to confront her with the fact that she was playing a martyr's role; to change the subject, a ploy which he had tried without success; to tell her firmly that he had no intention of coming night after night to a torrent of complaints; to retreat. Being a pleasant, rather passive individual, he chose the last alternative. His wife accordingly complained that her husband never talked to her.

Another reason for the uncommunicative male is that after two persons have lived together for some years, they are "all talked out." This is much more true of the husband than of the wife. Men tend to deal largely in terms of ideas, concepts, facts, and opinions. After they have talked these out, there is, for some men, little to share. Women, on the other hand, are much more in touch with their feelings, more interested in persons and their surroundings. Consequently, they have more to talk about.

In a restaurant it is quite easy to pick out the married couples. Quite apart from the age factor, married people are easily spotted by the simple fact that there is usually little exchange of conversation. What there is is usually desultory. Engaged couples, viewing this phenomenon while they engage in vivacious conversation, usually vow that their marriage will never become so dull and uninteresting.

One husband said, "My wife sometimes shakes me awake and says, 'Talk to me!' "

"Talk to you! What about?"

"Anything. Just talk to me."

"But I have nothing to talk about."

"What are you feeling?"

"Feeling? I feel tired. Sleepy. A little hostile because you won't let me alone."

"Good. That is a feeling. Tell me some more. What are you *really* feeling?"

Eventually, he said, he broke down under her insistency and admitted that he had been feeling considerable anxiety over the possibility of losing his job. She was gratified that he would tell her, so that she could share in his life. A day or two later she kept pressing to know what he felt. Finally, feeling some irritation over her insistence, he admitted that he was afraid of people. They talked about this for an hour.

"What is it," he asked me, "that makes women want to pry into your innermost secrets? What is it they want?"

"They want to know their husbands," I said. "Your wife felt she didn't know you, really. You told her only what you wanted her to know and kept your fears and anxieties to yourself. She sensed this, and wanted you to share yourself with her."

"I didn't want to bother her with my personal anxieties," he said.

"You mean you didn't want her to discover how scared you were?"

"Yes, I suppose that's it. I needed to preserve the image of the strong, silent, totally competent male. I think I felt I'd be vulnerable if I revealed my weaknesses to her."

"How did she take it when you told her how scared you were?"

"She loved it."

During courtship and the early years of marriage, there is much to talk about. Both partners assume that this situation will continue. They are learning to adjust to each other and exchange opinions on almost everything. In time, however, most topics have been discussed, all aspects of their lives have been explored, and there just isn't much to talk about unless they develop some mutual interests or share at a feeling level.

A wife says, "My husband gives me opinions, or grunts, or monosyllabic responses, and I never know how he really feels. I'd rather he got mad or hit me—anything except be his unemotional, placid, deadly self. He doesn't seem real because he never shows any emotion."

This comment points up one of the main differences between the sexes. Women perceive a person or thing by feeling it and identifying with it. Men take the more prosaic approach of analyzing persons, things, or circumstances.

Some women, with a high degree of tolerance and understanding, regard their uncommunicative husbands with amused affection. Others are frustrated and hostile. They feel cheated in their marriage, which they had envisioned as a half-century of blissful togetherness. All wives of such husbands, however, would prefer to have more communication.

One husband, after enduring for twenty years what he termed "a barrage of minutiae" every evening upon entering the door, finally said, "Look, dear, when I come home, I'm tired and really couldn't be interested in anything less than an all-out catastrophe. If you'll give me half an hour to pull myself together and keep the kids out of my hair, I'll listen to you. Right now, I'm shot. I don't want to *have* to take an interest in your day, which is what I've done for twenty years. I want to listen with genuine interest, and I can if I may have just thirty minutes of uninterrupted peace."

She said, "Do you mean to tell me you've just managed to endure all of my conversation for twenty years? Why didn't you tell me? I don't know whether you have been too polite and considerate, or too dumb to express your needs. If you need half an hour, or an hour, to pull yourself together so you can play the husband-father role, great! I'm all for it. I'm glad you told me." She kissed him, and he grinned sheepishly. "I just didn't want to hurt your feelings."

She turned back to her dinner preparations. "These men!" she muttered.

The problem becomes somewhat more complex when a husband simply cannot communicate. Men are often unable to express themselves as well as their wives and sometimes feel "out-gunned." In our culture men learn, as little boys, to suppress their feelings. One result is that the male is often incapable of communication, particularly if he feels that the conversation may involve emotions. He may then retreat into himself as a means of self-protection, to avoid anything having to do with feelings.

The man with a Don Juan complex poses a serious problem. The true Don Juan is sexually promiscuous, unmarried, and incapable of experiencing real love. However, in actual practice he often turns out to be married, since, as one put it, "One needs a base of operations." Such a man was usually his mother's only or preferred child and was considered a "pretty baby." As an adult he usually has a certain superficial charm which he uses to win women. His constant search for conquests is an effort to reassure himself that he is loved, desired, and truly masculine. However, he is incapable of true love. At a deeper level, he is punishing his mother for having shared her love with his father, thus depriving him of her sole love and attention. He is basically out to win every desirable woman. He is not motivated primarily by either love or sex, but by a need for continual conquest. He can feel secure only when he conquers a woman. The true Don Juan is relatively rare and builds such a reputation that any alert woman is usually forewarned; but his need for conquest and charm is so great that many women disregard all warnings and succumb.

The middle-aged syndrome is somewhat less easy to understand or detect. Interestingly enough, for purposes of definition, we must set middle age as anywhere from thirty-five to sixty-five, though the forties prove the greatest period of danger. Sometimes a trace of Don Juanism, lying dormant, can await the onset of middle age before it manifests itself. To complicate the picture still further, there is a considerable body of evidence to indicate that there is at least some latent trace of promiscuity in everyone. This can be attributed partly to the fact that no one person can ever satisfy completely all of our varied emotional, spiritual, intellectual, and physical needs.

Albert was still in his early thirties when he showed signs of wandering. He loved his wife but felt some vague, indefinable need to relate to other women. It was almost a compulsion. Sometimes the relationship involved no more than conversation, but often it went much farther. His wife was understandably disturbed. As I conferred with them, together and separately, we sought to resolve the problem. Albert stated that he frankly felt he was not "wired" for marriage, that marriage just did not offer him enough to make it worthwhile.

We looked into his childhood. He had had a succession of four or five stepfathers and he could not relate well to any of them. His mother worked long hours and he could remember periods of feeling intense loneliness and isolation. Feeling rejected by his mother, and with no suitable father figure with whom to identify, Albert did well to function as normally as he did. Eventually, as the result of intensive counseling, he achieved a spiritual breakthrough in which he sought to know and do the whole will of God. He sensed, at a deep feeling level, that there was more of fulfillment and happiness available to him in seeking the will of God than he could ever discover by himself.

However, as soon as Albert abandoned his old ways, his wife lost interest in a reconciliation and filed for divorce. She had been able to endure his unfaithfulness without too much difficulty, but she found herself unable to accept him with his new set of values. Before the divorce became final, she began to see a great deal of a friend of her husband, who had precisely the same set of moral values Albert had once had. She thus revealed her own masochistic tendencies. The relationship with her husband's friend did not last long, however, and she continued seeking, without much success, to reconcile her conscious need for a faithful husband, and her unconscious need to experience rejection by someone.

A typical victim of the middle-age syndrome may be motivated partially by a need to be reassured of his masculinity; partly by the knowledge that he lost his youth and fears middle age; partly by an unconscious need to relive some of his adolescence. If he did not rebel in adolescence, some of his unresolved hostility toward authority may now emerge in the form of rebellion against his wife-mother.

Even when a woman's intuition tells her (if her friends have not) that a man is a poor risk, her vanity may make her feel that she is the only one who can understand this charming man and change him.

A delightful and intelligent woman was married for twelve or fifteen years to a man with whom she was deeply in love. They each declared their love for the other, verbally and otherwise. It was a close, satisfying relationship. He had been married four times before, and each marriage had ended in disaster. For the first time in his life, he said, he was supremely, completely satisfied. They had common interests, and there was no lack of communication. There was every reason to believe that their marriage would last. One day, however, he told her that he wanted a divorce. He had found someone else with whom he had fallen deeply in love. She had not suspected until that moment that he was unhappy or had been seeing another woman. Whether we classify him as a Don Juan, a victim of the middle-age crisis, or a philandering male, the fact remains that he was a bad risk. His four previous marriages demonstrated his difficulty in forming and maintaining an enduring relationship. She had felt, of course, that he had just not met "the right woman."

There is a "male climacteric" which corresponds to the menopause in women. However, it is largely if not entirely emotional, rather than physiological. The late thirties and early forties constitute a danger period for both men and women. It is during this "middle-escent" age when many men and women begin to experience what one man termed "a kind of free-floating itch." A husband's preoccupation with his work may make his wife feel unloved, and she may react with complaints and demands which drive him still further into his work. In such a mood he is more susceptible than usual to any kindness or sympathy shown him by some "understanding" woman.

In 1850 the average life expectancy was forty for both sexes. In 1900 it was forty-eight for men and fifty-one for women. Today the life expectancy for men is sixty-six, and seventy-four for women. Old age has been postponed. Today forty (give or take a few years) is the middle ground between childhood and old age. At forty we are abandoning some of the unrealistic hopes and aspirations of youth; simultaneously, we begin to wonder where all the rich rewards are, the ones we dreamed of in youth. Life has settled down to a routine. We discover that happiness is not a perpetual thing, but consists of fleeting moments, with much of life somewhat on the gray side. If goals have been achieved, they do not always give us the intense satisfaction we had anticipated. If they have not been attained, we are disenchanted. A man's career may not provide him with the satisfaction he envisioned. Marriage, to the wife, has not presented her with the unending bliss she dreamed of as a young girl. Small wonder, then, that the forties are critical years for many men and women.

A husband in his early forties described his feelings about his marriage. "I walk into the house five evenings a week and look around at a complete shambles. The place always looks as if it had been hit by a cyclone. Actually, it's just our three kids. I pick my way through the junk and debris and my wife hits me with a barrage of trivia—what the kids did, how badly they acted, what the neighbor kids did to *our* kids; how busy and harrassed she's been all day; and I find myself thinking of the calm, efficient, well-organized young women in my department at the office.

"I know," he went on, "that it isn't fair to compare those sweet young things at the office with my wife, or compare our efficiently run office with a house and three kids. But the contrast is almost too great for me, particularly when I am met with a great big dose of complaints, when what I really need is a little consolation for my bruised ego."

He thought for a moment. "To be really honest with you, there is one girl at the office who is looking better and better to me all the time. She is sweet and understanding. She never goes into a flap no matter what happens. She is efficient, well-organized, and views life with amused tolerance. After I'm around her all day, believe me, my disorganized, complaining wife doesn't look nearly as good as she did when I married her."

The following week his wife was in a for a conference. "Our three kids came pretty fast," she said. "I guess I wasn't prepared for all that motherhood entailed. At times I have felt put upon and abused. For some years I was penned up all day with small youngsters, and when my husband came home, I wanted some adult conversation. All I got were grunts. I guess I pushed pretty hard, trying to get some sort of response from him. Maybe I just succeeded in driving him farther away. But what can you do?

"Now the kids are older, but in adolescence they can be even more of a problem. I have to make most of the decisions on my own. If I ask my husband for some assistance, he just says, 'I've had it. You settle these minor problems.' I'd like some co-operation in rearing the kids. They need a father, as well as a mother."

In the course of our counseling sessions, we managed to establish a basis for communication. They found it easier to discuss some of the painful areas of their relationship in my presence than at home, where she often dissolved in tears, or he retreated into hostile silence. Each became able to understand the needs of the other; both began to make an effort to meet the needs of the other, instead of demanding that their own needs be met.

In one of our groups, a husband recounted an experience which illustrates a problem peculiar to men. He was doing some repair work on the hall floor and was kneeling on a piece of rug left over from the carpeting of their bedroom.

"My wife saw the rug I was kneeling on and shouted at me, 'Don't you dare use that new piece carpeting. I'm saving that. You'll get it all dirty!' I got up in a blind rage and threw it across the room. I said something pretty hostile to her, I don't remember what, and there was silence around the house for two or three days. During that time I began to realize that I had overreacted. She sounded exactly like my mother, and like all of the women teachers in the private boys' school I attended. For the moment she had been the hostile, strident, mother-teacher authority figure I knew as a child. I do think she was out of line, too; but the only person I can change is myself. So, in due time I went and got the piece of carpeting, knelt on it, and finished the job. When she started to say something, I just said, 'Look, I'm not going to damage this small piece of carpeting. If I do, that will be time enough to complain. Just be quiet and forget it.' In so doing, I reclaimed my manhood, and gave up reacting like a small child chided by his mother."

There is a great and dangerous fallacy in our culture, summed up in the phrase, "He's such a *good* boy." By this the parents and relatives mean that he causes no trouble, is compliant and obedient. He learns early in life to repress his hostility. He will be loved only if he is "good"; that is, quiet, makes no trouble, and never talks back. But in forcing him to be a "good boy" we are laying the roots for later rebellion in adulthood, or neurosis of some kind. Every child needs the right to express his hostility without being punished for it. Anger is a God-given emotion, a survival factor, and unless one is allowed to express it in appropriate ways in childhood, it will emerge in inappropriate ways later in life. Repressed anger can erupt in a hundred ways—ranging from criminality to asthma or heart attacks.

An eminent psychologist said, "I am not interested in trying to make my children 'good.' I want them to be happy, and then they will act in appropriate ways. It is always the unhappy, frustrated child who gets into trouble." By this he did not mean to imply that he granted their every whim. He set limits and stuck to them. Children are unhappy without limits, though they will always test them.

A man who was not allowed to express his anger as a boy may express it in adult life by retreating into silence, out of fear of his violent anger; or may explode in senseless rages; or the repressed anger may simply take the form of some psychosomatic illness: ulcers, asthma, arthritis, colitis, neurodermatis, heart ailments, or any of a score of others.

A great deal has been written in recent years about the "feminization" of men in our culture. In many cases men expect, at an unconscious level, to be dominated by their wives, just as they were by their mothers, while at a conscious level they may proclaim their desire to be the strong, self-reliant male. A passive-aggressive male, one who is both passive and hostile, may need his wife to assume the dominant role but resent it bitterly when she does. Charles was such a man. He was excessively passive and felt vulnerable at two points: his ability to earn a living and to function sexually. He could not assume leadership in the home, but when his wife provided direction for the children, his sole contribution was to countermand her instructions. He argued for virtual total permissiveness, chiefly because he saw his dominant mother in his wife. In a sense he became another one of the children, rebelling against mother. There were conferences in which it was understood that they would try to agree on rules for the children, and that neither would countermand the instructions of the other. He was unable to comply, for unconsciously he identifed with the children in every instance. He had been so emasculated by his early childhood conditioning that he felt inwardly much more like a child than a man. Unable to endure a situation in which he felt so much like one of the children, doubting his own masculinity, he finally elected to end the marriage.

A dominant, controlling mother tends to produce passive sons and dominant daughters. The passive sons, in turn, tend to marry dominant wives, while the aggressive daughters usually marry passive males, thus perpetuating this vicious circle.

There are men who have great difficulty in deciding to marry. Clifford was in his forties and had been going with a woman about his own age for five years. In counseling sessions he sought to work out his ambivalent feelings toward his mother. He was almost certain that he had "cut the cord," but I could see many evidences of a deep emotional attachment. He interpreted his hostility toward his mother as evidence of his emancipation. The fact that he wanted to marry, but was unable to arrive at a definite decision, convinced me that he was deeply attached to his mother. It required two years of counseling with him and the women (whose hostility toward her father gave her a similar problem) before the situation was resolved. Eventually they agreed on a date for the wedding.

It was to be a simple wedding, with only the family and a few close friends attending. When the groom's mother apepared, I could see why it had taken him so long to cut the cord. She tottered in, murmuring anxious sounds to no one in particular, then saw the bride. Her face clouded, and she said petulantly, "Oh, you've changed, haven't you? Well, I suppose it will turn out all right." She gave a martyr-like sigh which seemed to say, "Son, after all I've done for you, and now you've betrayed me." After the wedding she managed to ignore the bride, while puttering about interfering with virtually everything. Under the circumstances, I felt that the groom had done rather well to be able to throw off the shackles even in his early forties. It proved to be a happy marriage despite the mother's reluctance to have it so.

A woman is vulnerable at the point of being able to find a suitable husband, create a home, and be successful in bearing and rearing children. A man is vulnerable in the areas of finding a suitable life-work, succeeding in earning a living, and fulfilling his sexual role as father and husband. As a man should never criticize a woman at the points where she is most vulnerable, neither should a man be criticized at his points of vulnerability. Comparisons are odious! No woman could possibly react other than with resentment at having her cooking compared with that of her husband's mother. Any man would react with hostility if his earning capacity was compared with that of his father-in-law or the man down the street.

In fact, criticism at any point is the poorest form of communication and the most destructive.

The art of communication is much more complex than learning to drive an automobile, or to type, yet we expect young people in their late teens or early twenties to be able to establish a happy marriage and know how to communicate without the slightest preparation. The human personality is much more complex than an electronic computer, yet we would not dream of turning a totally inexperienced person loose in a room with a battery of computers, suggesting that he would learn how to operate one successfully by trial and error! Society has failed miserably in preparing us for marriage.

The vast majority of wives tend to mother their husbands in some degree. Freud expressed the opinion that this is probably a necessary ingredient in any successful marriage, as pointed out earlier. This may be partly true because of the maternal instinct in women, but it can also be attributed to the fact that in our culture men demand it, usually without being aware of it. Most men grew up in homes where mother was usually the controlling factor, and in our increasingly matriarchal society, this becomes more pronounced.

There is still a third factor, which is often overlooked. Women have a strong, innate need to please their husbands. Altruism is too weak a word for it. If a woman feels loved and secure, and if she is a reasonably mature individual, she will feel within herself a strong desire to please, to serve, to mother her husband. An excessively passive male may need vast amounts of this and accept it as his due. An immature male may become insatiable in his need for love in this form.

An aggressive man, on the other hand, strongly independent, may react with some suspicion to his wife's need to please. With some caution he may permit her to minister to him, but if she turns her kindness off and on and is unpredictable, he will retreat and refuse to let her express her love in such ways. A man's strongly self-assertive, independent spirit is usually born out of a feeling that he is on his own and will have to face life unaided. He may be slightly suspicious of the motives of someone who seeks to express tenderness.

One such man reported that his wife often brought him something to drink when he was doing gardening on a hot day. It became a regular custom. One hot Saturday afternoon when he was mowing the lawn and his wife was reading in the shade, he asked her if she would bring him something to drink. She replied, "I'm right in the middle of this. Get it yourself."

Thereafter, he said, when she offered to bring him a drink, no matter how much he wanted it, he would refuse. "I know it was childish," he said, "but I suppose I'm pretty sensitive to rejection. I got plenty of rejection as a child, and I don't need any more. Each time I feel rejection, my total, all-out independence emerges and I refuse help or love or anything else from people—no matter who it is."

It is surprising to many women that men can be so sensitive. Because they are bigger, physically stronger, and appear to be more stalwart, women imagine that men should be less sensitive. It is probable that men are equally as sensitive as women, with two variables: they tend to conceal their hurts better, and they are often hurt by things which would not disturb many women.

The war between the sexes has been going on for thousands of years. We find evidence of it, for instance, in the thinly veiled hostility of many of the jokes and cartoons which emerge in a constant stream from some unknown source. Though the authorship of the jokes is usually unknown, one can be reasonably sure that the authors are men. For instance, here are three typical comments, or jokes, which bear the unmistakable mark of the male mind: "There are three words a woman loves to hear. She never tires of hearing them from her husband. They are: 'I was wrong.'" Another: "Behind every successful man stands a surprised mother-in-law." The third concerns a feminist leader of a bygone era, whose chief assistant complained of having a severe headache. The feminist leader said, "Dearie, you just go home and pray. Tell God all about it—*she'll* understand!" Such jokes provide a fairly harmless safety valve for the underlying hostility between the sexes.

Just as many women doubt their femininity, there are countless men who have grave doubts concerning their masculinity. Without being consciously aware of what is entailed in achieving a male identity, a man may doubt himself. He wonders whether he is "all man," either consciously or unconsciously. His doubts may manifest themselves in a variety of ways. If he is timid and withdrawn, he will try to retreat still further in order to avoid the pain of being noticed. He may have a secret dream of achieving something so significant that an astounded world will heap its praises upon him, but in his heart he knows it is a remote possibility.

If he is more aggressive he may overcompensate for his feelings of inferiority by swearing, talking loudly and aggressively, or boasting. He may become a compulsive talker, demanding complete attention. With more gifted persons, the compensation may take the form of a drive to achieve. Alfred Adler believed that a sense of inferiority is the strongest possible drive, that the "will to power" is the basis of all significant achievement.

One husband, quite emotionally immature, manifested his extreme sense of masculine inferiority by demanding absolute obedience in the home. He got along well at work, where his irascible temper was held in check, but at home he was contemptuous of all opinions but his own. No one dared disagree with him. His children were violently berated and punished for the slightest infraction of his rules. He tyrannized the entire family.

When his wife threatened divorce and announced that she had seen an attorney, he appeared hurt and surprised that she would do such a thing. He agreed to exercise more restraint in the home if she would give up her foolish idea of seeking a divorce, and for about three months he acted the part of a reasonably mature person. Then he reverted to his old self, and his rages were more violent. Eventually he agreed, under duress, to undertake group therapy, but dropped out after a few sessions. The threat of looking at himself proved too great.

This illustration brings into focus another male attribute. Men are much more reluctant to seek help for a faltering marriage than women. In seven out of eight instances, the wife first seeks help or proposes it. The male ego is usually threatened at the prospect of airing domestic problems with a marriage counselor or psychiatrist. I can think of only two instances out of hundreds in which the husband first sought help. In one case, the wife had already made up her mind to end the marriage. The other case involved a passive man married to a strongly dominant woman. When we eventually succeeded in having her come in for a discussion, she proved hostile and uncooperative. In all other instances, over a period of nearly forty years, the wife first sought help.

A man will take his car to a mechanic, have a dentist take care of his teeth, call a competent repairman to fix his television set, but when his wife suggests that they consult a counselor about a marital problem, the typical response is, "No! We're adults; we'll work this out ourselves. What can one of those head shrinkers tell us that we don't know already?"

The human personality is roughly a hundred thousand times as complex as a television set, and the marriage relationship is much more complex than

88

any other. It is a totally unrealistic, fear-ridden response on the part of the husband which causes him to reject professional help. In this, as in certain other areas, the woman is much more realistic.

Men tend to be "solution oriented" except where the marriage is concerned; when a wife is emotionally upset, the male mind automatically seeks a solution. In an effort to stop her tears he may utter such banal and unacceptable solutions as, "Don't take it so hard, honey. It isn't all *that* bad." This, of course, is a rejection of her feelings and of her.

Or he may try to get her to stop crying, because she makes him nervous or upset. No one has told him, of course, how to handle this situation, and all of his automatic responses are likely to be wrong. If he could learn to validate her feelings, he could go a long way toward resolving the problem. Validating her emotions calls for some response such as, "Tell me all about it, dear. What happened?"

Then, having heard her story (whether she is weeping or livid with rage) he could validate her feelings still further by saying, "Yes, I think under the circumstances, if I were you, I'd feel the same way." At this point she doesn't want solutions, but understanding and emotional support.

It is normal and instinctive on the part of a woman to try to change a husband. Each of us would like to change our environment and the people in it, so that life will be more pleasant. If we can get others to conform to our ideas, we make life more endurable for ourselves. Women may have somewhat more of a tendency in this direction due to the instinctive maternal role, which causes them to control and nurture children. Some women are guilty of unconscious manipulation. One highly manipulative wife, who would have been indignant had she been accused of seeking to control her husband, would say, sweetly and with deep sincerity, "Well, it's *right,* isn't it?" when her manipulation was being challenged. If it was right, as she saw it, then it must be right to cause all others to conform! And she did not sense in the slightest that she was manipulative.

Husbands react in different ways to being manipulated. Some know they are being quietly manipulated and go along indulgently most of the time, balking only when there is some issue at stake which seems worth fighting over. A completely passive man will comply, without sensing any difference from the manipulation of his mother, which made him passive.

An aggressive husband may tend to go along with manipulation, unconsciously accumulating material for his next explosion. His wife then wonders at his overreaction to some relatively insignificant event. Quite often a husband will respond with silence. Unable or unwilling to make a big issue out of a minor matter of being manipulated, he simply retreats into his own thoughtful silence, and shuts out his wife. Still another response, wholly unconscious, is illness. Virtually all illnesses, in the opinion of authorities in the field of psychosomatic medicine, bear a relation to our emotions. The illness or operation of today may be related to the accumulation of unconscious hostility over an earlier period of years. The individual, when his organism reaches the saturation point, simply responds with some physical symptom. The organism is saying, "I've had it!" whether it be asthma, a heart attack, ulcers, an operation, or almost any illness. The accumulation of tension and anxiety at work and at home; the self-condemnation for not being man enough to stand up to one's wife; the sense of guilt and failure common to all mankind in some degree—these all take their toll and may manifest themselves in a hundred different ways—physically, emotionally, or in terms of accident-proneness.

There appeared to be virtually no basis for communication between Jerry and Helen. He was a pleasant, humorless man in his early forties. He hated his passivity, and when Helen pushed him he tended to erupt with a violent outburst. In a group which they attended they always tended to resort to accusations and countercharges. Neither could be induced to deal with their own individual problems. He wanted out of this hostile relationship, but could not bring himself to break up the home, for the sake of the children. She was sick of the relationship and kept hoping he would change. It was an impasse, with neither willing to change.

The situation was temporarily resolved when he went to the hospital with a heart attack. For a time things were better as the family rallied around and gave him the attention demanded by his condition. As soon as he was fully recovered and back at work, the old pattern was resumed, and relations were again strained to the breaking point. A few months later he had another attack from which he died. There is, of course, no possible way of determining a positive relationship between the intolerable conditions at home and his heart attack, but it is becoming abundantly clear that stress plays some part in virtually every illness. Jerry's organism simply took what was for him the only acceptable way out of an impossible situation.

No one ever receives enough love. Everyone, without exception, needs love in great quantities. The human psyche is engineered by God to function best when it feels loved. Listen to your radio: virtually every song deals with love. In drama, opera, fiction, the great themes deal with love in some form. We are preoccupied with love simply because it is so vital to our well-being.

We are all looking for love. We want someone to love us—to love us unconditionally. A young woman admittedly a hundred pounds overweight said plaintively, "I've always wanted people to love me just for myself." Someone in the group said, "Honey, there's a lot of you to love—maybe one hundred pounds too much for an average man." She was hurt. Yet we all want the same thing—to be loved just as we are, faults and all. But we can never have unconditional love all of the time. Society demands a certain standard of performance before it deems us lovable or even acceptable.

The only way to receive love is to give it. Jesus said, "Give and it will be given unto you . . ." (Luke 6:38). This applies in many areas of life, but supremely in the matter of love.

If you want to be loved, you must begin to give love. I am referring to much more than romantic love, of course. But even romantic love comes most often, and in a most satisfying way, to those able to give *agape*-love, which in the words of the New Testament, "does not insist on its own way" (I Cor. 13:5).

Instead of waiting for someone to love you, make it your task to give love. Discover the need of another and fill it. Some people accept love in one form, some in another. There are individuals who find difficulty in accepting love in any form, and these can be the most challenging. Try to find a way to manifest love to others in such a way that they can accept it.

A loving person is a "giving out" sort of individual, ready to say "Yes!" to every legitimate request. This does not suggest buying love with deeds of kindness. Giving love must be without any thought of return. We do not count the deeds done or weigh the amount of energy expended on behalf of this one or that one, and wonder if we shall be repaid. One becomes truly loving when there is so much tenderness, concern, compassion within that it simply overflows into the lives of other people. Love does not calculate—asking if the recipient is "worthy," if we shall be repaid, if the act will be appreciated. "Love never ends," the Apostle Paul tells us (I Cor. 13:8). He means that if we have the capacity to give love, we will never fail to exhibit it, instinctively and without thought. It could be said, then, that if we are truly loving persons, "Love will never fail to manifest itself."

One wife who endured a rather difficult marital relationship determined to show love to her husband, at the instigation of the group, instead of trying to change him. At the next meeting, a week later, she reported, "Well, it didn't work. I showed that man nothing but love for a solid week, and he didn't show the slightest appreciation. It didn't work!" Someone said, thoughtfully, "I suppose you told him off." She said, "I sure did, but good!"

One of the women in the group said, "Katie, you weren't exhibiting love. You were trying to bribe him, and when he couldn't be bribed with sweetness and light, you got angry. He saw through you and knew that you were just trying another means of manipulation. The Apostle Paul said, 'Love does not insist on its own way.' I think you probably were trying to get your own way; however laudable that may be, you did the right things from the wrong motive."

Katie thought it over and eventually admitted that her "love" had been just a form of manipulation. She then agreed to exhibit love indefinitely, win or lose.

She reported week by week. Sometimes she failed, but as time wore on she learned the inner satisfaction of expressing love even to an unloving person; ultimately there was a gradual, cautious response from the husband. In time a good marriage resulted—but not until she became able to make love unconditional.

CONFLICTS

5 \ ## THAT MAR

MARRIAGES

> What's so remarkable about love at first sight? It's
> when people have been looking at each other for
> years that it becomes remarkable.   —*Anonymous*

A woman related an incident involving the six-year-old daughter of a neighbor who had just heard the story of Cinderella for the first time. The little girl retold the story up to the climax, and then asked, "Do you know what happened then?"

The woman said, "They lived happily ever after."

"No, they didn't. They got married!" her little friend replied.

As the child seemed to sense, getting married and living happily ever after are not necessarily synonymous. There are innumerable barriers to surmount before most persons can achieve a satisfying marriage.

One thing that mars many marriages is the effort to try to make marriage partners fit some preconceived pattern. In a group session Glenda's dissatisfaction with her husband centered chiefly on his lack of interest in doing household repairs. She referred to a screen door that had needed attention for six months, a window latch that she had asked him to fix weeks before, and half a dozen other uncompleted household tasks which he had neglected. Bill looked vaguely guilty as she listed her complaints.

"I'm not much of a handyman," he said. "I'm all thumbs when it comes to fixing things."

"But you would take care of these simple little things if you were really interested in the home," Glenda retorted. "Any ten-year-old boy could; I don't know why you take refuge behind your alleged incompetence."

Someone said, "Glenda, tell us about your father."

"Well, he was a wonderful man. I adored him. He cared about the home, unlike my husband, whose interests seem limited to his job, television, and his books. . . ."

"It's your father we want to hear about, Glenda," someone else said.

"All right! Dad was a whiz at anything he undertook—a success in business, active in the church, president of his service club, and yet he always found time to take an active interest in the home. He had a workshop in the garage, and I can still remember him working around the house weekends, doing things for mother and making furniture for her in his workshop."

"So," someone said, "Daddy ran around the house weekends with a box of tools and you imagined that this is the way all men are supposed to act. My father couldn't have built a bird house that any self-respecting bird would have lived in, and I was pleasantly surprised to find that my husband could fix a leaky faucet. I wonder, Glenda, if you aren't trying to make Bill over in the image of your beloved Daddy. Forget it! If Bill supports you and the kids, loves you, and is kind, why don't you get off his back and stop trying to make him over?"

Glenda thought for a moment. In the silence Bill responded. "It just occurred to me that if Glenda would get off my back and stop sounding like my mother, and give up trying to make me over, I might feel more like attempting to meet some of her needs."

Glenda said, "All right, I'll stop nagging you and we'll see what happens."

"No," someone retorted, "your attitude is all wrong. You're still trying to manipulate him. You'll have to take him as he is, whether he tries to be an eager handyman or not."

A few weeks later, when the discussion got around to the couple again, Glenda reported, "You know what happened? I stopped nagging Bill and just gave up. I decided to take him as he is, and all of a sudden he began to show an interest in the home. He actually fixed five of the seven things I had listed for him to do. Maybe when I stopped pushing, he felt more willing to comply."

Bill got into the discussion. "I just discovered something. It wasn't the repairs my wife was so bothered about. I think what she really needed was some manifestation of my interest in the home. The house is her nest, and apparently she feels that if I love her I'll show it the way her father did. I'm not very mechanical, but I'm beginning to see that love is more than romance—it's giving a woman a sense of security. I hadn't realized how much security a woman gets from having her husband interested in the nest."

"Any wife could have told you that," one of the women said. "Men are so dumb."

This little drama, enacted with many variations in thousands of homes, illustrates the female need for security; and one way a wife receives this security is from the assurance that the husband is deeply concerned about her *and* the home. It also illustrates the deeply buried and totally unconscious tendency of husbands and wives to try to fit the marriage partner into some preconceived mold.

In a counseling session with a couple, one of the issues raised was by the husband, who complained that his wife was a poor housekeeper. "The house is a shambles," he said. "Laundry is piled up everywhere, the kids' toys are scattered all over the living room, and at night when I come home I have to move a pile of magazines or unfinished ironing before I can find a place to sit down."

His mother, I discovered, had been a meticulous housekeeper. He was an only child, whereas his wife had four small children. His mother had no outside interests. The home was her sole concern. His wife, on the other hand, was deeply involved in church and civic interests, with three or four hobbies.

He had brought to marriage the preconceived notion that there was just one kind of wife and mother: the kind who devoted her entire attention to the home. I asked him if he would prefer his wife to devote her entire attention to housekeeping or remain the outgoing, spontaneous, active person she obviously was. He said, "Why, I love my wife for these attributes. She's a wonderful mother and has lots of varied interests. I suppose I have been trying to make her over in the image of my mother, forgetting the other traits she had, which are the ones that caused me to fall in love with her."

His wife said, "I am a lousy housekeeper, and I hate myself for it. But with four small children and all my outside activities, I just never seem to get caught up."

She was thoughtful for a moment, then asked: "Could it be that I am overextended and need to cut out one or two of my outside activities?" I looked at her husband.

"Honey," he said, "you handle it any way you want. As an engineer I imagine I'm a perfectionist, which I have been told is a little neurotic, especially if I bring it into the home. Suppose I stop trying to make you over. I like you the way you are. I guess I can get used to the mess in the house. . . ."

"Jack," she said, "it *is* a mess . . . I think perhaps I've always resented the fact that your mother was such a wonderful housekeeper and cook. I never could measure up to her. Perhaps I've overcompensated for my inferiority feelings by being involved in too many things. I'm going to drop one or two activities and devote more time to being a housekeeper."

"Okay, honey," Jack replied. "But don't stop being yourself. I didn't marry you just to keep house. Incidentally, I think I can control my perfectionistic tendencies around home. I'll leave my slide rule at the office."

One common difficulty in marriage is the disillusionment which often comes when a young couple discovers that their romantic dreams of perpetual bliss simply cannot be realized. The typical bride anticipates a continuation of the courtship, and lasting, loving attention from the man she marries. He expects the same warm response and idealized love he received during courtship. Both are disillusioned when the harsh realities of marriage begin to appear. He is no longer as attentive. The young man who catered to her whims now turns out to be something less than a Latin lover. He looks quite different slumped in front of the television set watching a ball game, and his memory of the lovely creature whom he courted, and who was tenderly affectionate, fades a bit as he gazes upon her in the early morning light, her head a mass of curlers and her face something less than alluring without makeup.

Each begins to discover in the other certain irritating traits they had never suspected before. He may be less gallant, more demanding, less considerate. She can be less affectionate, sometimes selfish, occasionally petulant, given to crying spells or other manifestations of discontent.

"You never take me anyplace," is a commonplace complaint of many wives, who had rather expected the courtship to continue unabated. He may come home tired and want to rest. She would like to get out of the house, or at least have some communication. One husband said, "All I want to do as I enter the front door is to go sit down, take off my head, and hold it tenderly in my lap, while I pull the tattered edges of my soul together. If my wife would greet me at the door, it would help; but usually I no sooner get seated than there comes a demand that I do something—take out the dog, feed the cat, or empty the garbage pail. There must be something about a seated or prone male that infuriates a woman beyond endurance, and she bends every effort to get him into motion." This was not precisely the picture of marriage he had entertained.

A young wife, who was employed, said, "I work just as many hours as my husband does, but when I get home, he's already sacked out on the sofa. I am expected to get dinner, set the table, and wash dishes after dinner, while he, lord and master of all he surveys, pushes back his chair from the table and retires to the television set. This isn't my idea of a fifty-fifty marriage partnership.

Another common difficulty encountered in the field of marital relations concerns the fact that women, in general, are becoming more dominant, while men are becoming more passive. By dominance we do not necessarily mean "to be domineering." Dominance merely means "to control." One may control in a score of ways—by manipulation, with a heavy hand or a gentle touch, through tears or martyr-like tactics, with threats, through condemnation, or by silent withdrawal. Any effort, overt or seemingly passive, by which we seek to control persons or circumstances, is dominance.

All of us would prefer to control our environment, which means essentially people and events. It is much safer and more comfortable if we are in control and can have our way. The less mature one is, the more he may seek to bring others under his control. The egocentric individual expects the world to cater to his needs. The spoiled child who grows up and marries, continues to be a spoiled child in the marital relationship.

In our culture women do many things today which were formerly solely in the male domain. A generation or two ago it was relatively rare to see women driving a taxi, playing golf, belonging to bowling teams, or employed in hundreds of different kinds of jobs formerly held only by men. This new freedom possessed by women has both liberated and confused them. Working with men in office, factory, and shop, they have tended to absorb many so-called masculine "feeling tones." This, coupled with "the masculine protest" described so ably by Jung, has resulted in the defeminization of women. The masculine protest is a woman's feeling, often unconscious, that "this is a man's world," and that men are bent on holding women in restraint. It springs in part from the tendency of many women to feel resentful of male assumption and superiority. One astute male felt that women in business and industry tend to imitate men's worst characteristics and demean their own virtues. In business, particularly if she achieves an administrative position, a woman tends to give up her own sense of real values and adopts man's—position, money, and power. "Money," he said, "doesn't seem to hurt women, but power and authority are seldom becoming. Women in power are mean to each other, thinking probably they are doing it the man's way. Almost always they use more authority than is necessary to accomplish the job."

Psychological tests reveal that more than half of the wives tested are more dominant than their husbands. It is not uncommon to discover in such tests that a wife will score in the eighties or nineties on dominance, while the husband's score may be in the twenties or thirties. A young wife who had taken the test discovered to her chagrin that her score on dominance was ninety-six. Her husband scored twenty-four. She said, "I knew I was high, but this is ridiculous!" She and her husband talked it out, both in the group and privately. The wife said, flatly, "I am not going to be a dominant wife. Something in me wants to control. Perhaps it is out of fear, but I am going to give it up. My husband is going to be in charge."

Asked if she meant that she would let him control her, she said, "Oh, no! I don't want anyone to control me and I don't want to control anyone else. It's just that I want him to be the head of this corporation. *Somebody* has to steer the ship through the matrimonial seas, and we've decided, together, it is to be him. I'm first mate." Her mild, quiet husband said firmly, "I hate my passivity as much as she hates her dominance. These traits can be changed, and we intend to change them."

Subsequent observations tended to confirm the idea that they could change these tendencies. He became more outgoing and aggressive, while she let him take the lead in areas where they felt he should be in charge.

I have observed radical changes take place in marriages if both husband and wife were anxious to work toward a happier marriage. Sometimes much was accomplished when only one of the two worked at it. In one case a couple achieved a beautiful relationship, after a bad start, in less than a year. In another instance a middle-aged couple devoted four and a half years to group therapy and private counseling before they achieved a significant breakthrough. But what they did was beautiful! The task seemed endless to them at times, but the love and harmony which they now experience is a vast improvement over the constant hostility and bickering which marred their relationship for twenty-five years or more.

I told a woman of forty that it might take two or three years to resolve her marital problem. She said, "Three years! I'd be forty-three by then." I asked, "And if you *don't* do anything about your marriage, how old will you be in three years?" She laughed and said, "Let's begin!"

A marital problem frequently encountered involves the sending of "coded messages." A coded message is a communication, verbal or otherwise, which must be decoded before it can be properly understood. For instance, in a group session a wife said, "I'd had a bad day, and when my husband came home, I needed some reassurance or support or some indication that he loved me. He asked how things had gone. I burst into tears, and he said 'What's the matter?' I said, 'Go away. Don't bother me.' What I really wanted was for him to put his arms around me and do something to comfort me."

Her husband spoke up. "I'm no mind reader. When she told me to go away, I did just that, feeling frustrated and rejected. Then we both spent the evening feeling rejected and unhappy."

It is quite a common experience for both men and women to send these coded messages, expecting the other to decode, interpret, and act so as to meet the implied need. Women, with their variable moods, send perhaps the larger number of coded messages, but men do so, too. Women know what they mean and are often frustrated because their husbands do not understand an obscure message. Men have their own faulty type of communication, which can often be just as confusing to their wives.

The coded message is, in a sense, a plea for someone to meet our needs, to take the trouble to understand us, to care enough to probe, pull, push, interpret, and finally get the real meaning. But this is as unrealistic as expecting someone to understand Arabic without having studied it. Communication demands an honest expression of one's feelings and needs.

A typical marital impasse was illustrated by the account of a man who said, "I travel a great deal. When I get home my wife questions me in considerable detail about where I went, what I did, what

I had to eat. Once I'm home I don't recall precisely what I did on Tuesday night, or what I ate. She thinks of me out in the big, gay, wonderful world, eating in fancy restaurants, having a blast, meeting interesting people, living the life of Riley, while she's home with the kids eating her own cooking. All I want to do is to get home and forget the rat race. I think I resent her assumption that it's all one big, glorious, frenzied round of gay activity out there. It's murder, as a matter of fact. I know she has a rough time of it with the kids and her boring routine, but no one has it easy."

His wife, on the other hand, unaware of the frustrations her husband encounters daily, feels that her life is circumscribed. When he returns from a trip, she would like for him to take her out to dinner, to offer his companionship, while all he wants to do is retire to his castle and relax.

This poses a basic incompatibility of interests; the only solution is to be found in the kind of love and understanding which asks not, "How can my needs be met?" but, "How can I meet the needs of my marriage partner?" Obviously this question needs to be asked by *both* partners, in sympathetic understanding, not just by one. A solution presupposes that both will seek a formula simultaneously. Many couples are finding their answers in such dilemmas through participation in a sharing group, where the basic built-in incompatibilities of husbands and wives can be discussed freely. Many find their solutions through a marriage counselor, but unfortunately many men are reluctant to consider such a proposal until disaster threatens.

Jealousy and possessiveness constitute another pitfall. One young wife shared with her group the fact that when she was first married she felt literally abandoned when her husband went to work each morning. "I was immature and overdependent," she said, "and I realize it now. I resented his job just as

I would have been jealous of another woman. But now that I have become less dependent I find myself less interested in him. I don't know whether I married him because I was in love with him or just terribly dependent."

A husband shared in a counseling session his sense of frustration over his wife's extreme possessiveness. "If I visit a friend in the same apartment building and I am not back in twenty minutes, she rushes down to drag me back. She won't go anywhere without me. What's the matter with her? Or am I overreacting?"

I asked him, "What was her relationship with her father? Were her parents divorced, or was he away a great deal?" He said, "Interesting that you should ask. Her father abandoned the family when she was quite young. Could that have anything to do with her problem?"

I assured him that in all probability it did. Being abandoned and feeling rejected in childhood creates deep insecurities in a child. These can later manifest themselves in various neurotic behavior patterns. Extreme jealousy or possessiveness usually stems from some emotional deprivation in early childhood.

Husbands have been known to become insanely jealous if their wives appear to show the slightest interest in another man. One wife complained that her husband accused her of flirting with store clerks and questioned her as to her whereabouts every time she left the house. She wanted to know whether this was normal behavior for a husband. I assured her that it was abnormal and undoubtedly had its roots in a deep sense of insecurity. I also told her that any hope of eradicating his jealousy was slight, unless he could get professional help. Unfortunately he was much too insecure to be willing to see a psychologist, a minister, or to join a therapy group. He had no problem, as he saw it. He felt the only difficulty was with his wife. She had a number of alternatives: to live as his prisoner the rest of her life, deliver an ultimatum that they both see a competent counselor, or she could seek divine guidance and delay action until she felt, inwardly, a definite sense of direction.

Often emotional opposites marry each other. A typical case involved a highly extroverted, gregarious, spontaneous wife who was married to a rather pedantic, decimal-point-minded type of husband. He was a cautious perfectionist. Of course, they had been drawn to each other, in a sense, because unconsciously each sought to find in the other things they lacked within themselves. He envied her spontaneity. If he could not have it within himself, he would marry it. If she did not have an orderly, methodical, logical mind, then she would get it by marrying it. All of these decisions, of course, take place far below the level of consciousness.

Eventually, she became deeply depressed. They had begun to reach the time of life—the thirties and early forties—when frustration often begins to take its toll. It is at this point that genuine spiritual and emotional growth can take place. External challenges have been met, and now internal emotional needs present themselves with genuine force. Through counseling she came to understand herself somewhat better and thus was enabled to accept herself more fully. A course of reading and counseling helped her to discover unsuspected and untapped resources within. A few sessions with her husband helped him to understand himself and his wife. Theirs was not a serious marital problem. In their case it was simply a matter of understanding themselves better, learning to communicate more effectively, and pursuing a course of study and counseling.

One young couple, just beginning to experience the built-in frustration common to almost any marriage relationship, told their group how they had worked out some of their conflicts. He was rather passive, and his wife dominant, but both were seeking to correct this imbalance. At home they had talked about the fact that neither was having their expectations fulfilled. They agreed that they would each write out a list of what they expected from the other, and discuss it a week later. He said, "I could see her making notes all week long. I almost panicked when I thought of the reams and reams of things she would demand of me. I just knew I could never fulfill all of her needs and expectations."

He made some notes, too, during the week, and when the time came for the confrontation, they exchanged lists. The young husband said, "I was flabbergasted to discover that she had listed only four or five things. I had expected hundreds! I feel I can gradually learn to fulfill these needs of hers, and I know she feels competent to meet my list of expectations."

This was a creative form of communication, involving down-to-earth realism and honesty in revealing true feelings. They had learned this kind of honesty in a group experience with eight or ten others, meeting weekly to deal, not with intellectual concepts, but with feelings.

A fairly common irritant is found in the case of couples where one is an owl and the other a lark. One likes to sit up and watch the late, late show, and then sleeps late; the other wants to go to bed early and is up bright-eyed and cheerful at an early hour. "How do you resolve a basic conflict like this?" asked one frustrated couple.

I told them of the home owner who had written to a gardening authority asking what could be done about crab grass. He received the answer, "Learn to love it."

Properly interpreted, this is not too bad an answer. We must learn to accept a given problem before we can solve it. Acceptance does not imply liking, but rather, seeing the situation as a fact, without hostility. The problem of owls and larks is simply a basic personality, or metabolic, incompatibility. Hence, one must learn to live with it. Thousands of couples have. It involves raising the level of one's tolerance for frustration. There *are* human differences we must learn to live with. There are innumerable emotional incompatibilities in men and women. When one is faced with a problem of personal differences, obviously a compromise must be made. We cannot always bend others to our wishes. It is childish to assume that everyone should be "wired up" as we are, emotionally or temperamentally. Whether it is a matter of early rising, very late rising, going to church, which television show to watch, or personal preferences of any kind, one thing which always helps is to *raise the level of our tolerance to frustration.* Anything we do which makes us more tolerant of others is in the right direction. We are then more open to compromise solutions.

Our level of tolerance for frustration can be raised in a number of ways:

1. *By seeking physical and emotional well-being.* A young wife and mother joined one of our groups complaining of dizziness for which her physician could find no organic basis. She had lost interest in life, snapped at her husband and children, and appeared generally frustrated. We inquired into her daily routine and deduced that she was emotionally exhausted. Group members suggested that she get away from her home and children one day a week. Rather reluctantly and feeling somewhat guilty at first, she and a neighboring mother worked out an arrangement to take each other's children one day each week. Within two weeks or less she was feeling vastly better and able to cope with life.

Part of her cure came from sharing her bottled-up frustrations within the group. Finding a responsive, nonjudgmental group where she could share her feelings gave her immense relief. She became able to accept herself better when she discovered the total, unconditional acceptance of the group.

2. *By gaining new spiritual resources.* Man is made in the spiritual image of God, and to function properly he needs to seek the fellowship of the Creator. There is but one Mind, divine Mind, and we are each using as much of that Mind as we choose to appropriate. This Mind is universal, cosmic, divine. Jesus Christ was the supreme revelation of this Mind. "Let this mind be in you, which was also in Christ," is the admonition of the New Testament. When we tune in, through prayer and meditation, we are letting this Mind fill us and guide us. "It is God who is at work within you, seeking both to will and to do of his good pleasure" (Phil. 2:13).

One hour of worship a week was never intended to provide sufficient spiritual resources for us to maintain our spiritual, physical, and mental well-being. In addition to some form of public worship, many are discovering today the need for small fellowship groups where they can be open and honest and learn new techniques for meeting life's issues, through appropriating divine resources.

Another common irritant was brought into focus by a wife who complained that her husband was always late. "No matter what we plan to do, or how early we begin preparing to go someplace, he always finds something to do at the last minute. We always arrive at our destination from ten minutes to an hour late. What's the matter with him?"

Those who are compulsively late, or those who must always be early, are both basically insecure. In addition, the individual may be poorly organized. To complicate this problem still further, he may be unresponsive to the needs of others, so preoccupied with himself and his own interests that he simply disregards the well-being of others. This can be a holdover from childhood, an inability to accept adult responsibilities.

Such an individual sometimes is testing, as though to say, "If you really love me, you will put up with my behavior. How much will you *really* condone?" Occasionally we discover that a person who is compulsively late is sensitive to authority and perceives the need to be on time as a kind of abstract authority figure. He thus resists the authority of the clock and of appointments. Such an individual is usually overly sensitive to coercion and interprets any effort to get him to hurry up as an effort to control or coerce him. By resisting in some way he is unconsciously attempting to assert his autonomy.

Marriage does not resolve personal problems, and it is no cure for emotional ills. Marriage actually complicates the lives of people with emotional problems. It is rare that a marriage counselor or psychologist hears someone say, "I'm not fulfilling the needs of my marriage partner!" Almost invariably the complaint is to the effect that it is the other who needs help.

Basically, we cannot change another person, either by direct, overt action, or through manipulation. It may be possible to change the *actions* of another person through various means, but we never change them fundamentally by advice, correction, or criticism. In fact, criticism is perhaps the worst possible approach. All of us react negatively to criticism and tend to feel defensive. Frequently we counterattack.

If the lines of communication can be kept open, many issues can be resolved without a major crisis. However, it is not always easy to communicate. Men and women are simply on different wave lengths, and discussions often bog down in a welter of confusion. Part of the problem stems from the fact that men and women approach a problem from different points of view. This was illustrated by the comment of a prominent layman at a religious convention where delegates were voting on whether to permit women to vote in their assembly. A leading layman opposed granting votes to women delegates on the grounds that "if you challenge a man's idea, you challenge his opinion. If you challenge a woman's idea, you challenge *her*."

In essence, this is true. Women tend to take things personally. They run ideas and reactions through the fine mesh of their own emotions. They tend to live in a world of people and feelings, while men in general live in a realm of ideas and intellectual concepts. This does not in any sense disparage the intellectual capabilities of women. It is simply that men are more likely to attach importance to concepts and ideas than to feelings.

One of the values inherent in a small group experience is that women are enabled to discover how a man's mind works, and men learn some of the subtleties of the feminine makeup. A woman may discover that she is not married to an obstinate, obtuse, uncomprehending male with no concern for her well-being, but to a standard brand male, much like other men. Husbands often discover for the first time that their wives are not the overly emotional, illogical persons they had thought, but women whose minds operate on a different wave length.

All of us are on our best behavior during courtship and in the early days of marriage. A wife minimizes her husband's faults and magnifies his virtues during this period. He does the same with regard to her. Little by little the slow attrition of daily living wears off the romantic sheen. They become their real selves, and areas of immaturity begin to show up. Romantic love spurred each to be his best self, a self difficult to maintain in day-to-day living. When a wife feels insecure, her need for attention grows, but she may be less lovable at a time when she needs more love. She shows a side of her nature her husband has not seen before. His reaction may be one of rejection, hostility, or silent withdrawal. He may begin to stay away more, finding escape in work, recreation, or old friends. She can feel equally disappointed when his less-than-ideal self emerges.

A confused young couple came to see me about the sad state of their marriage. We discussed the symptoms at considerable length. There was evidence that he was beginning to retreat and that he would retreat into divorce if the situation could not be improved. Though his problems were as great as hers, she seemed to be the one who was "pushing red buttons," as he expressed it. I sensed her deep insecurity, amounting almost to panic. I decided to see her for a few sessions, since women normally tend to be more responsive and are usually more willing to accept responsibility for the emotional climate of the home.

The problems were not deep. There were simply some faulty techniques on the part of both. In her case, she was so much in need of reassurance and emotional support that she was pushing him right out of the home. Her approach was all wrong. I told her that the principle of Jesus, "Give and it will be given to you" (Mark 6:38), is a universal, cosmic law applicable to any situation. She was encouraged to start trying to meet his needs, rather than demand that he meet hers. Specifically she began to meet him at the door with a warm greeting instead of waiting for him to look her up. She sought for other ways in which she could give instead of asking, and worked at it diligently.

Within a month, she reported that he had given up his practice of spending a day or two away from home each week, and was far more attentive. "I've stopped pushing his red buttons," she said, "and started trying to meet his needs. Now he seems much more intent on trying to please me. This idea of giving works."

More than ninety percent of divorced men remarry. Approximately fifty percent of divorced women remarry. Divorced women are equally anxious to remarry, but the shortage of marriageable men makes it impossible for them to do so. Granted that there are situations where divorce appears to be the only solution to an intolerable situation, it behooves the wife in most instances to look into the principle enunciated by Jesus concerning giving. This does not imply that one should become a martyred doormat, but that she should seek a positive solution. Whining, self-pity, martyr-like tactics, and demands are all inappropriate devices. Few men stop drinking because of these tactics. In fact, lectures and threats usually produce the opposite effect. The same applies to almost any other male attitude which the wife finds objectionable.

A young, unmarried woman related to her group an experience at the office where she worked. During the coffee break all of her married friends told of the intolerable conditions at home. After listening for some months, she burst into tears, and said, "Look! You're all complaining, but I'll tell you what; I'll trade places with any one of you, and relieve you of your unhappiness. I'd break my neck to try to understand your husband and make him happy." There was a long, thoughtful silence. It was the last coffee break where the women shared their marital woes.

We begin marriage hoping for fulfillment, but often find frustration. Our own immature neurotic traits are magnified by the fact that the marriage partner had another set of neurotic tendencies. Instead of seeking fulfillment for ourselves, the primary goal should be to *fulfill the needs of one's partner*. It is thus that our own needs are met.

The fact that many "normal" persons marry for neurotic reasons is too well established a fact to require documentation. An illustration was found in the case of a lovely wife, the mother of several children. She was finding life intolerable with the man she had married, and we delved into the problem over a period of several months. It developed that her strict parents had wanted her to marry a non-drinking Protestant from a family with no foreign background.

He must be a college graduate with a future in some profession. She left home at an early age and married a moody Roman Catholic with a European background, a high-school dropout. He was also a bartender, and showed many signs of emotional immaturity.

I said, "Since you obviously are seeking my encouragement in getting a divorce, I'd like to ask you a question. Have you any idea why you married this particular man?"

She said, "I've asked myself that a thousand times. I wish I knew."

"Let's go back over your parents' concept of an ideal husband."

She thought for a moment. "He's exactly the opposite, isn't he?"

"Yes, But have you any idea why you unconsciously chose someone who is the precise opposite of what your parents had in mind?"

"Was I in rebellion against them? Punishing them?"

"Yes, and asserting your own sense of freedom and autonomy. You were saying to your parents, 'I reject your whole way of life, your rigidity, your demands, your control of my life.'"

"Then I married for totally neurotic reasons, didn't I?"

Her whole background was opposed to the idea of divorce. She eventually secured a divorce, however, after making a valiant attempt to build a creative relationship. She had spent fourteen years attempting the impossible: to achieve a workable marriage with an emotional and intellectual cripple.

No one believes in divorce as a happy solution, nor do I know of anyone who encourages the breaking of the marriage vows. But "Till death do us part" is a goal rather than a requirement, just as "You, therefore, must be perfect, as your heavenly Father is perfect" (Matthew 5:48) is a goal rather than an unbreakable requirement.

Every woman feels guilty over the breakup of her marriage, even when she is confident that she has done her best. She may know intellectually that she is not guilty, as when the husband becomes a hopeless alcoholic or a criminal; yet she still feels existentially guilty. There is a sense of "Where did I fail?" even when she knows that the blame is not exclusively hers.

A man facing divorce may feel a sense of devastation or anguish, or abandonment and rejection; but whatever mixture of feelings he may have, his devastation is seldom as deep as that of the woman involved. Occasionally a wife who has undergone years of frustration before securing a divorce may express a deep sense of relief that it is all over, but there is usually a sense of failure or guilt involved.

Many a marriage can be saved if both can learn to validate the feelings of the other. It is probably more important for the husband to learn this technique, since the male tends to deal in logical concepts rather than with feelings. A husband often feels vaguely uneasy and incompetent when confronted with the varied emotional states of his wife.

At work men are usually seeking solutions to problems. The male mind, confronted with a problem, automatically seeks to find a solution. The husband brings this into his marriage, and when his wife is upset, he instinctively tries to offer solutions, when usually she wants reassurance or simply to have her feelings validated.

A young wife said, "I was upset the other day, and my husband said, 'You shouldn't be that upset over such a minor issue.' He was telling me that I was childish, and I felt rejected. All I wanted him to say was, 'Honey, tell me all about it,' and then after I had spouted about it for ten minutes, he could have said, 'Yes, I can see why you'd feel that way.'"

She would have felt that he understood, at least. She didn't want answers or solutions. She simply wanted the reassurance and emotional support provided by an understanding, sympathetic husband. If husbands could grasp this simple fact, they would go far toward resolving many a marital crisis.

A mother with five children reported that she was constantly frustrated, tired, and irritable. Her work was never done and she took out her frustration on her husband. She read in an advice column that husbands need love and attention, too. The columnist's advice had been to "quit feeling sorry for yourself and concentrate on your husband. No matter how many complaints you have, keep them to yourself and find something to compliment him on. Kill him with kindness."

The wife reported that at times she had felt like killing her husband, and decided to do it with kindness. "It worked," she said. "At first it was a real effort, but pretty soon he was sweeter to me and it got easier to be kind to him." A happy marriage resulted.

In the thirteenth chapter of I Corinthians the Apostle Paul, in his magnificent description of love, includes these words, "Love never ends" (v. 8). One should never abandon hope of a happier marriage until the basic principles embodied in this chapter have been applied.

INCOMPATIBILITY

6   **IN**

MARRIAGE

> Marriage is like a besieged fortress. Those who
> are outside want to get in; while those who are
> inside want out.   *—Anonymous*

A woman who described her husband as dull and
uncommunicative sought my counsel about the matter of divorce. "My husband never reads anything, he
doesn't talk to me; he just sits and watches television.
My suggestions about doing things together are met
with a disinterested grunt. The prospect of living with
a man like this for the rest of my life appalls me.

"Then I met a man at work during the coffee break
who was able to communicate. He is a fascinating
conversationalist. We found that we had much in
common—an interest in music, books, sports. It began
in a perfectly innocent manner, and I never admitted
to myself for a long time that I was unconsciously
comparing him with my dull, unresponsive husband.
I was famished for some companionship, someone
to talk to; and one day when he suggested that we
might go to dinner together, I made some excuse to
my husband and met him at a restaurant. I had
nothing in mind except to enjoy his company for
the evening; but perhaps unconsciously I longed for
something more.

"Anyway, I met him several other times, and finally

it happened. I suppose it was inevitable, after I made the fatal initial mistake of meeting him for dinner. We discovered that we were in love with each other."

She was a Christian with the highest moral values, but in her loneliness and sense of isolation she had let herself become trapped in a situation which was now producing a sense of remorse and inner conflict. She wanted help and guidance. Should she try to revive some interest in the husband whom she had ceased to love and respect? She recoiled from the idea of spending the rest of her life with such a dull, unimaginative person; yet the prospect of renouncing her marriage vows and divorcing him created all manner of conflict within her.

There is, of course, no simple or painless solution to such a dilemma. If you button the first button of your coat wrong, all the others will be buttoned wrong as a consequence. There were many factors involved: her feeling that divorce was "wrong" and the pain of contemplating forty or fifty years of marriage with a man with whom she had virtually nothing in common and whom she no longer loved. And, would the other man, in whom she was interested, ultimately prove to have traits which she would find equally unacceptable?

Under the circumstances I counseled her to delay any decision. I told her that God was concerned about every aspect of her life—mental, physical, spiritual, emotional, and domestic, and that a biblical promise states, "In all thy ways acknowledge him, and he will direct thy paths." In the search for God's perfect will, which involves our highest happiness and well-being, we find our answers. Most of us, like children, want instant gratification, quick, easy answers, and ready-made solutions. God is concerned that we shall discover our true identity. He sorrows over our pain and disappointment, but lures us toward spiritual and emotional maturity. When we have achieved spiritual maturity we come to know, deep within, the answers to our questions. "...if any man's will is to do his will, he shall know..." (John 7:17).

I told her that if she would say to herself a dozen times a day, "I *want* to want the perfect will of God," in time she could know His will; that it would come as a gentle urging, a sense of oughtness, of rightness. However, we often need to check our sense of divine guidance with a trusted friend or competent counselor to make sure that we are hearing the voice of God and not simply the voice of our own selfish desires.

Subsequently, through private counseling and participation in a small group she discovered that she had certain personality traits which inevitably caused men to reject her in time. Gradually the truth dawned upon her that her husband had simply retreated from certain characteristics which he found objectionable. Using the group as a mirror, she saw herself clearly for the first time. Her formerly unresponsive husband began to respond to the change in her, and a successful marriage resulted.

At a four-day retreat session a man asked if we could take a walk together after one of the sessions. He was terribly depressed over his marriage and was considering divorce, which could mean the end of his professional life for a number of valid reasons.

He was intensely hostile toward his overly possessive wife and described in considerable detail how she dominated him and the entire family. The situation sounded hopeless. He could not imagine ever feeling the slightest affection for his wife again under any set of conditions.

He was a sensitive, rather passive individual, and he admitted that he had never talked his problem out with his wife nor shared his feelings with her. He agreed that this was necessary, whatever course of action he followed thereafter. A few days after he had arrived home, I received this letter from him:

The old witch I left at home isn't there any more! I simply told her what had happened to me, and how I was no longer afraid of her possessiveness. I told her that I felt as if I were being strangled by an octopus when she hugged me, and how she had gotten angry when I was embraced at the beach by a pretty girl whom we both knew. I told her how I had been loved, and had loved, many persons besides her, both men and women.

As we talked I found out some things about her I never knew. The woman who terrified me needs *me* to keep her from being afraid! Things are different! No tranquilizers, and no fear, no panic, just love!

A week later another letter came:

The miracles never end! The tiger is a pussy cat. She doesn't wear the pants in our house any more, and doesn't even want to. The atmosphere at our home has become so serene it is unbelievable. We are communicating with one another as we have never been able to before. . . . If you ever need a testimony to the effectiveness of small personal groups in dealing with emotional hurts, just let me know! I am a confirmed believer in miracles.

Love, Henry

There are many reasons for the breakup of marriages, but the most common one is never mentioned in divorce complaints: both of the marriage partners are waiting for the other to meet their needs.

Paul and Jennifer are a case in point. Paul was taciturn, placid, and unemotional until, as he put it, "She pushes my red button, then I go into a towering rage." Paul believed in keeping his feelings to himself, but Jennifer felt a great need for communication at a feeling level. She pleaded, reasoned, coaxed, and finally stormed at him in an effort to get him to express some feelings. He eventually agreed to join a small group where they could learn to communicate.

In one session she voiced her complaints, which were that he paid her little or no attention and seldom shared any of his feelings. He said, "I knew this was coming, and I have made some notes here which may explain why I seem aloof and disinterested in your needs. I, too, have needs. For instance, I told you last week that I would need to have dinner precisely at six o'clock so I could catch a plane. You had nothing to do all day except routine housework, but dinner was served at 6:25 p.m. You have a compulsion to be late when it concerns me, but I notice you are not late when you attend functions in which you are interested. A second incident concerns a similiar instance last Sunday. I told you that I had to leave immediately after church to get home in time for a conference with some men. It was an important conference which had to be held before Monday. Five men were waiting for me. But you delayed twenty minutes talking gaily to friends in the narthex of the church despite my insistence that I had to get home. At one point you said, 'Oh, be quiet!'

"The third instance has to do with your oft-repeated criticism of the way I keep the garage. It isn't neat and never will be. I have no interest in keeping it neat and orderly. I admit it is cluttered, and I intend for it to remain that way. I am not going to spend my life tidying up a garage. If you want it all neat and orderly, you are free to fix it up, but I have no interest in whether you do or not."

At this point Jennifer burst into tears. When she had regained her composure she said, "I remember fussing about the garage, but I have no recollection of the other incidents."

Paul said, "Of course not. You have an unconscious need to punish me in just those ways for my alleged failure to 'emote' when you want me to. Well, I'm 'emoting' right now. I'm just plain hostile."

Here was a clear-cut case of incompatible needs. Jennifer wanted a warm, responsive husband and had married a calm, unemotional man who was virtually incapable of dredging up his deeper feelings. She was demanding that he meet her needs by learning how to communicate at a feeling level.

120

Paul, on the other hand, was demanding that she meet his needs; however, because her needs were not being met, she had unconsciously tuned him out and failed to hear or remember his requests.

A situation like this can be satisfactorily resolved in two ways: through divorce, or by the husband and wife agreeing to stop making demands upon the other and concentrating their efforts on *meeting the needs of the other*. Selfishness cries, "Meet my needs! Love me! Love me even when I am unlovable, hysterical, or uncommunicative, or impossible." Love says, "Let me try to meet your needs. Tell me what it is that you want or need, and I will do my best to comply. If I cannot do so at the moment, I will explain why, as patiently as I can; but *I will try to meet your needs to the best of my ability*."

There are two basic needs which every individual possesses: to love and be loved, and to feel worthwhile. Anything we can do to meet these basic needs is an act of love. Failure to meet them results in heartache, disillusionment, despair, and often, divorce.

Studies have shown that in fifty percent of marriages, either the husband or wife commits adultery at least once. One out of every five wives is having an affair; the proportion of men is larger. Some of these marriages end in divorce, but the majority of them do not.

A husband who had been married for well over thirty years shared his feelings on the subject:

"My wife and I would be considered happily married, but for my part, I am not particularly happy. I don't think I have ever fully forgiven her for being unfaithful. I have tried hard to forgive her, and most of the time I think I have succeeded, but eventually the old feeling returns."

"What kind of feeling?" I asked.

"Well, just the feeling that I don't want too much to do with her, or more generally, a reluctance to have a close warm relationship."

"Have you discussed the matter of her unfaithfulness with her?"

"Yes, and of course she denied it, but I don't believe her. There was far too much evidence to the contrary. Besides the overwhelming evidence, there was a long period of time when she went to great pains to inform me of her goings and comings, though I never inquired, but she was simultaneously broadcasting a blatant furtiveness which belied her apparent openness about her activities. She overestimates her acting ability and underestimates my powers of observation. She has no idea how transparent she is."

"Could you be a little paranoid, overly suspicious?"

"I've given a lot of thought to that possibility, but I always run head-on into the evidence. She handles secretiveness very poorly. Her efforts at deception are almost ludicrous. Eventually I just lost interest, and I didn't care whether she was having an affair or not. This shocked me, that I didn't care anymore. We went on living as before; but if I were to come home and find her in a passionate embrace with some man, stranger or friend, it would not interest me one way or the other."

I asked, "Is your passivity standing in the way of resolving the barrier? Do you find it difficult to sit down and talk out your feelings with your wife?"

"Yes, to some extent I do. I've had a go at it a time or two, but we never get anywhere. She would never in a thousand years admit that she had done anything wrong. I could forgive her and go on as usual if she would be open and honest about it. As it is, we have a third- or fourth-rate marriage. I am not miserably unhappy, though I would greatly enjoy an open relationship in which there is nothing to hide. On her part, she is supremely happy. She has all of the material things a woman wants and a reasonably attentive husband. When we have one of the rare discussions touching on this painful subject, she wins the battle, but she lost the war long ago."

"How did she lose the war?"

"In that I no longer have any genuine interest in her except as a human being. I feel what might be called Christian love, but affection—no."

"What can I do to help in this situation?" I asked.

"You've already done it. You've listened, and I got rid of some of my pent-up hostility; you've listened to my confession of guilt feelings—guilt because I can't love my wife as I'd like to; guilt because we have nothing approximating communication besides, 'the grass needs mowing,' 'there are a lot of birds out today,' 'we'll have to get the bills paid in the next few days'—mundane things like that. But I feel better for having talked about it. Thanks."

This picture of a third- or four-rate marriage, by his evaluation, is typical of many marriages. Change the scenery slightly, alter the details a bit, and you have a picture of millions of marriages which appear serene on the outside, but are lacking the basic ingredients of a truly satisfactory marriage.

Husbands and wives have affairs for any number of reasons. There are both men and women who feel that they must have the approval, the love, and the conquest of others in order to reassure themselves that they are attractive. The triumph gives them a temporary gratification.

A wife who thinks her husband is carrying on an illicit romance may be tempted to retaliate, to prove to herself that she has not lost her appeal. A man may be motivated by the same drive.

An oft-neglected area of this matter of illicit romance concerns the need for consequent self-punishment. Persons with a well-developed conscience will find some way to punish themselves for wrongdoing. Self-punishment is a wholly unconscious process and may take the form accident-proneness, failure-proneness, or a tendency toward physical or emotional symptoms. Obviously there are many other reasons for masochism, the term for self-punishment or unconscious need to expiate guilt through illness or disaster.

Many automobile accidents are undeniably related to an unconscious need on the part of the individual to seek punishment for wrongdoing. No one knows why one person unconsciously chooses an accident, while another becomes physically or emotionally ill as a form of self-punishment, but the evidence is incontrovertible. We do tend to punish ourselves in some way for our misdeeds. Sometimes one big accident, or a succession of minor ones, or a rash of minor illnesses will suffice to cause the inner judicial system to feel that the sin has been "paid for," at least temporarily.

The Christian, who believes that sins have been atoned for, and who can accept at a deep feeling level the forgiveness of God, will not experience any unconscious need for self-punishment; but unfortunately, what the mind believes, the soul does not always receive. I have observed an incredible number of situations in which staunch believers endured years of self-punishment for unresolved guilt. The individual knows he has been forgiven by God, but he cannot forgive himself and consequently feels an inner need to expiate his guilt through self-punishment.

Debra came to see me about her marital situation. She was young, attractive, and vivacious. She described her husband as intelligent, ambitious, thoughtful, but uninteresting. At least, he now appeared uninteresting when she compared him with the man with whom she had fallen in love.

The "other man," whom we will call Gilbert, was thirty years older than she, but she described him as being the fulfillment of all her dreams. Of course we delved into her relationship with her father, but at this point she was emotionally uninterested in anything other than finding a way to leave her husband without hurting him, and marrying Gilbert without hurting his wife! There were seven children involved in the two families. This passionate love affair had been going on for several years. At our counseling sessions it became apparent to her that the only possible solution was for her to break off the illicit relationship and try to rebuild her own marriage. However, Debra could not accept this course emotionally, and she stopped coming to see me.

Six months later she phoned for an appointment. I was scarcely prepared for the change in her. She looked haggard and worn and had lost much of her charm and vitality. She was obviously on the verge of an emotional crackup. In our discussion I went over the options which we had discussed before. Among other things I said, "With your moral convictions and Christian background, if you do leave your husband and children, I think it is a foregone conclusion that you will find some way to punish yourself. You will either have an emotional breakdown, become accident-prone, or find some other way to punish yourself."

She looked startled, "I've just completely wrecked our car in an accident, I feel right now as if I were ready for a mental hospital."

I said, "If you want out of your conflict, if you want to survive, then the only way is for you to break off this relationship. I know it will be painful, but it is your only hope."

She brought Gilbert in the following week, and I told him much the same thing—that the relationship was destroying Debra, and if he loved her, he would have to give her up. It was a painful hour for both of them, but eventually he agreed that he would not try to see her again; Debra agreed, through her tears, that in order to survive she would have to give him up.

At this point I could not have reached her with an appeal to her moral and spiritual values. She could hear me intellectually, but her emotional need for a father figure-lover was so great that she was out of contact with her lifelong moral values. That the love sprang from a neurotic need was beside the point, as far as she was concerned. She was trying to find her father, and Gilbert was trying to recapture his youth.

Many a woman endures untold anguish when she discovers that she is married to an alcoholic. Usually such a wife is torn between the desire to help her husband resolve his problem and save the marriage, and the knowledge that the task is virtually hopeless. Only a small percentage of problem drinkers can admit that they are alcoholics. The alcoholic has a vested interest in preserving the myth that he can take or leave his liquor. I have known men who were drunk virtually every day for ten or twenty years who refused to face the fact that they were alcoholics and needed help. Experience and the findings of Alcoholics Anonymous reveal that an alcoholic can never be helped unless he is willing to take that first all-important step: to admit that he is an alcoholic and is powerless to save himself. The next step, of course, is to seek help from Alcoholics Anonymous or some other available resource.

Scolding, nagging, advice, tears, recrimination, threats—all these are worse than wasted on the alcoholic. He is actually powerless to help himself. Alcoholism is not his basic problem, but rather it is a symptom of a serious emotional and spiritual difficulty. Even if, by some miraculous exertion of will power he were able to stop drinking on his own, he still retains the personality problem which drove him to alcohol in the first place. Alcoholics are basically passive, dependent individuals with deep feelings of inferiority and guilt. Lectures and threats simply compound their sense of guilt. A woman married to an alcoholic can normally expect a solution only if her husband decides to join AA and attends regularly. There are exceptions, but they are rare.

In many cases a woman marries a man with alcoholic tendencies partly because of his gentleness and passivity. The gentleness usually vanishes when he comes home drunk. When he sobers up, is "himself" again, and promises he will never get drunk again, she feels temporarily encouraged. When it happens again and again, she is then faced with the need to extricate herself from an intolerable situation, which means abandoning her husband, which makes her feel guilty. Or, she can remain and take his abuse or neglect. Neither alternative is particularly alluring. It is an axiom that an alcoholic will never seek help until he has "hit bottom," which for some is the loss of his job; for others, it is the loss of home and friends; for others, it is the loss of health. Each person has a different "bottom."

The wife of an alcoholic has these alternatives:

1. She can stay with him, endure the abuse and deprivation, criticize and lecture him, and rest assured that the chances for a cure under these circumstances are minimal. Such a woman usually is strongly masochistic.

2. She can make it clear that unless he seeks such help as is offered by Alcoholics Anonymous, or professional help, and stays with it, she is leaving. It must not be in the nature of a threat, but a simple announcement, and she must make good on it.

3. She can go on living with him and resolve her own personal problems. Emily did this in a remarkable way. She spent several years in a therapy group trying to discover her real identity. She found that she was, to use her own terms, "West Coast distributor for masochism, a first rate injustice collector." She discovered that she had married initially out of an unconscious need to be punished. In the course of her own spiritual rebirth she gained sufficient emotional strength so that she could say, "Whether he makes it or not is not my basic problem. I pray that he will. But I am going to survive whether he does or not. I do not nag him anymore; most of the

time I manage not react to his abuse when he is drunk." She had become a strong, self-reliant person who chose to go on living with her alcoholic husband, but not out of any unconscious need for punishment, or in the vain hope of saving him herself.

No one "believes in divorce" in the sense of encouraging it, any more than one believes in the desirability of disease, yet there are obviously instances in which divorce is the only alternative to an intolerable situation.

Hazel was the wife of a man who was possessed of charm and intelligence. She discovered one day that he was having a serious affair with a woman in the neighborhood. She forgave him and resolved never to mention the episode again. In the next ten years he had nine other affairs with different women. The various love affairs were an effort to prove to himself that he was desirable and masculine. After ten years, during which time her husband experienced at least two psychotic episodes, Hazel filed for divorce. She did so only after she had given him every chance to change and after she had exhausted every possible solution to the problem.

A wife came to see me in an effort to resolve the problem confronting her. She was married to a man with no interests outside his work. They had little or nothing in common. "I'm not even sure that I loved him when we were married," she said, "but of course I thought I was in love." Now, ten years and four children later, she had told him she wanted a divorce. He was astounded. So far as he knew, theirs was a happy marriage. She was not in the least interested in trying to work out a reconciliation. She had no love for him and wanted nothing to do with him. She hated to hurt him and agonized over the fact that she was depriving her children of a father. It was nothing that he did. It was, she said, simply that she married a man she had never loved and had just now admitted it to herself. This is one of those tragedies in which everyone involved is deeply hurt, for which there appears no immediate solution.

Studies have shown that approximately fifty percent of all adult males between the ages of twenty-one and fifty either are or have been sexually permissive at one time or another. The promiscuity of the unmarried male is only slightly higher than that of the married male.

It will be even more shocking for some to discover that thirty-four percent of all adult women between the ages of eighteen and forty-five have been or are sexually permissive.

A woman usually gives the explanation that she "was in love" and refuses to admit that she is sexually permissive, whereas the man will generally admit that he is. The United Nations Congress on the Prevention of Crime and the Treatment of Offenders points out that sexually promiscuous women generally fall into two categories. The first type feels an unconscious hostility toward the opposite sex and seeks through sexual relations to "conquer" the male and discharge her hostility, while at the same time convincing herself of her desirability. The second type, the report points out, is masochistic and "allows" herself to be seduced, then wallows in her own guilt and suffering.

There are other variables, however. Some overly permissive women are unconsciously seeking the love denied them in their homes as children. A succession of illicit romances, however, never succeeds in alleviating permanently the pain of having received too little love in childhood. Such a woman needs to learn how to give and receive mature love. She must learn to accept herself, to like herself, to love herself properly. She cannot do so easily or quickly, but it can be accomplished with patience.

It can be stated dogmatically that the woman who flaunts her sexuality, the sexually permissive woman, and the nymphomaniac, are unconsciously hostile to men, and at the same time doubt their own femininity. The same holds true for the man who indulges in a succession of sexual adventures and experiences a need to conquer women. He has serious doubts about his masculinity, which is temporarily assuaged after a conquest. Such people are emotional and spiritual cripples and in need of help. To reject them as "immoral" or consider them outcasts is to run counter to the example of Jesus, whose associates included just such people. To one He said, "Neither do I condemn you, go, and do not sin again" (John 8:11). Of another He said, "Her sins, which are many, are forgiven" (Luke 7:47).

Each situation differs, but there are many instances in which a husband or wife has engaged in extra-marital affairs because the marriage partner was either too possessive or indifferent. A woman who feels unloved or taken for granted can be rendered more susceptible to the charms of some man who, for his part, may feel smothered at home by a possessive wife.

In one of those rare instances of a husband and wife coming together for an initial counseling session, the husband complained that his young wife seemed to be emotionally immature. "She bursts into tears if she can't have her own way; she will fly out of the house and race around town in the car until three in the morning, then come home and weep; or she threatens to leave me and go home to her mother."

Her complaints were that he disappeared for long weekends without telling her where he was going and without ever inviting her to go along.

After seeing them separately a time or two, I began to see the wife at regular weekly intervals. Far from being the emotional mess I had expected, she proved to be a highly intelligent young woman who simply did not know any other way of getting her husband's attention. There were no deep emotional scars, and I proceeded to give her some pertinent advice on how to live with a man. I said, "You are driving him out of his mind, and possibly out of your life, with these tantrums and threats." Acknowledging that he had an equal responsibility to keep their marriage intact, I pointed out that a wife has more to gain from a good marriage, and more to lose from a bad one. She was to take the initiative. I urged her to meet him at the door with a kiss; to find ways to please him instead of nagging him. "If you ever succeed in changing him," I said, "it will be done with love, not threats and demands."

Within less than a month she reported that their life was much better, and it continued to get better. Eventually she reported that theirs could not be a happier relationship. She had simply stopped making demands and had started expressing love in ways that her husband could understand.

The solution is not always that simple. Sometimes there are emotional scars originating in childhood, traumatic events which have left their mark in terms of neurotic behavior patterns. Some of these situations can be resolved only through intensive counseling.

Women who try to make over their husbands, or husbands who attempt to change their wives, are doomed to disappointment. By the time an individual has reached marriageable age, personality patterns are formed. Surface changes can be effected; some basic attitudes can be altered, but the basic personality will remain much the same. However, virtually any marriage can be radically improved if both husband and wife are determined to work at it.

For instance, a young couple consulted me about a marital problem, which, on the surface, seemed relatively minor, yet it appeared to be threatening the whole marriage. She felt that they were living beyond their means, in a neighborhood that was "too good" for them, and that he refused to communicate. She also insisted that he was not handling their money wisely. He had no particular complaint except that she made him feel guilty when he bought a new stereo or a tape recorder.

As they talked in my study, I discovered that for the first time they were able to express their true feelings to each other. She had grown up in a poor section of town and had a "poverty complex"; she was feeling guilty about living in a home which they could well afford. It further developed that they could easily afford the items her husband was buying for himself and for the home.

"But we need things for the children instead of these luxuries," she said. He looked surprised. "Then buy them. I've told you a dozen times to get anything you want. You know where the checkbook is." She looked shocked. "I guess I never heard you," she said. Her poverty complex had rendered her literally deaf to his insistence that she could buy anything she needed within reason.

His lack of ability to communicate posed somewhat of a problem, for he had learned to control all of his emotions. His wife said, "I never know whether he is happy or sad, thrilled or disgusted. I don't think I even know him, because he never displays any emotion."

He began to see that a happy marriage involves the exchange of feelings as well as ideas, and that in bottling up all of his feelings, he was shutting her out of his life. He agreed to work on this problem, through counseling and otherwise, and she began the task of ridding herself of her lifelong poverty complex. It will take time, but the fact that both are working at it makes it almost a certainty that they can work out a highly satisfactory marriage. She had feared that their lack of communication and divergent views of how to spend money would wreck their marriage. Their problems were actually minor once they could be brought out into the open.

I had supposed that Carolyn and Jack were happily

married. He was a likeable, successful professional man in his early thirties. She was sweet, quiet, rather passive. They had several children and to all intents and purposes appeared to have a better than average marriage.

One day, out of the blue, he told Carolyn that he was in love with a young divorcee, whom he planned to marry. He wanted a divorce. There were no recriminations or complaints of any kind. It was simply that he had fallen in love with someone else. He was deeply grieved over the situation and the pain it caused her. They discussed frankly what the divorce would do to her and to the children, but the inescapable fact remained that he wanted to marry the other woman. No man can possibly imagine how lonely a woman feels when she has been abandoned by the man she loves. She was devastated.

Carolyn came to see me a number of times, and on the third visit I sensed through her anguished bewilderment a new quality she had not demonstrated before. It was an unsuspected strength neither she nor I knew that she possessed. The "little girl" quality in her was being superseded by a maturity forged out of pain and determination. She had been more hurt than angry, for she was not a hostile person. She could not find it in her heart to condemn him, even when he moved out of the house and proceeded with his plans for a divorce. Nor did she attack or criticize the other woman. She gradually became a new person, determined to face life on her own if she had to, to endure the breakup of her home if necessary, but at the same time she showed remarkable poise and strength when she talked to Jack about what he was doing to himself, to her, and to the children. It has often been said that we make no significant change in personality except as the result of stress or suffering. This truth was evident in the case of Carolyn and Jack.

Through months of painful discussion Carolyn began to discover that unconsciously Jack had been needing a wife who was not a passive little girl-wife, but a stronger, more self-assertive type of person. She gradually became this kind of a person as the result of their struggle to find an answer. Eventually Jack began to weaken in his determination to secure a divorce. Within a year or less he was back home, and a delightful new chapter in their lives began. Theirs is now a far better marriage than before, for both have changed. It would be difficult to pinpoint the moment when the change began to take place, or what brought about the reconciliation except that through counseling and the establishing of a deeper level of communication, some dramatic growth took place in both of them.

7

ALMOST ANY
MARRIAGE CAN
BE IMPROVED

> There is little less trouble in governing a private
> family than a whole kingdom.   —*Montaigne*

There are undoubtedly some marriages which were
doomed from the start. There are individuals whose
basic personalities are so fixed and rigid, or whose
behavior patterns are so neurotic, that it is difficult
to imagine their achieving a satisfactory marriage
relationship with anyone.

But nearly all marriages can be improved, and the
vast majority of divorces could be prevented by an
appropriate course of counseling or group therapy.
Those who expect marriage to solve their personality
problems are hopelessly unrealistic. In fact, marriage
intensifies neurotic tendencies.

One problem encountered in marriage is that of
defining "spheres of influence." There are many variables, of course, but in a typical home the wife may
have the final responsibility for the house, furniture,
gardening, cooking, and the day to day responsibility of the children. In areas which represent the
"nest" she will usually want to express her own taste
in the furnishings of the home, but she will want
her husband's approval. If he shows relative indif-
ference, she perceives this as a rejection of her, since
the home is an extension of her personality. If he is

insistent upon making final decisions in matters pertaining to the selection of furniture or other details of the home, his wife will feel a loss of identity. She will become either hostile or frustrated. If she represses her anger, she may tend to become depressed.

A young couple, discussing their wedding plans with me, mentioned the fact that they had already selected their furniture. I asked how they arrived at the decision to purchase the particular style of furniture they had chosen. She was a gentle, quiet, nonassertive type of individual and deferred to him consistently. He, somewhat more aggressive, said, "Well, the kind of furniture she wanted would have been nice, but I held out for something more durable. We finally settled on a sturdy type that will stand up through the years." I asked her if she was happy with the selection. She insisted that it was quite acceptable with her, and I think it was—at that particular moment. She was deeply in love and had the instinctive feminine desire to please her husband.

But she will spend a great deal more time looking at that furniture than her practical husband will, and every time she dusts it she will remember that it was his choice, not hers; in time, whether she admits it to consciousness or not, she will detest the sturdy furniture which he picked out. She will take out her frustration on him, either in some direct or subtle manner, or if she is masochistic, she will turn her hostility inward and suffer from some physical or emotional symptom.

I said to them, "You will find greater happiness if you discover various 'spheres of influence.' For instance, if the wife can have the veto power around the house, and the husband can exercise his veto power in areas pertaining to his job, the car, and finances, you may have less conflict. These areas will vary from couple to couple, but we should avoid imposing our opinions on each other in too many areas."

A woman who is deprived of the right to exercise

her own judgment in matters pertaining to her home can experience a definite loss of identity. It is not so important whether her taste or his is better. She should have the final say-so about the areas of the home which seem of vital importance to her. This may include the gardening, if she enjoys it. In one home, the husband loved gardening, and his wife was only too happy to have him assume total responsibility for the yard. She rejoiced in his love of flowers, and she did not feel that this was an intrusion into her domain.

I have never particularly liked gardening. In fact, I despise it; but for some perverse reason, perhaps involving some subtle form of masochism, I kept at it for the first twenty years or so of marriage. One day I suddenly realized how utterly stupid it was of me to do the gardening when I hated every minute of it. I told my wife, "You're in charge of gardening hereafter. You can do it yourself, since you enjoy some aspects of it, or you can hire it done. I've just graduated. It is an extension of the house, and it's all yours."

And it has been so ever since. We did not arrive at the decision through lengthy discussion. It was a unilateral decision, but of course I knew that she would not find it unacceptable, She was quite content to take over this added responsibility.

Earning a living is the fundamental responsibility of the husband, even though in our present culture millions of women work in order to supplement the family income, or because they desire some activity outside the home. When a married woman takes a job, however, it is seldom an end in itself, but a means to an end. She may want to help pay off the mortgage, or save for the children's education, or buy some additional furniture.

Since the financial end of the marriage is primarily, if not exclusively, a male responsibility, it is usually the husband who handles the finances. There are husbands who are good at it, and others who do a horrible job. I find wives who feel superior to their husbands in this area, and who set up a rigid budget, allocating a precise amount for their husbands to spend for lunch, recreation, and personal expenses. One such wife, who was actually more practical in the handling of money, came to see that her husband was feeling emasculated. He had tentatively suggested a number of times, that he take back the checkbook, but his sloppy performance in the past caused her some hesitation. She asked, "Should I let him take it back?"

I said, "You sound like mother asking if she should let junior take out the family car. If he wants to try it again, why should he have to ask you? Are you playing the mother role and he the little boy role?"

Rather hesitantly she handed him the checkbook a few days later and said, "I'm tired of this mess. Why don't you take it over?" She put the checkbook and the bills on his dresser. He took them rather casually and proceeded to do thereafter a creditable job, except that he would occasionally let some bills run two months or more.

His wife asked, "What shall I do if he keeps on letting bills go like that? It may ruin our credit."

"How will you ever find out if you don't keep your hands off and let him worry about it? If his education in this area has been neglected, he may as well learn how to go about becoming a responsible male. However," I said, "if the time ever comes when he makes a mess and actually wants to take over this responsibility, and you do it at his request, that will be another matter."

In one home with several children, there was a certain amount of wrangling over whether disciplinary measures were too severe. In a typical incident, the mother had sent one of the teen-age children to her room. She appealed tearfully to her father whom she thought would support her. He said, "Honey, I think perhaps mother was a bit hard on

138

you, but that's her ruling. You'll have to do as she says. There's nothing I intend doing about her decisions." A short time later mother cooled off and called the daughter to come down and join the family. All was serene.

Similarly, when the father issued some seemingly overly stern mandate, and the children appealed to the mother for sympathy and support, her response was that it was Daddy's ruling and they would have to work it out with him. This type of approach prevented the playing of one parent against the other. Sometimes a child will take advantage of an unresolved conflict between mother and father. If there is some smoldering resentment present, a child can appeal to one of the parents and get support, which in a sense is one parent's way of striking back at the other.

There are innumerable sources of conflict in a typical marriage, but the common denominator in working out a satisfactory relationship between the marriage partners is for both to seek spiritual and emotional maturity. In the achieving of this goal there are certain basic assumptions which must be dealt with:

First, no one person can satisfy all of one's needs. Each of us is a many-faceted person, and to expect some other individual to match each mood, satisfy every demand, and fulfill all of one's needs, is simply unrealistic. Every individual is different, and one's needs differ from day to day and week to week. In addition, the inescapable differences of the sexes compound the problem.

Our basic human self-centeredness is responsible for the fact that we keep hoping that the marriage partner will perceive our emotional needs, perhaps by extrasensory perception, and unselfishly set out to meet them. The inner child, always in residence within us, waits expectantly for the perfect fulfillment of all our dreams.

The only possible approach to this innate egocentricity of ours is to apply literally the formula of Jesus: "Give, and it shall be given unto you" (Luke 6:38). Instead of demanding, or expecting, that another will fulfill our needs, we must become mature enough to ask, "How can I discover and satisfy the needs of my partner?" If some of them are unrealistic or selfish or childish, then at this point one may say, "This is a need of yours which I cannot, in all good conscience, fulfill." There need be no explosion (though such an explosion is not necessarily fatal).

The beautiful young wife of a struggling young husband had always dreamed of the home she would have someday. It would be spacious, filled with lovely furniture, and surrounded by a rolling lawn. Her adolescent dreams of entertaining in this beautiful home were all shattered when they moved into their first home—a tiny, cramped one-bedroom house. Her tears flowed for months. "This isn't the way I had thought it would be at all," she cried over and over. She turned her frustration and anger upon her husband. When, in a counseling session, I pointed out that her dreams could not be realized for some years, she vented her hostility upon me. One would have thought that the young husband and I had conspired to frustrate all of her dreams and aspirations. We had wrecked her doll house. It took three or four years for her to grow up emotionally and discover that her childish dreams could not be fulfilled by a magic wand or a marriage ceremony. In time she became a poised, emotionally mature young woman, accepting the realities of life, willing to abandon her unrealistic adolescent fantasies.

I had occasion to counsel with another young couple concerning some of their marital problems. In this instance the husband had never grown up completely. He had been reared in a home where nothing was demanded of him. He had never done any yard work or assumed any family responsibilities. It was not that he was selfish. It was simply that no one had ever required anything of him. Now the marriage was foundering, and we were able to trace many of their disagreements to the fact that Charles refused to do anything around the house. He had agreed to put up some coat hangers in the hall closet months before, but had forgotten to. To a woman, neglect of the home is neglect of her as a person. The home is an extension of her own personality. His wife was outraged that he cared so little for her that he would not remember to put up the coat hangers.

His wife could easily have put them up, but she wanted him involved. Refusal to accept household responsibilities was evidence to her that he did not care about her. Gradually it dawned upon Charles that he had been pampered as a child and that his responsibility as a husband involved more than earning a living.

The second basic assumption is that in the marriage relationship, instead of waiting for our needs to be met, we must seek to meet the needs of the other. The more emotionally mature we are, the fewer demands we make upon others, and the more capable we are of being concerned about others and their needs.

The proper question to ask is not, "How can I have all of my needs fulfilled in this marriage?" but "How much love can I express in meeting the needs of this person I married?"

Individuals differ in their needs. To one husband the way his shirts are ironed is a matter of major importance. To another this is trivial, but it is important to him that his wife not show up at the table looking as if she were all set to haunt houses. One husband enjoyed his wife's extraordinarily fine cooking but never wanted to eat the same thing twice. Another man complained that his wife, who was an excellent cook, had such a mania for variety that he could never get her to cook the same dish twice. Still another husband was relatively indifferent to food and seldom knew what he was eating.

One husband feels a need to go into the kitchen and greet his wife affectionately when he returns from work, but his wife, harried with cooking and children, usually brushes him off with, "Oh, Henry, not now. Can't you see I'm busy?" She is trying to meet his needs by preparing an elaborate meal, when what he really wants more than a good meal is affection. She is giving him what she *thinks* he wants without being sensitive to his actual needs.

A perceptive wife, anxious to express love by meeting the needs of her husband, will try to discover whether she has grown up with some misconceptions about male needs. Just because her father was indifferent to whether meals were served on time does not mean that her husband is wired the same way. The needs of human beings vary enormously. It behooves a wife to become sensitive to her husband's needs and seek to meet them within the limits of her capabilities.

A wife has the primary responsibility for the "climate" in the home. This is true partly because women are more innately sensitive to persons and their needs, and partly because the home means more to the wife than it does to her husband. A woman has much more to gain from a good marriage and more to lose from a bad one. She may resent this fact, but it is still an inescapable fact of life. It therefore behooves her to make a career of trying to discover ways to please her husband. Women have a built-in need to please, to serve, to minister to the needs of others. Unless a woman is still immature and childish, she will want to discover ways of gratifying her husband's desires.

Along with this she has an equal need to be loved, cherished, protected. She finds her security in feeling that her husband cares about her, is concerned for her welfare and happiness. In fact, at an unconscious level many women—perhaps most—actually invent ways of discovering whether their husbands actually care deeply about them. Their deep insecurity requires constant reassurance.

A husband, whose primary responsibility is to provide for the financial welfare of the family, may come home from work with his physical and psychic energy depleted, to find that his wife has a list of things she wants to talk about. She may have accumulated a number of tasks for him to do around the house; or she is sick unto death of having children underfoot all day, and wants to turn them over to him. Now they are in trouble! They have incompatible needs. She wants his help in taking care of the children; or she wants adult conversation, and he is too tired to be concerned for the moment about her needs. As man and woman they are basically incompatible in many areas to begin with, and now their momentary incompatibility has compounded this problem.

The general formula to be applied in this, or any similar impasse, is: don't expect too much of the persons around you, whether they be in-laws, children, or marriage partner. But if there are obvious things which you have a right to expect of others, the approach is all-important. A half-hostile, half-demanding manner is much less likely to get results than a gentle approach. A man is much more likely to yield to a gentle, seductive tone than to the "I'm fed up to here with these kids. You take over!" type of approach.

One young wife, whose marriage was, as she put it, "coming apart at the seams," discussed her hostility over the fact that her husband never assumed any responsibility around the house. The facts which finally emerged were these:

He was worried about his job, which he felt was threatened. He spent two hours a day commuting, eight hours on the job, and came home to brood about his worries, expecting affection and sympathy. As he put it, "She has one child and a small house to take care of. She can get out during the day and visit her friends when she wants to, or go shopping, and maybe squeeze in an hour or so of television if she feels like it. I have my nose to the grindstone eight full hours a day. I resent entering the door and being met with a barrage of complaints."

She countered with the complaint that he came home grumpy, seldom discussed anything with her, and refused any responsibility around the home. In reaction, she had become nervous and emotionally distraught. She could express no affection of any sort, for she felt unloved and neglected. Partly to escape from her complaints he was taking weekend fishing trips which caused her to feel still more neglected.

Not because she was any more to blame than he, but because she was more susceptible to change, I met with her weekly for several months. We agreed on a number of things which she could do to improve their marriage. I assured her that if she would take these steps, he would respond as soon as he found that she had actually changed.

She began to meet him at the door with a kiss instead of complaints. Instead of making demands or requiring an explanation as to where he went when he was away, she accepted him as he was. Rather than using tears to manipulate him, she began asking him what she could do to make him happy. She was an eager, intelligent young woman, and not once in our counseling did she ever resort to the "Yes, but—" habit. Within a few short months they had worked out a delightful marriage relationship. It was possible because the wife was willing to accept sole responsibility for initiating some changes in her own personality. Women are less obtuse in many ways and thus better equipped to initiate changes in the marriage relationship.

But men have responsibilities for the marriage, too. If the wife most often must take the initiative in improving the marriage, the husband bears an equal responsibility in responding to change in his wife's altered approach.

A typical wife with the usual number of standard complaints about an unresponsive husband joined a group of eight persons who were seeking solutions to various kinds of problems. She was told, upon entering the group, that we did not confess the faults of others. We were to share only our own deficiencies. She reported at one group session that her husband had said one evening after she returned home:

"Well, I suppose you gave them all the details about what a rotten husband I am."

She said, "No, on the contrary, we're not allowed to confess the sins of others. We just talk about what we can do to improve ourselves."

He made no comment. A few months later, when it became obvious to him that she was making a valiant attempt to correct some of her own faults, he said, "I suppose you'll be wanting me to join one of those groups."

She said, "No, that isn't my responsibility."

"You mean you don't want me in the group?"

"Oh, I suppose you could join a group if you wanted to, but it's purely voluntary."

A month or so later he said, "I might visit one of these stupid groups and see what goes on."

"No, they won't permit visitors. You have to join for at least three months."

"Are there other husbands in some of the groups?"

"Yes, quite a number."

"Whom do I talk to about joining a group?"

She told him, and rather hesitantly he asked to join a group. Before the first session was over, he was participating freely. At the end, he said, "I had actually intended to make this a one-night stand, but I've enjoyed it. There ought to be more places where people can be themselves and learn how to be honest. I'm going to keep coming."

In a group session a woman quoted, in a facetious vein: "He took it like a man—he blamed it on his wife." Actually there is an almost universal tendency to blame someone else for our problems. It began in the Garden of Eden, when God asked Adam about eating of the forbidden fruit. He said, "The woman . . . gave me the fruit of the tree, and I ate." Eve, unwilling to accept her guilt, said, "The serpent beguiled me" (Gen. 3:12, 13). Perhaps if the serpent could have been queried, he might have said, "My environment made me this way." Most of us are born buck-passers. We begin to achieve a measure of maturity only when we cease to blame others and accept the responsibility for change within ourselves.

There is a Negro spiritual which expresses a great truth:

'Tain't my brother nor my sister,
But it's me, O Lord, standing in the need of prayer.

The basic physical and emotional differences between men and women are great. Future generations may well read with astonishment that young people were once permitted to marry without a year or two of intensive study of the complexities involved in this, the most important of all human relationships. A man, for instance, can never know what it feels like to be pregnant, to nurse a baby, to experience the up and down moods that accompany the feminine cycle. No man can fully comprehend how a woman's inner calendar affects her moods and her consequent responses to him. Women in general rate higher on "nurturing," the desire to provide loving care for others. Men are generally more competitive and aggressive; even if they are not innately so, our culture tends to fit them into this mold. Men are usually less able to express their feelings and are often unaware of some of their deeper emotions. Consequently they can be uncomprehending or impatient with the more volatile emotions of their wives.

Neither sex fully understands the other. We view each other through a lattice of our own physical and emotional responses, expecting our varying emotional needs to be understood and met even though we may not be able to express them.

It is precisely at this point that communication becomes so vitally important. Communication is not "just talking." It involves the willingness and capacity to express our feelings to each other. Such feelings may not always be positive. Often they will be negative, involving anger or hurt or disappointment.

A common barrier to communication between husband and wife is the instinctive tendency to blame and attack. In a group session in which a husband and wife participated, the wife expressed dissatisfaction with her husband's inability to communicate. "He comes home, reads the paper until dinner time, gulps his food, then plants himself in front of the television set. He never takes me anywhere, never reads a book, never talks to me."

Her husband was showing signs of growing tension, which he sought to control. He was playing the strong, silent, uncomplaining role for the moment. He forced a grin, as his wife finished her tirade. "Yeah, that's the kind of bum I am, I guess. I never was much for talking. I'm tired at night, and I suppose I'm not a very good husband."

One of the men said, "Hank, you make me tired. Your wife has done nine-tenths of the talking since you two joined the group. She has berated you, downgraded you, condemned you on a dozen counts, and you just sit there absorbing all this punishment as though you deserved it. Maybe you do, in part, but you can't be the hopeless person she makes you out to be. Why don't you defend yourself? Wouldn't your mother ever let you talk back? Were you terrified of your mother, and now of your wife? For heaven's sake, stand up to this woman! She has a grievance, but you must have some of your own!"

147

Hank looked thoughtful. "You mentioned my mother. She was a pretty stern person, but she loved us all. I can't recall ever getting mad, or at least I never showed it. It wasn't allowed at our house. Mom and Dad didn't talk much between themselves, and I guess I just became a silent person in order to stay out of trouble. I've never had a verbal battle with anyone in my life, and I don't feel disposed to start at this late date. My wife will either have to get used to my silence or get another husband, I guess." He paused and looked grim for a moment. "And I just now realized for the first time that I don't care much which she does. I've about had it."

The group leader interrupted at this point and said, "I think we'll go into a role play session, with Hank as the husband and Marian as the wife. Marian, the setting is this: Hank is your 'role play' husband. He is silent, uncommunicaitve, out of touch with his feelings. You feel neglected and lonely. You've tried everything in the way of verbal taunts and abuse to no avail. Just now you've discovered that Hank has planned a three-day hunting trip with a friend, and you have decided to try to let him know how you feel about this. Remember, you cannot change Hank by direct action, or by manipulation, but you have a right to let him know how you feel."

Hank and Marian sat facing each other in the center of the circle, while Hank's wife looked on with a mixture of emotions. Marian began gently:

"Hank, could I talk with you for a few minutes?"

"Sure, why not?"

"Well, Hank, I've been thinking lately about what a nag I've become. About all I've said to you in the last year or two has been either petulant or nagging. And I don't want to go on being this kind of a person. I hate myself when I do this."

"Yeah? What brought you to this conclusion?"

"Oh, I just got to listening to myself. Don't you

agree that I've been sounding pretty much like a fish wife lately?"

"Yes, sort of."

"I suppose it's because in the home where I grew up everyone talked all the time, and I guess I imagined all families would be like that—talking things over, arguing, loving, fighting." She paused.

Hank said, "My father and mother didn't talk much to each other, except to yell. I hate yelling. I remember always going to my room when Mom and Dad argued."

"You retreated?"

"Yeah. I guess I still do, especially when you start sounding hostile."

"You've never told me about your family before, how hostile they were."

"You've never asked me."

"You're right. I suppose I brought to marriage some preconceived notions about how it would be. We'd sit and hold hands and talk, and share ... and when it didn't work out that way, I started feeling lonely, then rejected, and then abused."

"I'm sorry. I'm just not much of a talker. Maybe you married the wrong guy."

"No, I don't think so. I just made a mistake in imagining that all men would be like my dad; but you have a lot of traits I admire or I wouldn't have married you."

"So?"

"Look, Hank, I've been all wrong in trying to change you. I've criticized you and attacked you, and your natural response has been to retreat; I'm responsible. At least I'm responsible for attacking you."

"And I guess I'm responsible for the way I react. Maybe I could learn to be more communicative, but I just can't react with affection when you're hostile."

"Look, Hank, I want to stop trying to change you. You just be yourself, and I'll stop criticizing you. I do love you, and I don't want to drive you out of the house or into your silent self with my attacks."

"You don't drive me out of the house. I go of my own free will."

"Couldn't this hunting trip be partly an effort to escape from my tirades?"

Hank was silent for a long minute. "Maybe so. I just feel more at peace when I'm out in the woods with a friend. He and I don't criticize each other."

"Hank, I want you to know that after this I'll never complain when you go hunting, or anywhere else for that matter. I do feel lonely, I'll admit. I'd like to be with you and go places with you; but maybe I'm not very good company, the way I've been acting."

She reached out and took Hank's hand. He smiled. He was a passive male who had been retreating from a demanding, hostile, aggrieved wife. Marian's tenderness reached into some hidden recess of his soul, and he responded. He was no longer playing a role. He squeezed her hand.

"Honey, I don't think I'll go on that hunting trip. I'd rather stay here with you. Perhaps we could do something . . . maybe dinner and a show?"

"I'd love that." Marian got up and kissed him tenderly on the cheek. Hank stood up and hugged her.

Hank and Marian resumed their seats in the circle. Hank's wife was weeping silently. When she had regained her composure, she said, "I saw myself for the first time for the nagging, demanding wife I am, and hate myself for it. I saw Hank melt when he was confronted with an understanding wife. I have been battering him, not loving him. I have been confessing his faults, instead of my own. I've done it all backward."

Hank walked over to her and said, "Honey, I'm an uncommunicative slob. I don't think I've tried very hard to overcome my lifelong hangup about talking. But I think I can do better. I see that it's not a passion for hunting, but an effort to escape from having to communicate or face your anger."

"Hank," she said, "I talk faster and more than you, but I can see now that I'm no better at communicating than you. Suppose we keep on trying, at home and in this group, to learn more about real communication."

They did not become proficient overnight, but in time they both learned to express their deeper feelings. There were moments of hurt and hostility, but they rode over these and learned that even anger can be creative at times. He learned to face and express his feelings, and she discovered that love and patience work miracles.

Most married couples send "coded messages" quite unconsciously. They hope the other will decode the message and give an appropriate reply. Here is a typical series of coded messages, with their real meanings in parentheses:

Wife: "I've had a terrible day. The kids were perfectly awful, and I've got a splitting headache." (I'd like for you to put your arms around me and tell me you love me and that you understand how rough I have it; and maybe you could take us all out to a drive-in for dinner.)

Husband: You've had a terrible day! Wait 'til you hear what happened to me. There was an accident on the freeway, and I was a half hour late to work. The boss bawled me out and wouldn't let me explain. Then my secretary was home sick, and I had a whole mess of correspondence that had to go out. On top of that I goofed up a sales contract and the sales manager gave me a bad time. Good grief. What a day!" (You can stay home and watch television if you feel like it, or visit with your friends, or go shopping, while I knock myself out trying to earn a living for this family. What I need is some peace and quiet while I pull myself together. Maybe a little understanding would help, too, and all I hear is complaints. What do you *do* all day?)

Wife: "Honey, will you take these kids off my hands and get them out of the kitchen while I try to get some dinner on the table?" (I've had these kids all day, and I deserve a little peace. You never really do anything with our kids. You're not a very good father, to tell the truth.)

Husband: "Sure, sure. Kids, all of you get out of the kitchen. Go clean up the living room and wash up for dinner." (What a mess this house is. It looks like a cyclone had hit it. Why can't you keep this place picked up a little or teach the kids some responsibility? Where can I go to get away from all this racket, and pull myself together?)

At dinner:

Wife: "The washing machine broke down today. Would you take a look at it after dinner?" (It would give me a feeling of security or something if you'd take a little interest in what goes on around this house.)

Husband: "Yeah. I'll look at it, but I doubt if I can fix it. Those things are pretty complicated." (Why can't you call the repairman? I'm not a mechanic. I need some rest after a hectic day, and I come home to a bunch of screaming kids and a broken washing machine. I have no intention of spending the evening sitting on the floor looking at the insides of a busted appliance I don't know a thing about.)

After dinner:

Wife: "Jimmy's teacher called today. She says he's a disruptive element in the class and shows signs of emotional disturbance. She thinks one of us ought to go and talk to her about it." (I want some help in raising this brood. If you'd just take a serious interest in these things, I'd feel much better. In fact if you'd just give me some undivided attention while I talk about it instead of sneaking looks at that newspaper, I'd feel that you really cared about us.)

Husband: "Okay. Maybe you'd better drop in and see his teacher tomorrow. I'll talk to Jimmy in a day or so and tell him to shape up. He's really getting out of hand. But I guess it isn't too serious. My teachers were always sending notes home about me when I was his age." (Why can't you handle a little session with the kid's teacher? One would think this was a major catastrophe. I handle fifty issues a day more important than this. Why are women so helpless? I wish I could read the evening paper without all of this rehash of the day's minor issues.)

At breakfast:

Wife: "Oh, dear, I forgot to tell you mother is coming to visit us for a few days. You'll have to clear your fishing gear out of the guest room. She's coming this afternoon. Could you do it before you leave for the office?" (I hated to tell you this while you were tired last night. For some reason you have this unreasonable hostility toward my mother. I know she can be a little difficult and overtalkative at times, but after all, she is my mother. I hope you'll be nicer to her than you were the last time she was here.)

Husband: "Oh? She's coming this afternoon? Well, I guess it won't be too terrible if I'm late two days in a row. I'll skip the rest of my breakfast and get that fishing gear stowed away." (Old Vesuvius is coming again! The last time she came for a few weeks, she stayed three months, and by the time she left the kids were out of control, and all of us were at each other's throats. Why must she descend on us and wreck what little peace we have? She's always resented me, and frankly I can't stand having her around. She takes over the house, spoils the kids, and runs things to suit herself. She treats us all as if we were idiots incapable of handling our own lives. I'll try to be polite, but it isn't going to be easy. You don't like her visits any better than I do, but you're too loyal to dear old Mom to admit it, even to yourself!)

And so it goes. In millions of homes the coded messages are sent back and forth day after day, year after year, while silently the tensions mount, until when some minor issue arises, one or the other explodes in what would seem to be a senseless display of anger. The explosion, whether verbal in the form of muffled underground rumbling, or silent withdrawal, can usually be attributed to the daily accumulation of unresolved irritations because they were unexpressed and thus unresolved.

The alternatives would seem to be, at first glance, to keep on sending polite coded messages or to talk the problem out explosively. The first alternative involves temporary peace at the price of slowly accumulating hostility. The second choice, speaking one's mind honestly and freely, all too often results in wounded feelings and failure to resolve the basic difficulty. "Speaking the truth in love" is generally a better solution than blurting out the honest and hurtful truth. To be loving is more important than to be honest, yet to be loving involves facing, at times, the fact that one must speak honestly.

There are times when true feelings must be shared, provided that the marriage partner is able to face and accept the truth. We have no moral right to unload all of our hostile feelings on another who may be emotionally unequipped to deal with that much anger.

In small groups in the past few years, several thousand husbands and wives have worked through, and resolved, basic marital problems. Yokefellow groups, as they are called, are not solely "therapy groups," yet this is often one vital aspect of their activity. It is usually easier to work through a difficult marital problem in a small sharing group than it is at home. Very often husband and wives learn for the first time how to communicate within the circle of a group of people with similar problems. The group does not seek so much to deal with the symptom, but to find the basic cause of the problem.

A seriously depressed wife came to me for counseling. She had always been a happy person, she said, until the past year. Gradually she had become depressed and unhappy, yet there was nothing significant in her story to account for her morbid depression. The children were not too happy in their new home, and her husband appeared to be somewhat rigid, but none of this seemed sufficient to explain her mental condition. After a number of private sessions, I suggested that we might get to the root of the problem more readily if she and her husband would join a group. He came with her to the first meeting with serious reservations. He proved to be a quiet, somewhat reticent person. As he said later, he had no intention of washing his dirty linen in public, but he had agreed to come to "see what it was all about," and because his wife urged him to do so.

There was no one single problem to resolve. He discovered that he was much out of touch with his emotions and became exceedingly angry over seeming trifles. He was basically compliant and agreed to his wife's suggestions, though often with buried hostility. She feared his angry outbursts, whether directed at her or a neighbor, and had begun to withdraw. As the result of burying her true feelings, she turned her resentment inward upon herself, and depression was the result.

They shared nothing sordid or intimate, yet each seemed able to express real feelings in the group more readily than at home. There was a certain safety in the group. Others had similar or identical problems. The atmosphere of total acceptance made it easier to be honest and open.

Within a relatively short time both husband and wife reported significant dividends. He said, "I find myself able to function better at work, with less hostility toward fellow workers. I am not so irritable, either at work or at home. I guess I was a very hostile person, and didn't realize it. I'm learning how to handle my anger in a more creative way."

She said, "My depression has diminished greatly, now that I'm able to say, in the group, what I feel. At home I often feared to say what I felt for fear I would hurt my husband's feelings, or because he might become angry. The children must have picked up some of my depression, and perhaps some of his hostility, because they were out of focus. They are now reacting differently, probably because *we* are different."

I have no desire to oversimplify the matter of communication or to suggest that a few months in such a group always will quickly resolve difficult problems of long standing. But it can happen.

8

TEN
COMMANDMENTS
FOR WIVES

> Keep thy eyes wide open before marriage; and half
> shut afterward.   —*Thomas Fuller*

There is a story about a young unmarried psychologist who wrote a book with the title *Ten Commandments for Parents*. A few years later he married, and in due course a baby was born. When the child was about five, the father rewrote his book and had it published under the title *Ten Suggestions for Parents*. After the fourth child was born some years later, he rewrote his book and it was published with the title *Ten Possible Hints for Parents*.

After forty years of marriage and after having counseled with several thousand married people, I still feel understandably presumptuous in setting down ten absolutes, or commandments, for husbands and wives. Perhaps these could be considered "Guide Lines," general principles which, if followed with some degree of consistency, will tend to make a better marriage.

Here are the Ten Commandments for Wives in brief form:

    I. Learn the *Real* Meaning of Love.
   II. Give Up Your Dreams of a "Perfect Marriage" and Work Toward a "Good Marriage."

III. Discover Your Husband's Personal, Unique Needs and Try to Meet Them.

IV. Abandon All Dependency Upon *Your* Parents and All Criticism of *His* Relatives.

V. Give Praise and Appreciation Instead of Seeking It.

VI. Surrender Possessiveness and Jealousy.

VII. Greet Your Husband With Affection Instead of Complaints or Demands.

VIII. Abandon All Hope of Changing Your Husband Through Criticism or Attack.

IX. Outgrow the Princess Syndrome.

X. Pray for Patience.

When you married, you probably brought to marriage certain preconceived ideas of how life was going to be—perhaps a kind of perpetual romance, a continuation of the honeymoon. Then came grim reality. It wasn't the way you had dreamed it. He changed, didn't he? And without realizing it, you weren't always the same loving, patient, starry-eyed, adoring young woman he married. You both changed. Now let's see how we can go about restoring some of the star dust. Taking the Ten Commandments one by one, let's see what they imply:

1. *Learn the Real Meaning of Love.* You thought you were in love, and no doubt you were. Since then you may have wondered if you were *really* in love. Were there times when you wondered if you should have married someone else? Maybe it was all a terrible mistake.

Well, love isn't what you thought it was when you were in your teens. It is much, much more, and far more complex. *If you want to be loved, you must make yourself lovable*—not for a day or a week, but on a permanent basis. This may involve a radical change of attitude on your part. You want your husband to change, of course; undoubtedly there are many areas in which he needs to change. But you will never change him without a mature love. "Love never fails," said the Apostle Paul in his first letter to the Corinthians. That is, if you are going to make a success of your marriage, you will do it with a mature love, not with demands, criticism, or tears.

Love is not adolescent infatuation or even sexual attraction, important as this is. Love is basically love of life, love of God, proper love of oneself, love of others, and the expressing of this love in manifold ways. *Almost no one ever receives enough love.* If you would be loved, learn to give mature love in a form your husband can accept. Some men who grew up in homes where affection was not freely expressed are undemonstrative. A young wife whose parents were demonstrative and affectionate complained that her husband resisted her attempts to express affection.

"He expresses love by buying me things and taking me places, but he won't tell me he loves me," she complained. "He will do things for me; but why can't he *tell* me he loves me?" she asked. I explained that his environment had "wired him up" that way and that she would have to accept, for the time being, the fact that he was not demonstrative.

"Give him two or five or ten years," I said, "and if you are patient, he can learn as an adult what he never learned as a child. Meanwhile try to accept his manner of expressing love."

Love is not just a sentimental feeling, nor is it simply affection. It is also an act of the will—a determination to give love in a form the other can accept. Love can be expressed through patience, tolerance for the failings of your husband, meeting his needs, and by avoiding criticism. Love does not demand, it gives. Your own need for love can make you unlovable if it is expressed in a demanding or martyred manner.

II. *Give Up Your Dreams of a "Perfect Marriage" and Work Toward a "Good Marriage."* There are no perfect marriages for the simple reason that there are no perfect people. Teen-age expectations of an idealized marriage are unrealistic. There are some more or less ideal marriages, but they are generally the ones which have been worked out through the years.

When you have shaken the rice out of your hair, you have just started on a journey which may involve "debt, drudgery, and diapers," as one wife expressed it. Now begins the long hard pull toward the goal of a workable marriage. You begin to discover that your young knight has faults you had never discovered during the courtship. (He's discovering some things about you which he never expected, too.) He is not quite the person you had dreamed of, but then, neither are you the person he thought he was marrying. Irritations set in, differences appear that you had not counted on. Marriage is the most difficult and complex of all human relationships, and it requires patience, skill, tact, emotional and spiritual growth. You can "grow a good marriage" if you are willing to work at it.

III. *Discover Your Husband's Personal, Unique Needs and Try to Meet Them.* He is not precisely like any other person on earth. He, like you, is unique. He has needs and preferences, failures and weaknesses, virtues and strengths, in a combination unlike anyone else. Give up any preconceived notions you had as to how to please a man. You have, as a woman, a strong desire to please him. But the way you want to please him may not satisfy his needs at all.

You may have heard, for instance, that "the way to a man's heart is through his stomach." This may or may not be true of the particular male you married. It is more likely that his basic need is for gentleness and affection. He may be a meticulous person who likes everything in its place and feels irritated by a cluttered house; or he may be relatively indifferent to neat housekeeping and be passionately fond of sports, in which he wants you to take part. He may be spontaneous and unpredictable and want you to react to life in the same way; or he may have more of a slide rule mentality, preferring stability and an orderly, planned life.

Abandon any preconceived ideas as to what men are like and discover what *your* man is like. You will be unable, at first, to meet all of his needs. *No one person can meet all of the needs of another individual.* Don't feel that you have failed in your marriage if you are unable to gratify all of his needs and preferences, or that he is a failure as a husband because he cannot meet all of your needs. However, as you discover the unique, special requirements of your husband, you can work toward the goal of seeking to meet them. If he makes totally unrealistic, or neurotic, demands upon you, you have a perfect right to maintain your own integrity by expressing your feelings. You need not become a doormat or a household slave. You can seek to meet his needs out of a strong love, rather than out of weakness or a need to "buy" his love.

IV. *Abandon All Dependency Upon Your Parents and All Criticism of His Relatives.* You spent eighteen or twenty years or more in close relationship with your parents. During the first few years of your life you were totally dependent upon them for everything. Growth and maturity demanded a gradual lessening of this dependency, until finally the cord was cut and you were on your own. Many parents consciously want to give their daughters freedom, but at an unconscious level fear to "lose" them. This fear can manifest itself in many ways—through the giving of unsolicited advice (which may be quite valid and wise), or it may take the form of trying to run your life. They want to prevent you from making mistakes. I have known women of thirty or forty years of age, who, upon visiting their parents, were made to feel like little girls again.

"I always feel like an eight-year-old girl when I visit my mother," complained one wife of thirty-eight. "She takes over my children, tells me how to treat my husband, and what I ought not to do. I love her, but she refuses to let me grow up. Even after I get back home my mother writes lengthy letters of advice. I wish she'd let me alone and permit me to make my own mistakes, and learn from them."

In her complaint, however, I detected not only a mother's possessiveness and dominance, but the inability of the wife to cut the tie for good. She wanted, consciously, to be on her own, but at an unconscious level she still felt immature and dependent, unable to tell her mother quietly and firmly to give up her meddling. Many a mother will protest that she wants to give her daughter complete freedom, but her innate "need to be needed" often will not allow her to cut the cord.

A basic rule in marriage is to never, *never* criticize the relatives of your marriage partner! Your husband may offer criticism of his parents or brothers and sisters, but you should never join in. Even though he may feel hostility toward some relative, he will generally not appreciate *your* criticism. It's all right for him to express resentment of his parents, but your attitude should be one of tolerance. Nor does he have a right to criticize your relatives. You may do so if you wish, but he should not.

V. *Give Praise and Appreciation Instead of Seeking It.* Women generally need somewhat more reassurance, and desire it oftener than men, but husbands need it, too. You may have done your best to prepare a delicious meal and may expect some appreciative comment. But some men are unaware of a wife's need for frequent appreciation and praise. One husband said, "My wife is always complaining because I don't appreciate her efforts. She says I don't comment on a new dress or tell her how nice she looks. When she spends a whole day cleaning up the house and has it looking just right, she feels put out because I don't praise her for doing what, to me, is her normal everyday job. Good grief! When I bring home a paycheck, she doesn't squeal with delight and praise me for being a loyal, hard-working dependable husband. Why should I be expected to go into raptures over an omelet or a good meal or a new hairdo! Isn't that her job, just as it is mine to knock myself out every day at the office?"

I explained to him that women need more reassurance. Their self-identity needs to be restored through oft-repeated expressions of appreciation. Men are sometimes far less aware of their surroundings, what they are eating, or even of what their wives are wearing than a woman would be. They are less given to little expressions of approval.

You, as a wife, cannot command your husband's approval. You cannot make him more thoughtful by complaining. Such tactics may cause him to retreat or become hostile. Your task is to offer him the same sort of recognition and praise which you expect of him. If he is too egocentric or blandly unaware of his surroundings to discover your need for frequent expressions of appreciation, you can let him know gently, lovingly, that you need to hear him tell you these things. If you tell him in a complaining, martyr-like manner, however, you will only succeed in making him hostile. Don't sound like his mother reproving him for some childhood failure. No man likes being made to feel like a small boy. Love and tact can win when petulant demands fail.

Your husband will learn more by "osmosis"—through unconscious absorption of your attitudes—than if you make irritable demands upon him. It takes a wise and patient wife to make a good husband. They seldom come ready-made.

VI. *Surrender Possessiveness and Jealousy.* These

two traits are close relatives. Everyone has the capacity for jealousy, and some jealousy is normal. It is only when it becomes possessive and all-pervasive that it is destructive.

Extreme possessiveness stems from insecurity. A young man whose wedding was only a week away consulted me about his overly-possessive fiancée. She was eighteen, he twenty-two. She had vetoed his selection of a best man, whom she disliked. In fact, he said, she had stated that she would not allow his friend in the house. She had made certain other demands which indicated considerable insecurity. I said, "If you let her get away with this, you will have to give in a thousand times in the next few years, until you either have no freedom left, or you abandon the marriage. Ask her to come in with you so we talk it out." She refused at first, saying that as adults they ought to be able to work out their own personal problems. I advised him to tell her that unless she would agree to see some marriage counselor now, and after the marriage if necessary, he had no intention of going through with the marriage. He said, "Thanks for that! I wanted to do it, but felt guilty. The invitations are all out. But I feel I have regained my manhood in deciding to tell her that we must see a counselor when it seems necessary."

Of course she came in, though somewhat sullen and resentful. During the conference she tugged at his sleeve reprovingly when he didn't sit up straight in his chair. She frowned at him when he made a mild grammatical error. After listening to them for an hour, I said, "Your marriage has less than a fifty-fifty chance of surviving. But if you will both agree, willingly, to see a marriage counselor, or join a group where your problems can be resolved, I'd give it a ten to one chance of working out."

She would not agree. I said, "I sense that you must have had an impaired or broken relationship with your father."

She said, "My real father died when I was two, and of course I don't remember him. Then for a few years I had a stepfather. My mother divorced him. I don't feel that I ever had a father."

She had two counts against her, through no fault of her own. Having had no father to whom she could relate, and no brothers, she really didn't know the first thing about men or marriage. In addition, the loss of her father and stepfather had implanted in her unconscious mind the feeling: "Men abandon you. They go away. I must cling to this one or I may lose him as I lost the others." Her all-pervasive insecurity had an understandable origin.

As Freud pointed out many years ago, we act out in adult life the unresolved conflicts of childhood. If we are to live creative, happy lives, we must seek out the origin of our insecurities and try to resolve them rather than justify them.

Overpossessiveness will drive a man away or cause him to retreat into the cold gray castle of his own loneliness or into the arms of another woman. If you are unduly possessive, you are basically very insecure. You probably cannot resolve this deepseated condition all alone. You will need the help of a professional counselor, and it will take time.

VII. *Greet Your Husband With Affection Instead of Complaints or Demands.* You would appreciate some warmth and affection from your husband when he comes home. Your needs are valid. But if they are not being met, you can initiate response yourself. He too has needs. Perhaps he wonders why you don't greet him at the door with a warm hug and a kiss. Instead, you may greet him with the news that Jimmy has been bad, the washer is out of order, and the garbage needs to be taken out. "Oh, yes, and there's a notice from the bank that we're overdrawn." That does it!

Here we have some incompatible needs. Your needs are valid. You want someone to lean on, to share with—to take some of the responsibility off of your shoulders. You've had a bad day. If he grunts and shuts you out, it is not because he doesn't care, but because he, too, wanted something and didn't get it.

Delay the bad news until after dinner! Don't hit him with it the minute he walks into the house. Greet him with some affection whether you feel like it or not. It pays big dividends. "Give and it shall be given unto you. . . ." Perhaps he should be more understanding, more appreciative, more communicative. But he isn't. This is the man you married "for better or worse." It's worse than you thought? He could be thinking the same thing. He may be sitting in front of the TV set or reading, half wondering, "Why did I give up my freedom for this? Before I was married at least I had some peace and quiet. I wasn't met at the door with bad news and demands."

No one is right or wrong at this point. It is simply that one of the basic incompatibilities of marriage has shown its face. Both of you are asking, and no one is giving. Someone must break the impasse. Let it be the most mature, the most perceptive, the most loving. If you are this one, then begin to act that way. Give your husband appreciation and affection. Don't try to achieve results in three months. He may even be suspicious of your sudden change. "What's she up to now?" Be willing to invest a year or five years. Kill him with kindness and see what happens. Your marriage will be better.

VIII. *Abandon All Hope of Changing Your Husband Through Criticism or Attack*. Almost everyone is familiar with the basic threefold axiom: We can change no other person by direct action. We can change only ourselves; and when we change, others tend to change in reaction to us. If you want a better marriage, you must abandon, once and for all, any hope of changing your husband by direct action. The "now look here!" stance never works. It breeds hostility and often a counterattack. This applies not only to husbands, but to all other persons including children. Love changes people. Hostility breeds hostility, but love begets love.

You do have a right to express your feelings, within limits. Consider the probable reaction to these two different approaches:

"Henry, I've about had it! You never talk to me; you forgot our wedding anniversary, and you don't pay any attention to the kids. It's been months since you even thought of taking me out to dinner."

Or, "Dear, I have a problem. Maybe you can help me with it. I've been feeling depressed and out of sorts lately. At first I thought maybe I needed a physical checkup, but I think perhaps it's something else. Suddenly I began to realize I'm depressed. You look depressed, too, sometimes. I'm cooped up with the kids, and feel frustrated at times, but you have it hard, too. I know I've been demanding and critical. Maybe you feel I don't love you, but I do. If I've become a nag. I want you to tell me. I *don't* want to nag. You know, I just realized that I was a lot nicer to you before we were married than I am now. I didn't nag then.... Look, honey, how would it be if we sort of started all over? I'll try to be less critical. I have no right to change you, and I am going to quit trying. How would it be if we get a baby sitter some time this week or next and have dinner out, and perhaps go somewhere afterwards. Maybe we need a little time to ourselves. Huh?"

Friend Husband may or may not respond immediately. Or again he may. This approach should not be used as a manipulative device to get your own way, but only if you genuinely want to express love and affection, and if you want to give up making demands. He may respond instantly or a year later, depending upon whether he is a delayed reactor or a spontaneous type of personality. It's worth trying: give up making demands; abandon the martyr stance and stop trying to change him. Express love and patience.

IX. *Outgrow the Princess Syndrome.* Not every woman suffers from this, of course, but many do, just as many men grow up with the Prince Syndrome. In essence, the Princess Syndrome is the feeling that you are "special." No one is special; unique, yes; special, no. A little girl may have heard a hundred or a thousand times that she was pretty or cute. She absorbs this, when quite young, as her due. Her adoring subjects (parents, relatives, friends) pay homage to this lovely little creature with the beautiful smile and cute ways. If she is an only child of adoring parents, or the youngest child, she can become even more susceptible. If she is especially talented in some way, she may grow up to believe that she is, indeed, very special. Often such a girl learns instinctively how to manipulate others, beginning usually with Daddy.

A married woman of thirty once told me of her problem in this area. She had been the pride of her parents, who granted every wish. She became compliant and dutiful, learning that this was the easiest way to get what she wanted. Her mother always dressed her in the frilliest of dresses and showed her off proudly to adoring friends and relatives. She sat in the front row at school and got good grades. Great things were predicted for her. "Then," she said, "I married Carl. He's a nice, quiet, dependable person. He loves me, and we have two nice youngsters. But I can't quite get out of my head that I ought to be 'special.' Carl thinks I'm wonderful, but that doesn't satisfy me. It's as if I had really been a princess, or was treated as one, then lost my kingdom. People don't adore me and lavish praise on me. I'm just one of millions. Intellectually I know this is silly, but at a deep emotional level I feel cheated. I guess I'm still a little child at heart, wanting adoration and praise." She grinned. "It's awful to grow up thinking you're something special, and then find you're just one of three billion people, no more special than others." She sighed. "Can I ever grow up and abandon this Princess Syndrome?"

She was already on the way toward maturity through the very act of recognizing her immaturity.

All of us would like to be treated as "special." This narcissism is a holdover from childhood, a relic of the past. Emotional maturity cannot be achieved until we abandon this childhood behavior pattern.

A "princess" doesn't give. She asks, demands, becomes petulant when she cannot have her way. She buys luxuries with money that should be saved for necessities. She delivers ultimatums, or if she is subtle, manipulates to achieve her ends. If you see any of these traits in yourself, however small, begin now to abandon them as a holdover from childhood.

X. *Pray for Patience.* "I thought we could work out all those little things after we were married," said a wife who before marriage knew that her husband was a fairly heavy drinker. "He wasn't an alcoholic," she said, "and I was sure that if he loved me enough, he'd keep his drinking within bounds." Marriage, however, increased some of his inner tensions and he began to drink to excess.

Another wife, whose husband's passion for golf did not bother her before marriage, complained that he left her alone on weekends while he golfed with his male friends.

The urge to be married, establish a home, and have children is so strong in most women that they are often blind to faults which are only dimly perceived before marriage. There is a partly unconscious belief in the minds of most women that "love will surmount all." In most instances, the right kind of love *can* solve any marital problems. The right kind of love involves patience. "Love is patient and kind," we read in the New Testament (I Cor. 13:4). A mature love has this quality of patience. An immature love wants results right now. "Lord, give me patience, and give it to me right now," is the unconscious prayer of such persons.

"Love bears all things . . . hopes . . ." (I Cor. 13:7). Give up the tendency to complain, criticize, and control. You cannot control another human being even if you are entirely right in what you desire. The more you criticize and condemn, the more likely you are to drive your husband farther from you. If he drinks or golfs or watches television to excess; if he seems to ignore you, forgets anniversaries, and is in other ways thoughtless or inconsiderate, your petulant demands or hurt expression will seldom bring the desired results. It takes a great deal of patience to put up with unacceptable conduct, but good marriages are built on a foundation of patience.

This does not preclude the right to express your opinion. You need not give up your identity or become a doormat. A wife suffering from deep anxiety and depression came to see me about entering a group. She had been seeing a psychiatrist for five years and felt that little progress had been made. I arranged for her to join a group, but when she told her husband of her intent, he became very hostile. A furious argument resulted. Normally rather a passive individual, the wife had determined that she must have help, and she stood her ground. He was determined to control her, and she was equally insistent upon entering a group. As her husband became more and more angry and insistent, she finally threw a phone book at him, whereupon he seized her, pinned her hands behind her back and said, "You're sick!"

She said, "That's what I've been trying to tell you, and I'm going to get some help whether you like it or not." She joined the group and told, without rancor, of the battle with her husband. She had decided that she had to be a person in her own right, and that marriage did not give her husband the right to control all of her actions. Patience with another does not imply that we must lose our freedom of choice.

170

TEN
COMMANDMENTS
FOR HUSBANDS

9

Women forgive injuries but never forget slights.
—*Halliburton*

Here are the Ten Commandments for Husbands:

I. Treat Your Wife With Strength and Gentleness.
II. Give Ample Praise and Reassurance.
III. Define the Areas of Responsibility.
IV. Avoid Criticism.
V. Remember the Importance of "Little Things."
VI. Recognize Her Need for Togetherness.
VII. Give Her a Sense of Security.
VIII. Recognize the Validity of Her Moods.
IX. Cooperate With Her in Every Effort to Improve Your Marriage.
X. Discover Her Particular, Individual Needs and Try to Meet Them.

I. *Treat Your Wife With Strength and Gentleness.* No matter how self-reliant a woman may be, regardless of her intelligence, capability, and drive, even if she seems dominant, there is something within her which wants to "lean" on a man. Reduced to its basic elements, a woman wants to be "taken, and taken care of." She wants to feel that she has been chosen (even if she has actually done the initial choosing).

She would like to be swept off her feet, and then taken care of with gentleness and strength.

These two qualities are basic. Your wife may discover that you are not always as strong as she had hoped, nor as perfect, and sometimes perhaps not as gentle. If she married you taking your passivity for gentleness, and your quietness for strength, she will be disappointed.

In a group session a wife was complaining about her husband's passivity. She said, "He is very gentle and quiet—too quiet. He never has any ideas of his own. I make most of the decisions. I can have my way about almost anything. I don't *want* my way all the time. I want him to take the lead, to initiate and plan. I even plan our vacations. He lets me do about anything I want. I just wish he'd put his foot down once in a while and tell me I *couldn't* do something."

"Suppose you knew you were right," I said, "and he stubbornly put his foot down and insisted on having it done his way. Would you go for that?"

"I'd enjoy that," she replied. "I'm sick and tired of making all the decisions."

"But if he did start making decisions, you'd put up an argument, wouldn't you?"

"Sure, almost any woman would. But I don't really want to win. I want him to win part of the time. I want him to be stronger than I am."

"But you picked out a passive male," I said. "Something in you sensed his passivity, you wanted it, and now you are complaining."

She was thoughtful. "Well, I guess the human part of me wanted someone I could manage and control, but the feminine part of me wants a man who is strong enough to make me behave—even when I put up a fuss."

This confusing ambivalence on the part of a woman can be irritating or infuriating to a man who sees it as illogical. You, as a husband, might feel like saying to such a wife, "Look! If you want me to be in charge, stop putting up a battle over every issue. After knocking myself out at work, I don't want to have to come home and spend what little psychic energy I have left fighting a mock battle over some trivial issue. Maintain your identity in some other way, but don't give me an argument over each issue that arises." Even such a speech as that could, in a sense, indicate to your wife that you *are* taking charge.

Being in charge does not mean being "the boss" or becoming domineering. Only a very insecure man feels a need to force his will on others. Strength does not imply throwing your weight around, issuing orders, and demanding obedience of everyone within earshot.

This combination of strength and tenderness is not easily achieved if one does not possess it innately, but you can work at it. You may make mistakes, but with patience and determination you can satisfy your wife's inner need for emotional security with a quiet strength that is gentle and tender.

II. *Give Ample Praise and Reassurance.* For thousands of years women were in a subordinate position. Only in this century have they achieved equality in voting and property rights, and partial equality on the job. Their rights are newly won, and the ancient insecurities are still resident in the female emotional structure.

In addition, the role of mother renders the woman much more vulnerable and insecure. Instinctively she feels a need for someone to protect her and her children and to provide for the family. This generates a kind of all-pervasive insecurity which exists whether there are children or not, or after the children have left the nest. Some women are extremely reluctant to reveal to a man the extent of their insecurity and their desperate need for a husband to "lean" on. But it is there.

Because of this and other factors, women need considerable reassurance. It can be given in the form of praise, recognition, commendation, or simply by saying, "I love you!"—often. When a woman asks, "Do you love me?" she isn't asking for information. She is asking for reassurance.

One husband, who found it extremely difficult to express tenderness verbally, complained that his wife was always asking if he loved her.

"Of course I love her. She ought to know that! I bring home my paycheck and hand it over to her. I take care of her and the kids. If I didn't love her, would I be hanging around? The boss doesn't tell me every day what a fine job I'm doing. In fact, no one has complimented me on my work in twenty years, but I am pretty sure of a job. Why do women need all of this sentimental stuff?"

"That's the way they are," I said. "Women are simply made that way and you had better accept it as a fact. Since verbal expression of affection is a need of hers, go along with it whether you feel like it or not."

"But that would be hypocritical if I didn't happen to feel like it at the moment."

"Not at all," I replied. "It is never hypocritical to do the appropriate thing. In time you will discover that your feelings will catch up with your actions, and you won't feel so clumsy in expressing tenderness." He agreed to try.

III. *Define the Areas of Responsibility*. In a relationship between any two persons, there must be a tacit understanding of the areas of responsibility. If two men are in partnership, they must work out the spheres of activity and have them clearly defined. The same thing holds with equal force in a marriage relationship.

Some areas seem clearly enough defined. Your wife takes care of the house, cooks, and has the primary responsibility for the children, particularly when they are very young. You earn the living. But there are many other less clearly defined areas.

Who takes out the garbage? Who is responsible for

the lawn, choosing the new car, deciding where to spend the vacation? Who has the veto power on making investments or where to live? Who is primarily responsible for seeing the teacher when one of the children is having difficulty at school? Who decides when to buy a new washing machine or new furniture? Who casts the deciding vote concerning what to do on weekends—whether time will be spent with the children, with friends, or on some hobby?

A simplistic answer is: "Let the final decision rest with the one who is best qualified." Unfortunately this is a gross oversimplification. You, as husband, could easily abdicate responsibility by saying, "Look, dear, you're a lot better at that than I am. Why don't you just take care of it and not bother me with details?"

There is, to the male, a "peculiarity" of the feminine nature which—in most cases—wants the husband to participate. A wife often feels more "secure" if she can talk things over with her husband. She may choose a time to do this when you want to read, golf, or watch television. You can become grossly irritated over what may seem to you to be minor issues. But life consists not only of major decisions. Marriage is mostly "little things," which, to a male, can be an excruciating bore. But this is a part of marriage and of living.

A couple must find out for themselves where the various "spheres of influence" lie: who pays the bills, who casts the deciding vote on buying what house, renting which apartment, where to vacation. A selfish husband or wife may insist on rendering a final verdict on all decisions, major and minor; but marriage involves *resolving the incompatible needs of two different people*.

In general, a wife's decision about the house or apartment, the furniture, and details pertaining to the "nest" should be given priority. As a man's job is an extension of his personality, the home is an ex-

175

tension of the wife's even if she is employed. Her job, if she works, is only a means to an end, not a major part of her life.

"We'll decide these things together," said a young couple to me as we discussed their forthcoming marriage. At that point they could not even begin to envision the countless decisions concerning which they would have divergent views and needs. When there is a difference of opinion, the couple must decide whether this matter falls within his sphere or hers, and whether he or she has the veto power.

A husband who bought eight cars in five years exasperated his wife with his total disregard for the realities of their budget. She brought it up in a group session. She was extremely conservative concerning money, and he had no concept of how to live within a budget. They were always heavily in debt. His immaturity in the handling of money and in other areas had resulted in a separation. Now they were in a group trying to effect a reconciliation. Over a period of months he came to perceive that he had been acting in an immature fashion in certain areas, and said, "I'm a whiz at my job. I earn plenty of money, but I'm not very good at handling it. I'd like for Marie to take over the handling of our finances."

I asked, "Will this make you feel like a little boy, with 'Mother' allotting you so much to spend each week?"

"Not at all, at this point. It would have a year ago. I think I've matured enough to let her handle the finances." His wife was not a controlling type of individual, and in this instance the plan worked well.

IV. *Avoid Criticism.* A woman tends to lose her identity somewhat more readily than a man, other things being equal. A man who constantly criticizes and condemns his wife can produce numerous negative results in his wife. She may:

  A. Become deeply depressed through repressing her hostility.

176

B. Develop one or more physical symptoms, since the mind tends to hand its pain over to the body.

C. Become hostile, emotionally unresponsive, or sexually frigid.

D. Lose her identity through being contsantly beaten down.

E. Unload her resentment onto the children and cause emotional disturbances in them.

F. Decide to give up the marriage.

A regular barrage of criticism, even when warranted, is always destructive. In fact, almost all criticism is destructive. There is usually a better way to achieve results.

A woman who liked to read a great deal, and who had numerous outside activities, admitted in her group session that she was a poor housekeeper. Her husband complained from time to time about it. Finally he said, "My criticism of her housekeeping is getting us nowhere. I don't know what her block is. I'm not a perfectionist, but I would like to see the house halfway cleaned at least once a week. I'm embarrassed to have a house that looks like ours, and to have a wife who does such a sloppy job. I'm going to stop carping about it. But I have the same right to a decent house as she has to expect me to earn a decent living. I'm going to decide on some positive solution. Give me a week to think it out."

The next week he had his answer. "I told her quietly, and without hostility, that if she had a block about housekeeping, I'd handle my job and clean up the house, too, until she overcame her neurotic block. This week I have come home from work and started doing housework. I am trying not to play the martyr, though I do admit I'm not overly happy about this solution. I am going to do this until she gets sick of abdicating her responsibility. If it takes six months or ten years, I will do my job and hers, without comment. I know she has either a neurotic block or a total incapacity to keep house. When she gets tired of goofing off, or sick of her neurosis, she can take over the housekeeping."

This was said with some impatience, but also with a considerable measure of understanding. In their particular case, the procedure worked. She did have an emotional block. Her mother had been a fanatically meticulous housekeeper, and at an unconscious level she had resolved to be as unlike her mother as possible. She worked this block out in her group, and in a matter of months began to assume her household duties. When she slipped back into her old ways, as she did at times, her husband quietly took over again. In time she was able to function normally as a housekeeper.

Criticism in any area is inevitable in almost any human relationship, but the less there is, the more satisfactory the marriage will be. This does not rule out expressing one's feelings. There are, however, different ways of saying the same thing:

"Do you realize we have just about the same kind of meal day in and day out? Why can't you get some kind of variety into our meals?"

Or, "You know, dear, you're a good cook, and I enjoy your meals, but when I was a kid we had the same kind of food week in and week out. Mom wasn't a very good cook, and I resolved that when I got married, I'd have some variety in my meals. There's nothing wrong with this food, but I'd prefer a little variety. Just one of my idiosyncrasies."

"Can't you keep these kids quiet? Look, when I come home from work I deserve a little peace and quiet."

Or, "Honey, I've had a hard day, and I know you've had a rough time with the kids, too. They must get on your nerves. I expect you'd like to turn them over to someone else and get a little relief. Unfortunately I just haven't got much steam left when I get home. Tell you what: I'll try to get the kids under control when I come home, while you get dinner; and after dinner I'll go pull myself together for a bit. Then we can sit down and have a little time to ourselves. Okay?"

These are not suggested as "solutions," but simply as different ways of saying the same thing. Just because we are married we do not have the right to be insulting, or tactless and critical. The marriage license is not a license to insult.

V. *Remember the Importance of "Little Things."* Men are usually less sentimental than women and attach less importance to such things as birthdays, anniversaries, "little" gestures which mean much to women. Love is not just a feeling; it involves positive actions which can mean a great deal to a woman.

I have long been aware of the principle, but like a typical male, I had not let it filter down into the feeling level of my nature. I once asked my wife what she wanted for Christmas. Although, like any woman, she likes surprises, I felt that there was nothing I could get her in the nature of a surprise which would fill any particular need. She surprised me by saying that all she wanted for Christmas was to have a large tree cut down just outside our bedroom window. She had mentioned this numerous times, but I had delayed because of the considerable expense involved. I agreed and long before Christmas I found an opportunity to have the tree removed. Then Christmas arrived, and I felt a need to put something under the tree for her. Her physical needs and wants were, so far as I could see, well supplied. She could think of nothing she particularly wanted.

Christmas Eve came, and I still had no idea what I could get her. Sitting at my desk I began, rather halfheartedly, to work on a crazy—to me—little idea. I cut out a dozen three by five sheets of paper and stapled them together with a cover to form a coupon book.

On one I wrote: Good for One Dinner at a First-Class San Francisco Restaurant. The second one read:

Good for One Dinner at a Drive-In with Entertainment Afterwards. The third was for One Dinner at a Medium Priced Restaurant. The fourth was good for a dinner at a Chinese Restaurant. Another coupon entitled her to a meal at a steak house. One was for a dinner "at a first-class restaurant, to be earned by meritorious conduct beyond the call of duty," and so on. There were twelve in all, to be used at her discretion.

I felt rather sheepish about the whole deal. It was a crude little coupon book and involved only some dinners and fun which she had every right to expect anyway. To my surprise she was thrilled, because she could pull out a coupon on any free night I might have (rare enough in my case) and decide where we would go for dinner. Eating out in a restaurant is no great treat for me, and I knew this was not true for her, but I was not prepared for the great satisfaction it gave her to know that I was setting aside twelve evenings for dining out.

Men are nearly always surprised to discover how much "little things" (as they deem them to be) mean to a woman—an unexpected gift, a compliment on a new dress, or a sincere, "You look great with the new hairdo, Honey."

A husband who forgets a wedding anniversary has committed an almost unforgivable sin. Mother's Day, Easter, and Christmas all call for recognition. A young wife married to an unresponsive husband told me that she felt cheated by his lack of consideration of her needs. Part of her resentment was passed on to him in the form of criticism, and part to the children when he wasn't around.

Finally, realizing that direct criticism was useless and destructive, she sat down with him and explained her needs as a woman. She asked him gently to recognize her emotional needs. He just grunted and said he would think about it. But a week or two later he brought her an unexpected gift with a tender expression of love. He had not been unwilling, just uncomprehending. Her former tirades had evoked only hostility or silence. The quiet expression of her needs helped him understand for the first time, and enabled him to respond.

"I don't want to have to remind my husband of our anniversaries," one wife said. "That takes all the fun out of it; and I don't want to have to make all the suggestions about going out, or to dinner. I'd love it if just *once* he'd initiate something, take the lead, show me that he cares, plan something for us without asking me." This is a legitimate female need, and a husband must recognize it if he is to be an adequate marriage partner.

VI. *Recognize Her Need for Togetherness*. No two women are identical in their needs, of course, but in general women tend more often than men to require a sense of "togetherness." This term is much overworked, but the truth it involves cannot be ignored. There is the dependent, possessive, clinging, demanding wife who doesn't want her husband out of her sight. She is in need of counseling, for her neurotic needs spring out of a deep insecurity, but even a typical wife may often want more of her husband's time and attention than he feels like giving her.

Many husbands enjoy family outings. Some men enjoy all manner of activities with their wives, while others have a strong need for male companionship. A husband who wants to preserve a good marriage relationship will try to meet his wife's need for doing things together. If their recreational tastes differ, then a compromise is indicated.

I recall a summer when my wife expressed a desire to spend our vacation at a summer resort. I felt an urge to take a pack trip with some men. She detested camping, and I had no particular desire to sit around a resort with no opportunity for fishing. After a brief discussion, we arranged a compromise.

We had two weeks to spend, so I suggested that I would spend one week with her at the resort and one week on a pack trip into the mountains where I could get in some fly fishing. She agreed readily. It was an altogether satisfactory arrangement. She did not in the least mind being left alone for a week because she made friends readily.

A clinging, demanding, possessive wife could make such an arrangement difficult if not impossible. Virtually all husbands and wives have incompatible needs. Togetherness does not imply that we will go through life hand in hand, always enjoying identical things to the same degree. We are still individual humans with divergent needs and tastes. We must respect the needs of others and compromise cheerfully when necessary. Only the immature and childish demand to have their way under all circumstances.

VII. *Give Her a Sense of Security.* A woman's need for security is much greater than most men imagine. It can be provided by a husband who is strong, gentle, and considerate. But in specific areas women's needs vary. Many women derive a sense of security (often without being aware of it) from having a husband who does household repairs. This means that he is interested in the nest and thus interested in her. If he is all thumbs and cannot repair a leaky faucet, he may be at a disadvantage at this point. But any man can mow a lawn, which is also related to nest building, or rake leaves, or help move the furniture (if she is a "furniture mover"), or at least take an interest in her daily activities. Maybe you feel that you couldn't care less about the details she relates, but you are expressing love by the very act of listening, and thus reinforcing her sense of security.

Some women (as well as men) have what could be called the "pack rat syndrome." They like to save string, or magazines, or have little caches of money for some special event. If your wife derives a sense of security from having a bank account of her own, or her own savings account, go along with it. It may not make sense to you, but this is not as important as her sense of security. It need not be logical. Don't try to run your marriage on a steady diet of logic. Feelings are just as important as logic, often more so. Whatever gives your wife a feeling of security needs to be encouraged so long as it does not disrupt the budget or rob you of your masculine identity.

VIII. *Recognize the Validity of Her Moods.* All humans vary, of course, in their mood swings. Women, however, tend to have somewhat stronger mood variations than most men. Part of this can be attributed to the monthly cycle. With this a husband must learn to be patient and considerate. A woman can appear to be illogical and utterly irrational at times, at least to the male mind which wants things tidy and logical. You may as well accept her variations in mood as inevitable.

Some happy event can make a woman ecstatically happy, or something that has been said or done may plunge her into depression. A rigid or insecure husband can feel threatened by these up and down mood swings. You may prefer a steady pace with no fluctuations, sacrificing the euphoria if you can avoid the depression. Your wife may be constituted differently. Perhaps you married her because of her capacity for joyousness. But a joyous personality can sometimes experience deep depression. You need not ride up to the heights of her happiness if you are wired up differently, nor plunge into her depression. Perhaps one reason she married you was that unconsciously she desired your emotional stability. Don't be panicked or disturbed by mood swings. Ride them out with patience and kindly indulgence. *Don't take it personally* or tell her to "Snap out of it."

IX. *Cooperate With Her in Every Effort to Improve Your Marriage.* Women, as we have seen, are insatiable, and men are obtuse. They can be insatiable in their desire to make a better marriage. Your wife may want to read a book on marriage or communication or child rearing. Your male ego, if it is a bit weak, may reject this suggested reading, believing there is an implied criticism in her handing you the book to read.

Read it! What do you have to lose? You may even learn something. No one is automatically equipped by a marriage ceremony to function at maximum effectiveness in marriage. Any husband could read a dozen or two books on marriage and profit from the experience.

If she encourages you to visit a marriage counselor with her, or join a group, or go to a series of lectures on marriage or child rearing, by all means go. Marriage and the home involve an all-out activity for a typical woman. Don't be dismayed because she is always pushing for a better relationship. Go along with her graciously and good naturedly. A marriage counselor can cost a great deal less than a divorce and years and years of child support, besides saving a marriage and avoiding the tears and pain of divorce.

X. *Discover Her Particular, Individual Needs and Try to Meet Them.* No two wives are alike. The one you married is different from any other woman. She has her own particular set of likes and dislikes, moods, and emotional needs. Her needs may seem limitless at first, or unreasonable. Perhaps you cannot meet all of her needs at once, maybe never. But you can try to discover what she needs, wants, appreciates; you can seek to meet those needs within your capacity. This does not mean catering to childish whims, but it can mean going along with something that may seem illogical or unimportant to you. If it makes her happy, and gives her a sense of satisfaction, try to satisfy the need.

EIGHT TYPES

10 ## OF NEUROTIC

HUSBANDS

A perfect wife is one who doesn't expect a perfect
husband.   —*Anonymous*

It is important to recognize that each of these eight
behavior patterns is only a symptom of a basic underlying personality disorder. By attacking the symptom
you will almost certainly make it worse.

1. *The explosive, argumentative, domineering husband.* This type of man has some deep-seated feelings
of inferiority. He may have begun early in life to try
to control his environment by shouting or by being
overly argumentative. Because of immaturity he fears
to let anyone become an equal, lest he feel over-
whelmed and thus controlled. He must at all costs
maintain his fictional superiority. He must always be
right. He cannot endure the idea of having been
wrong about anything.

Such a man tyrannizes and dominates through fear
and sheer volume, or if somewhat quieter, through an
intensive argumentativeness that seems never to end
until he is confident that he has squelched all his
adversaries. Emotional immaturity and insecurity are
the basic difficulties in his case, and to argue back,
to attack or criticize, only antagonizes him further.
At whatever cost, however ridiculous or illogical he
may sound, he feels he must maintain his alleged position of superiority. He will risk alienating family,

friends, and fellow workers rather than admit an error; or, if he reserves his tirades for his family, as some men do, he is willing to make a resounding idiot of himself rather than admit that anyone else could be right. He must be in charge, or his minuscule ego will collapse.

The argumentative, domineering husband, because of his great insecurity, is usually reluctant to undertake any sort of therapy. He tends to resist the idea of seeing a marriage counselor, for this implies the possibility of change on his part. To alter his basic behavior pattern poses a greater threat than he cares to face. However, if he can be induced to undertake some form of group therapy in a group situation which is not too threatening, he can gradually make some changes in his personality.

The wife of such a man was in deep depression and came in for counseling. She had been beaten down until she felt worthless and hopeless. I encouraged her to give up all efforts to change him by direct action or through manipulation. She was invited to join a group of husbands and wives who were preparing to take a spiritual growth inventory consisting of a standardized psychological test, with weekly evaluation slips. I told her, however, that she could not join the group without her husband. (In some instances husband and wives are put in separate groups, but in their case I felt it desirable for them to belong to the same group.)

She told her husband, at my suggestion, that they could probably get to the root of her depression through such a process, but that it would be necessary for him to come with her, if for no other reason than to understand her better. She persuaded him to attend at least one group session. He came with great reluctance, solely in order to help his wife "get some sense into her head and snap out of her depression." He discovered a friendly atmosphere in the group, in which no one challenged or criticized him. He agreed somewhat reluctantly to take the inventory along with other members of the group. When the weekly evaluation slips began to arrive, he appeared very apprehensive, but when he discovered that others in the group were receiving similar slips, he felt less threatened. His wife received a slip indicating that her depression was the result of buried hostility. His first slip told him that as the result of a basic insecurity originating early in childhood, he had a tendency to seek to control others about him.

In the ensuing discussion he said little, but agreed that the slip might possibly have some slight validity. He remained in the group, curious as to what the remaining weekly slips would reveal. Gradually his tension and anxiety disappeared as he entered more and more into the spirit of the meetings. There was much laughter, which relieved the tension. No one criticized or attacked. Each group member was intent upon discovering his own areas of need.

Without any conscious effort to make a change in his behavior, the argumentative husband began to relax both in the group and at home. He had been accepted by the group just as he was. He observed that other husbands and wives had their problems, different from his but just as serious. In addition, he began to learn more about women than he had ever known before.

In one session he said, "I am beginning for the first time to see the many ways in which women differ from men in their emotional reactions. Things which I thought were neurotic or odd in my wife's attitude, I now see are perfectly normal. I'm beginning to understand how women feel and to accept their different emotional responses as perfectly valid. I never knew until I entered this group how greatly men and women differ in their emotional reactions to life." In the process he came to understand and accept himself much better. As his basic insecurity diminished, he felt less and less need to control his wife

Theirs became a greatly improved marriage, and his wife's depression vanished as she became able to express in the group feelings which would have precipitated a storm at home.

2. *The compulsive husband.* Compulsiveness takes many forms. One may be a compulsive eater, golfer, drinker, or television watcher. He may fall into the category of the compulsive worker, or be a compulsive talker.

Compulsiveness is a neurotic behavior problem which never—never!—yields to arguments, threats, pleas, tears, or any other form of persuasiveness. It is just what the name implies: a compulsion. Such a person feels literally *compelled* to act in a particular manner. You cannot shame a compulsive drinker or compulsive talker into changing. It is not that he is unwilling. He is unable. No one knows how many wives have learned to their sorrow that tears and threats are of no avail in dealing wtih a compulsive personality.

There is a basic insecurity involved in such an individual. He is not to blame for having this particular problem, and criticism is the worst possible approach, but he is responsible for doing something about himself.

A compulsive drinker is basically an insecure person usually possessed of a passive personality. His passivity does not rule out aggressive behavior, especially when he has been drinking. Such persons are usually amiable, kindly individuals when sober, but their promises "never to take another drink" are, of course, utterly meaningless. The wife of a problem drinker needs to get in touch with Alcoholics Anonymous and learn how to deal with her husband, as a first step. She will learn, probably, that almost everything she has been doing to solve the problem was completely wrong.

The compulsive worker has a kind of free-floating anxiety. An underlying insecurity motivates him to achieve, to be busy constantly. This is usually far less destructive a behavior pattern than many of the others, but it can be mildly to seriously destructive to the security of the family.

A man with this obsession may take infrequent vacations, working long hours, convincing himself with all manner of rationalizations that he simply does not have time for other activities than the work to which he devotes himself.

Quite often a man who feels threatened by close personal contact or who feels badgered, criticized, or "hemmed in" will retreat to some activity in an effort to escape into a less threatening situation. He may be avoiding close relationships with his wife or children. He is unconsciously—or consciously—seeking a socially acceptable way of getting away from conflict or tension. This is more of an escape mechanism than a compulsion, but it can frustrate a wife who wants more of her husband's time and attention. If a husband seems to fall into this escape category, a wife can ask herself what it is in their relationship or in the home which makes her husband feel unwanted, threatened, or simply uncomfortable. If he is attacked or criticized, degraded or ridiculed at home he may—if he is a passive type of individual—simply find some way of avoiding the situation. He can argue that he needs a hobby, that he must have some male companionship, or that he has work which must be finished. Instead of demands, tears, or ultimatums the wife of such a man must find a way to make the home a place where he feels comfortable and at ease.

3. *The uncommunicative husband.* "My husband never talks to me," is a common complaint of wives. There are numerous categories into which such men fall:

(a) The passive, shy male. As a child he was encouraged to be seen and not heard or was dominated by overstrict parents. As an adult he finds himself literally unable to carry on an extended conversation.

He is at loss for words with which to express himself and is usually out of touch with his feelings. Whatever the original cause, such men cannot be *compelled* to communicate. They feel ill at ease and inadequate in trying to express themselves. The wife of one of these uncommunicative individuals generally must resign herself to the situation and find outlets for her social needs, unless the husband will undertake some long-range therapy.

(b) The "strong, silent" husband. His wife may have been attracted to him initially because she mistook his silence for "silent strength." He may, indeed, have considerable inner strength which reveals itself on the job, yet be incapable of communicating at home. At home he does not talk about things in which his wife is interested. This type of man usually is "thing oriented"; that is, he tends to deal rather exclusively with things or ideas and feels himself at a disadvantage when confronted with feelings. Usually he will feel threatened by any emotional upset, for he prefers things to run smoothly, with no emotional ups and downs. Wives of such men are often prone to push, test, or manipulate in an effort to get some kind of an emotional response. The husband then reacts with an angry outburst, silent withdrawal, or quiet hostility.

(c) The limited conversation husband. He is capable of carrying on a conversation about almost anything so long as it does not involve feelings. He is not uncommunicative. He will talk, but he finds it extremely difficult to talk about feelings or to share any emotions.

There is a sense in which we do not know a person until we know what he feels. A typical wife wants to know her husband at a feeling level, to know how he feels about himself, about life, about her. A man who is incapable of sharing feelings cannot be known. In fact, he fears to be known or to know himself. He finds it much safer to deal with things, concepts, and tangibles. He feels uncomfortable dealing with emotions.

(d) The "'turned-off' husband. At one time, perhaps during courtship, there was considerable communication at a feeling level. Now he has grown morose, silent. This type of man is usually retreating from something he does not care to discuss. The wife may be a compulsive talker, and if her husband cannot turn her off, he can tune her out. His wife observes that he talks easily with friends but is uncommunicative at home, and she feels hurt and rejected. He may feel unable to tell her honestly what the difficulty is, for fear of an endless argument. Some such husbands feel rejected sexually and respond with a cold aloofness. They respond to sexual rejection by rejecting their wives in other ways.

A couple whose discussion at home always ended in hostile exchanges came to see me. The wife came first and stated her grievances. I told her, after several sessions, that it would be necessary for her husband to come in. She was surprised when he agreed to a series of conferences. They discovered that in my presence they could state their problems openly, without either erupting in anger. In fact, they learned for the first time that communication was possible, but it had to be learned in the presence of a third party. "I am for the marriage," I told them, "not for either one of you." In the course of time their differences were resolved, and they became able to carry on the discussions at home with more light and less heat. This also can happen as the result of a group experience, where quite often husbands and wives can learn to communicate at a deep level for the first time.

4. *The child husband.* This is the spoiled-child neurotic husband. In marriage he is seeking to recreate something similar to the relationship he had with his mother, from whom he was never fully able to detach himself. He is often passive and shuns re-

sponsibility. Such a personality is often the result of a weak or indifferent father and an overprotective mother. He requires much attention and "mothering," when he is ill, and may be prone to numerous vague or specific ailments. He lacks a sense of masculine identity and sometimes goes to ridiculous lengths to prove himself and to others that he is truly masculine. He can be petulant when he does not get his way. He has an inferiority complex for which he attempts to compensate in various ways. Marriage to such a man can succeed if the wife is able and willing to take up where his mother left off. She will need to mother him, pamper him, and put up with his unreasonable demands until he can grow up.

A variation of the child husband is the man with a mother fixation. He has never fully cut the cord joining him to a possessive mother. His mother, either because she was unhappy in her own marriage or was a widow, dotes on this particular son. If the man's mother is living, he will give her devoted attention, visit her as often as possible, and yield to her whims. He is psychically married to his mother, and his wife takes second place in his life. This is a frustrating experience for the wife, who can never feel that she has her husband's complete love and loyalty. Logic, arguments and ultimatums seldom if ever change such a man. Usually the only effective cure comes through some type of individual or group therapy.

5. *The hypochondriac husband.* This is usually a relatively harmless neurosis, so far as marriage is concerned, but the wife must be prepared to put up with a lifetime of pills, doctor's appointments, psychosomatic ills, and physical complaints. Such a man is no more to be blamed for this condition than a person is to be condemned for any other neurotic behavior pattern. We are each the product of early environment. It is utterly fruitless to try to argue a hypochondriac out of his obsessive attention to ill-

ness. Logic has little or no effect upon a neurotic behavior pattern. Unless the pattern is seriously disruptive, the wife of such a man would do well to say to herself, "I'll live with his pill bottles and physical complaints, and he can learn to live with some of my peculiarities." An amused, loving tolerance is a far better approach than the judgmental attitude.

6. *The passive, silent passive, or retreating husband.* An intelligent and highly competent wife consulted me about her husband's behavior several years ago. He refused to talk to her or to the children, and had refused to give her any money with which to run the house. She was at a loss to account for this erratic behavior. I knew him as a quiet, friendly, passive individual. She was outgoing, exceedingly frank and quite talkative. Her approach was direct and forthright. It was easy to discover that he was simply retreating from a situation with which he could not cope. Honesty, to her, meant telling a person exactly what she thought. She was not sensitive to his needs and failed to understand his silent withdrawal.

I suggested that counseling or a group experience could help them both discover the source of their difficulty. She was reluctant to undertake either. "He's the one that's sick. Get hold of him and try to straighten him out," she said.

With patience, tact, and understanding she could have saved her marriage, which finally ended in divorce. It could have taken six months or three years to resolve the difficulty, but it could almost certainly have been achieved had she been willing to try something other than the heavy-handed, direct, critical approach she used with him. He needed help badly. He felt condemned and rejected and did not know how to protect himself. His only recourse was that of silent retreat. In a futile effort to control the situation he cut off her household funds, forcing her to go to work to support herself. Her resentment grew into overt hostility, and there was the inevitable divorce. Who was at fault? Neither; both. Both were a product of early environment, yet they were responsible for taking steps which might have resulted in a creative solution.

7. *The playboy husband.* This interesting specimen may still be a boy at heart, resenting or resisting adult responsibilities. One such husband neglected his family responsibilities in favor of pursuing his hobby of motorcycle racing. Another collected and tinkered with old cars. One whom I counseled pursued his hobby of hunting and fishing to the neglect of his family.

Still another, representative of many, pursued women. He needed to confirm his maculinity by making as many conquests as possible. He could handle his lack of masculine identity only by having a series of affairs with numerous women. One typical philanderer had a collection of guns, which he seldom used, a boat he used only twice, a vast assortment of fishing rods, though he never went fishing. These were simply masculinity symbols. He engaged in an endless series of affairs with various women until his frustrated wife ended the marriage. His male identity was so weak that he was emotionally incapable of any sustained relationship with one woman.

Tinkering with the symptoms is usually fruitless. Emotional and spiritual growth is the only solution, and unless a husband with such a problem is willing to get help, there is little hope for the marriage.

8. *The neurotic tightwad.* The husband who seeks to control his wife or family with money is using the weapon he knows and loves best. He is, like most of the others in these categories, an extremely insecure individual, and money has become his chief source of security. He uses it to control those about him. A typical man of this type thought nothing of spending a hundred and fifty dollars on a suit for himself, but doled out a totally inadequate amount to clothe his wife and children. He demanded an

accounting of every dime he handed out. He had grown up in extreme poverty and was resolved that he would never again suffer from a lack of money. Understandably, his neurotic behavior alienated his family. He was quite willing to endure their hostility rather than part with any of the money which, as it turned out, was ultimately divided between his wife and himself when the marriage finally ended in divorce.

A confirmed tightwad is not necessarily mean. He is frightened of being without money. He can no more be argued out of his neurosis than one can be talked out of being five-feet-eight. It is an almost ineradicable part of his nature. Psychotherapy could help such a person, but the tightwad will seldom part with the money necessary to achieve a cure he doesn't want.

How to Live With a Neurotic Husband

We all marry an ideal. During courtship we each present to the other our best side. The ancient statement that love is blind is essentially true. The flow of pink sex hormones shuts off the flow of oxygen to the brain. This is almost literally the case, for during courtship we are "in love with love," and we tend to idealize the loved one, magnifying the virtues and minimizing the personality defects. There is a glow, an expectancy, a kind of euphoria which short-circuits the cortex, where rational judgment takes place. Then reality sets in. The euphoria disappears soon after the wedding veil is laid aside and the honeymoon is over. Now begins the task of working out a satisfactory marriage relationship.

A neurotic husband (and of course everyone is neurotic to some degree) needs precisely the very thing his wife feels incapable of giving him—loving tolerance. At the time he is the most unreasonable he is in need of the greatest amount of understanding and patience. When his ego has been bruised and he takes out his accumulated frustrations on his wife or children, he is in need of unconditional love, something that is difficult to give to an unreasonable, demanding, or hostile person.

Remember that his actions are not "thought out." They are compulsive, as are all neurotic reactions. He does not know why he does or says what he does any more than a child who is having tantrums. Almost any negative response will cause him to feel even more unloved. His unreasonable or frustrating actions evoke in his wife such a feeling of resentment that she is too busy hating him to give him the very thing he needs most, which is love.

He will not sound rational or reasonable simply because he is reacting emotionally in an effort to protect himself and keep his ego intact. If he is in need of nurturing, some form of tenderness, he feels instinctively that he cannot reveal his need lest he seem to be weak. He may, in consequence, respond to his wife with anger or retreat in silent rejection. He is usually not conscious of the fact that what he really needs is to be loved; by acting as he does he makes his wife less able to respond with affection.

It is difficult for many people to accept, but the truth is that the basic need of a woman is for security, and the fundamental need of the male is for affection. Her need for security may involve much more than material possessions. She can be made to feel secure by the knowledge that she is loved and cherished, that her husband is strong enough to take care of her, that he can be depended upon. She often tests unconsciously just to make sure that he has the strength she needs.

He, on the other hand, has a basic and fundamental need for affection. Some men feel embarrassed by outward demonstrations of affection, but the need is still there. He is desperately in need of tenderness, affection, gentleness, though the forms in which men can accept these emotional offerings varies greatly with the individual.

A neurotic husband, frustrated in his work may be unable to share his anxieties with his wife for fear of appearing weak. As a result he may turn to excessive drinking or abusive conduct, or seek to bolster his weakened ego by some kind of flirtation. He may seek refuge in sickness, the bottle, an affair, or in some kind of frenzied activity which gives him temporary relief.

To point out to him how irrational his behavior has become will only intensify his anger or self-rejection. His wife's arguments or admonitions remind him of his mother's exhortations about his homework or household chores. It is worse than futile to argue with a neurotic husband. The wife of such a man feels instinctively that her marriage is failing, and she usually begins to show him how wrong he is. A far more creative approach is to give him as much love and affection as possible and discover some outside activities for herself. If she feels neglected because of his neurotic or unreasonable behavior, she will feel tempted to point out that he has not taken her anyplace in weeks or months; that she has needs, too; that their marriage is falling apart; that they should see a marriage counselor—with the result that he either retreats still further into his silence or seeks to justify himself.

Women in general tend to want to engage in activities with their husbands. They like doing things together. Some husbands find home and hearth and television a safe refuge from a hectic or threatening world and seem uninterested in going out as often as their wives would like. Arguments are usually futile since they imply a judgment or criticism. A far better approach, if there is no other solution, is for the wife to find some activities of her own in which she can engage. If she cannot have a perfect marriage, she can have a satisfying one. Millions of unmarried women would settle for a *poor* marriage—"Even a warm body in the house, someone to talk to, would be better than the loneliness I endure," as one unmarried woman put it.

Besides, a husband is more likely to respond to a cheerful wife who has been busy with her own interest outside the home, than to a nagging wife. It is never a matter of *who* is right, but rather how to work out a creative relationship.

Some husbands, as opposed to the silent retreating type, play the game of "uproar." As the result of accumulated tensions they unconsciously feel a need to keep everything in a turmoil. One such husband vented his daily accumulation of anxieties by shouting at the children at dinner, correcting their eating habits and their grammar. He challenged their opinions and shouted them down. "Dinnertime at our house is sheer hell," his wife complained. "What can you do with such a man?"

Argument with a person in that frame of mind is fruitless. In fact, it is fatal. The wife of a neurotic husband must learn not to argue or attack when he is erupting. Later, when he is calmer, she can talk with him, making sure that she does not sound critical.

A wife came in for a counseling session and stated that she was just about ready to end her marriage, which had become intolerable. Her husband had refused to come with her. "If things do not get better, I want out," she said.

She was quite serious about her intent, so I said, "You have three choices: You can end your marriage now; you can continue with counseling and endeavor to sort out your emotions, in the hope that he may respond to some changes in you; you can, if you prefer, tell him that you intend getting a divorce unless the two of you together can see a counselor and work out a better relationship." She thought about it for a week or two, and at a subsequent session said, "I've told him, quietly but firmly, that unless he is willing to work at this marriage as hard as I am, I want a divorce. He finally agreed to come with me for a counseling session next week, but I don't think it will do any good. He's hostile and argumentative. He'll come once and that'll be it."

The two of them came in a few days later, and we had a reasonably good discussion. I encouraged them both to take a psychological test in order to discover areas of their personality in need of attention. He readily agreed, for to him it seemed less personal, and consequently less threatening. Both took one of the basic psychological tests and for eleven weeks each was given an evaluation slip, indicating some area of their personalities in need of attention. The weekly slips focused attention upon their own individual personality defects and they ceased arguing about who was right or wrong. Each discovered eleven things they needed to undertake in order to achieve a better marriage.

He reported, "You know, after that first session things seemed to calm down at home. I guess we got out some of the tension. Anyway, I can see some sense to this counseling ·business. It has helped already."

In their weekly sessions with me they each talked about their own individual slips. No one was being accused, and they did not find the evaluations too painful since they were simply the result of their own personality inventory. They worked out a thoroughly satisfactory marriage.

EIGHT TYPES

11 OF NEUROTIC

WIVES

> Love means to love that which is unlovable, or it
> is no virtue at all; forgiving means to pardon that
> which is unpardonable, or it is no virtue at all—
> and to hope means hoping when things are hope-
> less, or it is no virtue at all. —*G. K. Chesterton*

1. *The overly dominant wife.* The term dominant
as used here does not necessarily imply "domineering."
One can possess a dominant personality without being domineering. Dominance, as a personality characteristic, simply means an inner need to control other
people or one's surroundings. This tendency can be
expressed overtly or subtly, suppressed or channeled
into creative activity.

All of us feel safer when we can control our environment and those about us; there are many ways
by which we seek to do this. Some wives use a heavy
hand and a loud voice. Others, who are quieter, may
control through manipulation. Some women unconsciously seek to control those about them through the
use of illness, real or imaginary, or they may achieve
their goal by creating guilty feelings in others.

A man in one of our groups said, "It has just begun
to dawn on me how thoroughly mother controlled
the entire household with a strange mixture of love
and illness. She was tender and solicitous as long
as we obeyed, and as long as Dad did exactly what

she expected of him, but if anyone expressed any independence of thought or action, she would have a 'heart attack' or take to her bed with any one of a long list of illnesses. She lived to be ninety. Dad was passive and never sensed that he was being manipulated into total subservience. Mother always got her way by fair means or foul. Only lately have I sensed how she controlled the whole family through manipulation. Quiet arguments would come first. If that didn't work, she would cry. Then she'd become 'ill' as a last resort, and we'd all be made to feel that we brought about her illness. Then we'd feel guilty and give in."

It is important to remember that a controlling wife is seldom fully aware, if at all, of her dominance. She may think of herself as self-sacrificing and filled with love. Her feeling is, "If you really loved me, you'd do as I say." Failure to accede to all of her wishes is interpreted by her as a lack of love or consideration.

With a part of her nature such a wife wants a strong, loving, tender, dominant male. Another part of her wants her own way, and she feels unloved or rejected if she meets with any resistance.

2. *The narcissistic woman.* A narcissistic person is one who has an inordinate self-love. She is unduly preoccupied with her face, her body, and often with her own interests, which she perceives as an extension of herself.

Women who are possessed of great beauty often have difficulty achieving emotional maturity. They become accustomed, early in life, to receiving compliments on their beauty. It becomes their sole stock in trade. They have heard so often, as children, how beautiful they are that they come to feel that the world owes them a continual stream of compliments. Self-centeredness, narcissism, results. They learn to expect praise as their due.

Sometimes a young woman has been overpraised for a specific talent, and she learns to expect great things from life. If she showed some talent as a child, with a certain musical ability for instance, she comes to expect applause all through life. If her talent is just a bit above the ordinary and fatuous parents have overpraised her, she may develop ambition out of all proportion to her talent and end up a bitter, disappointed performer, one of many thousands who did not make the grade.

A man married to a narcissistic woman is in for trouble. If the world does not continue to praise her, and if he does not cater to her infantile whims, she may develop any number of physical or emotional symptoms. Her complaints against her husband and the world in general can lead her from doctor to doctor, seeking a cure for innumerable physical complaints. The mind, frustrated, turns its pain over to the body. With a physical or emotional illness she now has a ready-made excuse for having failed in her marriage or career.

A sensitive and perceptive wife in one of our groups said: "When I am out of focus I really want my husband to stand up to me, but he's too considerate and gentle to resist me. So I go on pushing and prodding him to get him to stop me. I wish he were more dominant; I want him stronger and able to handle me."

Her husband, unable to decode her messages and understand her nonrational behavior, tried to please her and, when he failed, became either silent and morose, or exploded in frustrated anger.

One such woman effectively controlled her family by a succession of weeping spells, threats, or retreats into "illness." She prevented her daughter from marrying and disrupted her own marriage. She lived to a ripe, bitter old age. Her husband was much too gentle to cope with her and left her after thirty years of marriage. The unmarried daughter, frustrated and unhappy, went on caring for her mother through endless spells of alternating illness and fits of anger. The mother was obviously a sick woman, but only in an emotional sense.

There is no simple, easy solution for a wife who is determined to have her own way in everything. Counseling can often help. A man married to such a woman must be firm. Efforts to solve the problem with arguments are usually doomed to failure, but some form of communication must be established. Such persons are basically self-centered and immature. They interpret any resistance as selfishness on the part of others.

Such an individual needs considerable therapy or a genuine religious experience. The supreme law, as given us by Jesus, is to love God with all our hearts and to love others as we love ourselves. This includes, of course, a *proper* self-love, as opposed to a neurotic preoccupation with oneself which excludes others.

A narcissistic woman constantly seeks to be the center of attention. She seeks flattery and is engaged in a constant battle for popularity. She is sometimes a "psychic scalp collector," flirting with men in order to prove to herself that she has not lost her attractiveness. She uses men, including her husband.

A twice-married woman said to me in a counseling session, "After my marriage broke up, I asked myself repeatedly what, if anything, I had done to cause my marriage to fail. In a quiet time one day I just sat and listened. Some inner voice said gently, 'It isn't anything you *did* that caused it to fail. You just didn't do anything to meet his needs.' Suddenly, in a flash, I saw that I had never really met *any* of his needs. I had not even tried to be aware of his needs spiritually, mentally, socially, or sexually. I had just assumed that we'd have a good marriage, but I had not really taken the trouble to understand him and his needs."

A narcissistic preoccupation with her own needs had blinded her to the fact that one must *give* in marriage, as well as *receive*.

3. *The adult-infantile wife.* I knew her first as a sweet, charming high school girl. She was perhaps overly compliant, but her behavior gave no indication of the terribly neurotic wife she became. She was married at nineteen to a handsome young man, and they settled down in a small apartment. During the first year or two of marriage she showed signs of depression and became petulant and demanding. Her adolescent dreams of unending romance were not being fulfilled by her gentle, rather unimaginative husband. His income was meager and they could not afford all of the luxuries of which she had dreamed. Their tiny apartment, and a few courses at junior college, did not give her enough to occupy her mind.

She became more and more demanding. In bewilderment he listened to her angry tirades about his modest income. When her outbursts became violent he brought her in for a conference. Instead of the sweet high school girl I had known, I found a hostile, demanding, utterly unreasonable young woman who had seemingly regressed back to childhood. She pouted, wept, demanded, threatened. The childishness of her demands appalled her stunned husband. She wanted, she said, to be taken care of, to have luxuries like other people. She wanted them *now.* I asked her to describe specifically what she expected her husband to provide for her. The list was astounding and utterly ridiculous. She had obviously become emotionally ill and was in need of intensive therapy. It required three years of intensive private therapy before she was able to achieve a degree of emotional maturity and lead a normal life.

A less glaring instance of the adult-infantile wife was provided by the case of a young minister's wife. They had married while he was still attending seminary, and they had worked out a relatively satisfactory relationship. He became the pastor of a small new church. The tiny congregation was meeting in a beautiful six-room home high on a hill with a magnificent view, and the young minister and his wife were to live in the residence temporarly, but the congregation utilized most of the rooms on Sunday. It was not precisely the thing a young bride dreams of, but she had married a minister, and he thought she had understood that initially there would be a fairly meager salary and probably some inconveniences.

After trying out the arrangement for a month, they came to see me. The young wife was livid with rage and weeping uncontrollably. She poured out her complaints about the intolerable living conditions, some of which seemed completely justified. Her real problem then came to the surface when she said, "I'd always dreamed of a seven-room house, filled with beautiful furniture, and wall-to-wall carpeting; and here we have this awful situation where the church people move in on us on Sunday, and we have no privacy at all. I just won't stand for it."

I asked Claudette if she had ever really wanted to be a minister's wife in the first place. "No," she said, "I wanted him, but here I've married a whole church, and I don't want any part of it."

She and her husband joined a group of young ministers and wives who met every Saturday morning as a Yokefellow group. They took a spiritual growth inventory, consisting of a psychological test with the usual weekly evaluation slips. She had ample opportunity to vent her petulant anger over her husband's preoccupation with a struggling young church. Other wives in the group had similar, if less violent, complaints. There was complete and utter honesty in the group. The couples learned how to communicate at a far deeper level than ever before. Laughter and anger, hilarity and seriousness marked the sessions. I met with them for two years and watched their amazing growth.

Honesty with oneself is the first essential step toward spiritual and emotional growth. Honesty with others is the second essential. Out of their openness there evolved a love and warmth which was wonderful to experience. Something reminiscent of the spirit of the early church seemed to be present. They had obeyed the biblical injunction to "confess your faults one to another, and pray for one another that you may be healed." Each of the marriages improved measurably as the result of the group, and Claudette grew up in the process.

Eventually when Claudette and her husband were able to move out of the original residence into their own home, she found this alone did not solve her problem. She discovered that her problems were within, and were involved in the complexities of married life. After a few years, when they moved to a larger church, she told me of the growth that had taken place in her; her whole personality now validated her self-appraisal. She had grown up.

On a lesser scale, many an adult-infantile wife manifests an emotional immaturity which makes life intolerable for a husband. Marriage does not solve emotional problems. It compounds them. Many a woman of twenty or forty is still emotionally unprepared for the role of wife. The infant within the adult is still making unreasonable demands, still expecting instant fulfillment of every wish. When an emotionally immature woman or man is married, the prognosis for a successful marriage is poor, unless the immature partner is willing to undertake a fairly long-range effort to grow up emotionally.

4. *The masculine-protest wife.* The term "masculine-protest" was first used by Carl Gustav Jung to describe a fairly large group of women who experience an unconscious ambivalence toward men. They love and hate them at the same time. The feelings are usually unconscious. A man married to such a woman is always engaged in a struggle for power. If he gives in she is jubilant but she also feels defeated because he was not strong enough to stand up to her.

"Men are so weak and ineffectual!" she will then say. Such a woman is basically argumentative, and will provoke an argument usually in an unconscious effort to keep the power struggle going.

The masculine protest stems from any of the following or a mixture of them:

(a) A father or brother who was idealized. No man will ever be able to measure up to the idealized male, who epitomizes what all men should be like.

(b) A weak, ineffectual, or alcoholic father whom the woman learned to despise as a girl. Hating the father, she unconsciously despises all men, or feels a need to punish all men for the failures of her father.

(c) An overly strict or domineering father can instill in a daughter the fear of being controlled. She wants a strong husband, but if he reminds her in any way of the father whom she feared, she may experience a "fear-anger" reaction and feel a need to attack. Or, if she is passive, she can become subtly manipulative. If her husband exhibits any of the undesirable traits of her father, whom she may have consciously loved and unconsciously rejected, she can react with unreasoning hostility.

All of these reactions, of course, are entirely unconscious. She can justify herself on a logical basis, but her problem is rooted in a deeply buried hostility toward men. Unfortunately, her children often become the targets of hostility which is really felt toward her husband.

Such women are often frigid, both emotionally and sexually. They are caught in a web not of their own making. A competent marriage counselor, or group therapy, can often provide valuable insights leading toward a solution.

5. *The martyr-wife.* The martyr-type is known technically as masochistic. That is, such individuals are unconsciously seeking punishment. They may be accident-prone, operation-prone, or simply prone to exercise bad judgment in an unconscious effort to be

defeated in life. Unable to find happiness or fulfillment in life, they derive a kind of obstinate satisfaction from the attention they get from being ill or depressed or in trouble of some kind. They cannot endure success or happiness, which they are consciously seeking. I recall one such woman who married a succession of five alcoholics. Another endured sixteen operations for a variety of causes, all quite valid. The "organism"—that is, the unconscious mind operating in cooperation with the body—found that in the hospital she could get attention, the only kind of love she knew how to accept.

There is another type of martyr who does not resort to such extreme measures. Her attention-getting device is simply that of verbal complaints. She is never satisfied. She plays a quiet game of "poor unfortunate me" in an unconscious effort to get attention. Attention is fourth cousin to love, which she is incapable of accepting. If she cannot get love, she will accept sympathy. If that is denied her, she will welcome pity. If she is the "uncomplaining martyr," she will suffer in silence, piteously waiting for some form of attention. If she is the "voluble, overtalkative" type she will turn any conversation into a recital of her ills. It is her sole stock in trade.

I wish it were possible to offer some simple solution for the martyr. Masochism, unfortunately, is a deeply rooted emotion originating in childhood. It is a "life style" which yields reluctantly to any form of therapy. I have known any number of individuals who could recognize the self-defeating lives they were living, but who seemed incapable of finding any creative solution. Deeply implanted in such persons is the will to fail. It is not impossible to eradicate this, but it is exceedingly difficult. Long-term therapy is usually indicated.

6. *The passive-aggressive wife.* No one is all "this" or "that." We all have various conflicting tendencies operating within us, usually at a totally unconscious

level. A passive-aggressive person is just what the term implies—both passive and submissive, with aggressive and hostile tendencies.

Belle was such a wife. Her aggressiveness took the form of seeking to control her husband and children, always for their own good, of course. As is often the case, because she was more aggressive than passive, she married a passive man. He was not as adept at handling finances as she, and she went to great pains to show him how inadequate he was. She was argumentative, overtalkative, with a kind of impatient tolerance for the weaknesses of her husband. When she had prodded him into a rage, she would become passive and retreat.

Unable to have children, she had proposed to her husband that they adopt several. He refused. She persisted, but without results. He was firm in his refusal.

She could not induce him to join a group or come in for counseling, so she came in alone over a period of several months. It became apparent that she was "aggressive-passive," while her husband was "passive-aggressive." That is, she was more aggressive, with passive tendencies, while he was basically passive, but could erupt into violent rages when pushed too far. There had been one particularly ugly experience in which she had prodded him beyond endurance and he struck her.

Over a period of several weeks we worked on just one thing: how to live with the particular male she had married, without loss of integrity or loss of her identity. She came to see, in time, what she had been doing that provoked his rages. We discovered what his "red buttons" were and how she could avoid pushing them. At first she felt that this would involve loss of identity, if she couldn't say everything she felt. I offered her the New Testament concept: "Speaking the truth in love" (Eph. 4:15), and added that it is not necessary or wise to say everything we think, at all times. As a compulsive talker, she found this difficult to grasp, but she did in time.

One day she came in looking radiantly happy. "Guess what! Things have been going a lot better since I learned not to push his red buttons, and yesterday right out of the blue, he said, 'Honey, you've always wanted to adopt some kids. I've decided that it might be a good idea. Let's do it.' I never thought he'd reverse himself so completely. He means it, too. I think he's just been resisting the idea of children because he's resenting my pushing and prodding. Now that I've let up, he's different in a lot of ways."

In most marriages there is, to some degree, a power struggle going on. It may be so subtle that neither is consciously aware of it, or it may erupt in frequent displays of temper. The struggle for mastery tends to disappear when honest, open communication can be established. "Love does not insist on its own way," declares Paul in his second letter to the Corinthians (13:15). When we truly love one another, we cease to seek having our own needs met and endeavor to discover how we can meet the needs of the other person. Ultimately, as a result, our own needs are usually met. "Love never ends," Paul concludes (I Cor. 13:8).

7. *The jealous-possessive wife.* Jealousy knows no sex. It afflicts both men and women. Everyone is capable of jealousy in some degree. God said to Israel, "I am a jealous God," meaning that He wanted to be their only God. The marriage ceremony contains the words, "Forsaking all others." The goal is for each to give complete loyalty and love to the other.

It is only when jealousy turns rancid that it becomes a neurotic manifestation. Overly possessive jealousy usually springs from a deep-seated insecurity. The case of Jeanne illustrates this type in its milder form. When she was quite young her father abandoned the family. Jeanne grew into a beautiful and charming young woman and married a man who became highly successful in business. She was poised and was loved by everyone who knew her, but the emotional scar caused by her father's disappearance revealed itself in her marriage. Her husband made frequent business trips around the country, and each time he returned home his wife questioned him for the next few days about his activities while away from home. It was done in a fairly subtle manner.

"And what did you do on Monday night, dear?" she would ask casually. He would try to recall and tell her. An hour or so later she would inquire, "And how did things go on Tuesday evening? Did you meet anyone interesting?" After this type of questioning would go on intermittently for several days, he would explode in irritation. "How can you expect me to recall every event that transpired during a perfectly routine business trip? Do you want me to carry a diary?" Despite the fact that he had never given her the slightest cause to doubt him, she kept this up during the forty-five years of their married life. Without at all understanding the origin of her jealousy, he managed to live with it.

A husband who shows a faint interest in a woman at a social function can arouse the most intense jealousy in an insecure wife. If she is pathologically jealous, like Katherine, the marriage can be threatened. Katherine's jealousy and possessiveness were so intense that if Jack came home an hour later than usual, he was always subjected to a barrage of questions. When he casually mentioned the name of some woman in the office where he worked, she insisted on knowing what their relationship was, what she looked like, how often he saw her. Jack told me, in utter desperation, of the hundreds of times he had been subjected to an inquisition. Life had become unbearable, he said. Katherine's possessiveness had become so extreme that she insisted on going with him to the store in the evening; or she would insist on his accompanying her if she went. She could not endure having him out of her sight except during the time he spent at work.

I said, "It seems probable that she had a terribly insecure childhood and that she must have lost her father or some beloved male figure early in life."

"Yes," he said, "her father died when she was a very small child, and an older brother died soon after. She idolized both of them."

It is far easier to deduce the cause of a neurotic behavior pattern than it is to cure it. In the case of Katherine, it required vast patience and understanding on the part of her husband, and intensive therapy for Katherine, before she could resolve the problem.

A wife who is beset by extreme jealousy must first realize that this springs out of a deep sense of insecurity, and second, that to give way to this possessiveness will almost certainly drive a husband farther away. It can become almost a self-fulfilling prophecy, whereby the fear of losing one's husband becomes a reality through focusing upon the fear.

8. *The depressed wife*. There are different kinds of depression, and different degrees. Most humans experience occasional depressed moods at one time or another. Unhappy events or disappointments can cause mild depression, which tends to vanish in time. Some depression originates in a chemical imbalance or as the result of physical illness.

Varying emotional states accompany the monthly cycle for many women, and most husbands learn, if they are at all perceptive, not to react to an emotional outburst at such a time.

There is one type of depression common to many wives about which a husband can do something constructive. A young mother with three small children came to see me in a highly emotional state. She had made the rounds of doctors, one of whom prescribed iron and vitamin shots. Another gave her tranquilizers, and a third urged her to "snap out of it." She told me that she was depressed much of the time, irritable with the children, and cried easily. She alternated between talking jags and depression so deep that she felt she could not even carry on a conversation with her husband.

Since physicians could find nothing organically wrong with her, and tranquilizers helped hardly at all, I surmised that she was suffering from nothing more acute than simple emotional and physical fatigue. She had her small children with her from twelve to fourteen hours a day. Her husband worked eight hours a day, came home and rested. I urged her to take a vacation from husband and children. "Every mother of small children," I told her, "deserves a day off every week. In your case I'd urge you to take a three- or four-day vacation now and take off a full day once a week." Like most emotionally upset and depressed persons, all she could see were difficulties. I helped her work these out, and she went away for a few days' rest. She returned looking and feeling wonderful. I urged her to get off by herself, or with a friend, one day a week, quoting to her "Six days you shall labor..." (Ex. 20:9). I pointed out to her that she could trade with another mother, and that if she had to pay for a sitter, the ultimate cost would be much less than weekly sessions with a psychiatrist over a period of months or years. In her case it worked.

Many husbands have no conception of what is involved in having one or more children underfoot ten to fifteen hours a day, unless they have taken over for a day or two when the mother is ill. Some husbands of working wives expect their wives to work all day and do housework until far into the night with little or no assistance.

But there are also wives who become professional moaners. Marriage is not just what they had dreamed it would be. Housework becomes an endless round of meaningless monotony to them. And indeed, much housework is just plain janitor work, and for a creative personality it can lack meaning. A wife who feels unfulfilled can become depressed and create an atmosphere in the home that makes the husband wish he were somewhere else. Creating the right emotional climate in the home is chiefly a wife's responsibility to discover what he can do to help her create a wholesome atmosphere.

A depressed, demanding, possessive, complaining wife—who may indeed have much to complain about —is setting the stage for marital discord. If she can, without anger or threats, make her needs known, she stands a better chance of working out a satisfactory marriage. If she cannot do this alone and unaided, she needs the help of a marriage counselor or some qualified person who can aid her in sorting out her feelings and finding a creative solution.

INCOMPATIBILITY

12

AND PARADOXES

IN MARRIAGE

> When the satisfaction or security of another person
> becomes as significant to one as one's own, then a
> state of love exists. So far as I know, under no
> other circumstances is a state of love present, re-
> gardless of popular usage. —*Harry Stack Sullivan*

Everyone likes a happy ending. Authors tend to use
for illustrative material case histories in which everything turns out well. But candor compels us to face
the reality of marital tangles for which there are
seemingly no solutions.

Earle and Gladys are a case in point. Gladys came
in for counseling over a period of a year or more.
They attended a group of husbands and wives for
nearly a year. I discovered that Gladys had two personalities. When her marriage first broke up her three
children turned against her and went to live with
their father. Feeling very much alone and rejected,
she came to see me. She was puzzled and hurt. She
could not see why they were all against her. It was
difficult at first for me to understand why this pleasant, gentle, attractive wife and mother had been so
totally rejected by her family.

When, at her insistence, her estranged husband
joined the group, I began to understand. The quiet,
gentle wife turned out to be, in the presence of her
husband, a hostile, attacking, critical person. Earle

proved to be a passive-aggressive individual. The two elements of passivity and aggression within his personality simply did not mesh with the traits which his wife possessed. There was a brief time when they got back together, but this was short-lived. I began to see the dynamics at work as they participated in the group. She was a psychic masochist, and he was a sadist. Unconsciously she needled him until he would explode in impotent rage. She would then become a martyr, pleading for sympathy and understanding. The masochist usually finds the sadist, and vice versa. One who feels an unconscious need to be punished or to suffer in some way will usually find a counterpart. I saw no hope for their marriage. It was a mistake in the first place. They were mismated, and, worse, neither was a good marriage risk with anyone because of their particular personality patterns which they seemed unwilling or unable to alter.

However, most marital tangles can be straightened out. There are situational differences which can cause major disturbances: relatives, money, and minor sexual incompatibility. These usually can be solved without too much difficulty if the two persons involved possess reasonable emotional maturity. However, such problems quite often require the help of a competent third party who can view the scene objectively.

There are deeper problems which are not situational, but which have their roots in a damaged personality structure. Denise joined one of our groups, determining to get the root of her emotional, physical, and domestic problems. Her husband opposed this step and forbade her to leave the house without his permission. Outside the home he was a meek and passive man, but in the marriage relationship he seemed determined to control every detail of her life. She risked his wrath for the first time in more than twenty years of marriage, joined a group, and began to gain considerable insight into herself and her problems.

At one point she related an instance when, as a small child, she came home and could not find her pet dog. Her mother said, "Your daddy killed your dog because you were bad." This episode left an indelible impression on her. If Mother said she was bad, then she must be. She had gone through life feeling guilty, though she could never discover what it was that she felt guilty about. One result was that she felt she had no rights. She could not defend herself or her opinions. Inevitably, she met and married a man who was her counterpart. Feeling that she had no rights, she found and married a man who was unwilling to grant her any rights or privileges. He controlled her life down to the smallest detail.

This is not a situational problem, but a personality problem. There would have been no point in trying to help this couple work out their financial or social problems or any other relationship issue without first helping the wife discover her true identity. She came to discover that she had normal human rights, that she could defend herself and express her opinions.

Normally, when a husband or wife makes significant personality changes, a mild to serious crisis is created in the marriage. Either the crisis awakens the other to the need for change or evokes a hostile reaction.

Rudy and Mary illustrate some of the problems encountered when two radically different types of personality seek their counterparts. Mary was quiet and subdued and took a rather serious view of life. She laughed seldom and seemed devoid of any sense of humor. Rudy, on the other hand, was gay, vivacious, boyish, and immature in many ways. Whereas Mary was conservative where money was concerned, Rudy was unperturbed when bills went unpaid or when they were overdrawn at the bank. He was financially irresponsible and did little around the home.

Her seriousness found a counterpart in his ebullience and spontaneity. His irresponsibility needed her stability. They had found their counterparts, but now they could not live at peace. They were poles apart in their concept of child rearing, finances, social life, and many other issues.

Eventually they were separated, and divorce proceedings were instituted. Mary came in for a number of counseling sessions and later joined a sharing group. Initially, all she could feel was that her husband acted like a totally irresponsible boy. Little by little she was able to see that her terribly serious approach to life was as extreme as his boyish immaturity. Some months after their divorce became final, they began to see each other again, and finally Rudy began to attend the group. Mary began to abandon some of her ultrasober concepts, and Rudy started settling down. Without feeling any loss of masculinity, he offered to let Mary handle the finances. He began to assume more responsibility around the home. They were ultimately remarried and now have a better-than-average marriage.

It has been said, "Marriage is a give and take proposition. You give up your freedom and take the consequences." In the case of a woman, she gives up her name, the security of her parental home (or job, as the case may be), her independence, and takes on the responsibilities of running a home and caring for a husband and children. Housework is repetitious, monotonous, and not very creative except for those few ultradomesticated women for whom it is an unending joy to make beds and biscuits and wash dishes. If there are children, the wife and mother is shut in with youngsters at the very time in life when she would like to be out "doing things." No matter how much she loves her children and home, she may miss being "out where things are happening." As one young mother expressed it, "I'm hemmed in by dishes, diapers, and drudgery."

Yet, paradoxically, this is just the sort of thing, minus the drudgery, of which a woman dreams: husband, home, children. It is all made worthwhile if she feels secure in her husband's love. If he appreciates her, listens to her, validates her feelings, takes an interest in the home, and shares some of her problems, then her life can be a joy.

One young wife expressed her incompatible needs: "I want to be the most important thing in my husband's life. However, I want him to have an all-consuming passion for his work. If he can have both passions at the same time, he's ideal. If he can hold both halfway, he's good. If he can hold neither, he's hopeless." Her paradoxical needs could frustrate a husband unless both learned to be tolerant.

A man, on the other hand, gives up his freedom and independence and takes on the responsibility—legal, moral, financial, and psychological—of a wife and children. This is intended to be a lifetime contract. If he comes home to a frustrated, hostile, complaining wife, a cluttered house, and a group of shouting children, he can begin to wonder if he made a mistake. However, if he is met by a loving wife at the door and is made to feel that this is his castle, a refuge from a hectic and demanding world, marriage can seem well worthwhile.

The paradoxes in marriage are at the root of many of the incompatibilities which prove so frustrating. A young wife said, "I want my husband to be decisive, masterful, and tender. He must be in charge, and wise enough to make the right decisions."

"What do you mean by 'right decisions'?" I asked.

"Ones that coincide with what I think is right," she replied, laughing. She saw the incongruity of this, but it was precisely what she wanted, and she accepted this as paradoxical but valid.

Someone has described the best combination of parents as a father who is gentle beneath his firmness, and a mother who is firm beneath her gentleness. Two people who can be this as parents would also have some of the basic ingredients of being good marriage partners.

There has been much speculation as to why women as a group live considerably longer than men. One theory holds that it is because women are more in touch with their feelings and do not repress their emotions. This in itself would make for better health. In addition to this as a probable cause, I believe that a more important factor is that women usually have their greatest responsibilities when they are young, while men tend to be given greater responsibilities as they get older. In her twenties, thirties, and forties a typical wife and mother has the responsibility of her children and the home. If she is employed, as many mothers are, she has a double responsibility, but it comes at the time of life when she is physically and psychically at her peak. Men, on the other hand, usually begin to have greater responsibilities in their forties and fifties, and in the early sixties.

Out of a genuine concern for her husband, and because of enlightened self-interest, a wife can contribute to her husband's well-being and her own if she will recognize this and do whatever seems indicated to lessen the strains within the home for her husband as he reaches the critical forties and fifties.

I recall an anguished wife in her fifties whose husband had just dropped dead of a heart attack. He had been a community leader, widely known and respected. She had come to me, in tears, to ask, "Do you think I caused my husband's death?" I asked why she thought this could be so.

She said, "Well, I suppose I was too demanding. I have robust health and couldn't understand why he always wanted to sit down and rest when he came home from work. I like a beautiful garden, and I insisted that he mow the lawn and do all the gardening."

I asked about their social life, and she said: "Yes,

I liked a lot of parties, and he used to complain that we went to too many social functions. He was always insisting that he was too tired, but I usually got my way. I guess I made too many demands, and now he's gone." She burst into tears. I found that she had made the rounds of several psychiatrists and had consulted her friends and associates, asking each if they thought she was responsible for his untimely death. Of course, she felt inwardly that she was at least a contributing factor and was hoping to get enough opinions to the contrary to assuage her guilt, but no amount of reassurance from her friends could console her. She knew the truth.

There is on record the case of a woman who said to a marriage counselor, "I hate my husband! I not only want to divorce him, but I want to make life as tough for him as I possibly can." The counselor told her, "I'll tell you how to proceed. Start showering him with compliments. Indulge every whim. Then just when he knows how much he needs you—start divorce proceedings. You'll fracture him."

The wife decided to accept the advice. Six months later the counselor met her at a social function, and asked, "How did things turn out? Did you divorce your husband?"

"Oh, no! I followed your advice, and we've never been happier. I love him with all my heart."

I related this at a retreat, and one rather hostile wife who was considering divorce said something testily, "You sound as if it was the wife's sole responsibility! The husband has some responsibility for the marriage, too!"

"Yes," I said, "he has equal responsibility; but just as someone has to take the initiative in starting divorce proceedings, one person must seize the initiative in instituting love and patience and good will."

The power of praise has perhaps never been fully explored in the marriage relationship. Mark Twain once said, "I can live for two whole months on one

221

good compliment." One would think that a famous novelist with a world-wide reputation would not need praise, but this is totally untrue. No one ever outgrows the need for honest, sincere praise and recognition.

Shakespeare wrote, "Our praises are our wages." Praise is like sunshine to the human spirit. We cannot flower and grow without it, but criticism is a cold and devastating wind that withers the spirit. Be liberal with praise and stingy with criticism. Any praise or commendation, to be genuinely helpful, must be deserved; otherwise it is mere flattery. Handing out sincere compliments to people is simply another way of distributing love and appreciation. There is nothing more distasteful than living with a person who is critical and disparaging. Many husbands and wives who have a seemingly valid basis for complaint turn out, upon further study, to be critical individuals, or demanding and hostile. The injustices of which they complain are often merely the inevitable harvest reaped from their critical attitude toward others.

How does one overcome the tendency to be negative and critical? To begin with, it is always easier to act your way into new thinking than to think your way into new acting. One must begin at some point, and a good point at which to start is by thinking of ways in which you can compliment your marriage partner. Some people find this exceedingly difficult because they do not really know how to express love in this way. They think of love as merely a feeling, failing to see that love must be expressed in tangible ways. Love is an action as well as an emotion.

Many marriages are failing simply because neither husband nor wife will take the trouble to pay sincere compliments to the other. We all need to be loved, and how shall we know that we are loved unless it is expressed? Psychiatrist William Glasser believes that all emotional illness springs from a failure to feel loved. Whether the patient is psychotic and running berserk or has a nervous headache, a common cause is the dual need to love and be loved, to feel worthwhile to ourselves and to others.

Each of us has a threefold drive: to be loved unconditionally, to change others so that life will be easier for us, and to have all of our needs met. At their core, these are childhood wishes to which the adult clings. They are unrealistic and can never be fully realized. Women are more likely to be idealistic than men (though this is, of course, not universally true) and consequently seek the ideal marriage, either consciously or unconsciously. It is not uncommon for an engaged couple to vow that their marriage will never deteriorate into a humdrum affair. It is usually the starry-eyed young woman who first voices this splendid ideal. George Washington once wrote a letter to his granddaughter, Eliza, then eighteen. She had asked for his picture as a birthday present, and along with the picture he sent her some unasked for advice about marriage: "Love is a mighty pretty thing," he wrote, "but like all other delicious things it is cloying when the first transports of passion begin to subside, which it will assuredly do.... Love is too dainty a food to live on alone, and ought not to be considered more than a necessary ingredient for that matrimonial happiness which results from a combination of causes." He advised her not to expect perfect felicity in marriage. "There is no truth more certain than that all our enjoyments fall short of our expectations," he warned her. It would be asking too much of marriage to expect that all of our dreams, hopes, and needs could be realized, at least in the initial stages of the relationship.

A typical wife wants a husband, home, children, security, affection and tenderness, companionship and strength. She is really asking for a kind of husband-father-lover-friend. Usually the young wife is expecting all this of a man much too young to be emotionally mature, and thus he is normally incapable of satisfying

223

all of her needs. Consequently she may feel frustrated and cheated.

A typical man wants affection, emotional support, sexual fulfillment, a companion, a hostess, a wife-mother-companion-friend. But the young woman whom he has chosen is, like him, usually too young and emotionally immature to be able to fulfill all of his needs.

When the realities of marriage set in, they try to change each other, either through criticism, manipulation, or some form of domestic blackmail. It is not uncommon for a wife to withhold affection as a form of punishment, and for the husband to seek to control or manipulate his wife through the use of money, or refusal to communicate.

A far more creative solution is for them both to sit down with a competent marriage counselor and learn to communicate about real problems. Long before they are likely to do this, however, she may have him cataloged as either manipulative stingy, sarcastic, or just plain difficult. And he may complain that she is a sloppy housekeeper, given to frequent temper tantrums, or sexually frigid. If they battle about these symptoms without ever getting down to the real basis of their problems, it is highly probable that they are headed for either a lifetime power struggle or the divorce court.

Married couples usually feel, after a few years of marriage or even before, that they know each other well. Often the opposite is true. Humans are many-faceted.

I saw an illustration of this in a group where six couples were having their first meeting together. I said to them, "We cannot change each other by direct actions, and after tonight we will abandon the effort as fruitless. But just for tonight you have a final opportunity to list three things that you would like to change about your husband or wife." There was some nervous laughter, but each person present, in the

224

next half hour, listed three important changes he would like to make in his mate.

· The first one, a husband, said gently, "I wish Marilyn would show the same affection that she revealed the first year of our marriage. She's begun to take me for granted. Second, I wish she would be neater around the house. Third, I would like for her to stop correcting me in public on minor matters."

His wife looked at him in astonishment. "Why Fred, you've never told me these things before! I wasn't aware that you felt this way. I thought you were perfectly happy. Why didn't you tell me?"

"Well," he said, "I have faults, too, and I felt that I had no right to criticize you." They discussed these items at some length. Marilyn was seeing herself for the first tme as her husband saw her. In the safety of a group it became possible for him to express his real feelings. And when her time came, she surprised him with her list—things which she had never mentioned to him before. She wanted him to let her know when he expected to be late for dinner; she was jealous of the attention he paid to a woman friend of hers; she felt hurt because he had never invited her to go along on his fishing trips. He, in turn, said in considerable surprise, "But Marilyn, you never expressed the slightest interest in fishing before. How was I to know?"

Communication is the keynote, the fundamental ingredient in any successful marriage. In some relationships the only communication that takes place deals with trivia; discussions may bog down in accusations and countercharges. Some marriage partners discover that there are certain things which cannot be discussed without a fight, and they carefully avoid these areas, leaving the issues to smolder unresolved. The important thing is to find a safe place where troublesome issues can be resolved. Normally this requires a trained counselor or an adequately led sharing group.

Not only do husbands and wives fail to understand each other, but few individuals understand themselves. We have a vested interest in not knowing ourselves at a deep level. When someone says, "Oh, I know myself pretty well," what is meant is, "I know some things about myself which I hope will never be discovered." Paul Tournier, the Swiss psychiatrist, has pointed out that no one really knows himself, and for that matter, that we can never completely understand ourselves, no matter how long we work at it.

Lucille was a case in point. I had known her when she was in college, but had not seen her for about twenty years. She came to see me about the deep depression from which she was suffering. Psychiatric consultation had provided her with some insight into her problem, but she was still depressed. She had been divorced for some years and was the sole support of two children, one of whom was completely out of hand. She was desperately unhappy and lonely, and, as we came to discover, she was caught in a bind. She wanted to remarry, but all of her relationships with men ended disastrously. Men would date her a time or two but inevitably drop her. One day she asked, "Is there something radically wrong with me?"

She was an attractive, intelligent woman, but three things stood out: she was entirely devoid of a sense of humor; she was pleasant but terribly serious; and it became gradually apparent that she was argumentative with men.

At first I suspected an unconscious hostility toward men, a not-uncommon double bind experienced by women who love, need, and hate men. We went into matter of her relationship with her father. He was an intellectual who loved to debate with his daughter, an only child. They argued animatedly over every conceivable topic—social, political, and psychological. She had been a straight A student, and her father was thrilled to have someone with whom he could match wits. She had learned as a child that the one

226

way to please her father was through intellectual attainment.

Her only satisfying relationship with a significant male had been argumentative. She engaged in arguments at the office where she was employed, especially with men. Besting a man in an argument was, so far as she knew, the only way to relate.

It was not an easy task to help a woman of forty to see that an argumentative woman is not a man's first choice. She even wanted to debate the matter with me. I refused to argue with her and became quite directive at this point: either she could give up her argumentativeness, or she could abandon any hope of establishing a satisfactory relationship with any normal man. Suffering is a powerful motivator. She began to accept my thesis that contentiousness and the pose of being an intellectual were her two chief drawbacks. Even so, there were occasional doubts. "I've often heard that men don't like intelligent women," she said. "Maybe that's my trouble."

"That argument," I replied, "is the last recourse of a hostile, emotionally immature woman. A typical man does not disparage a woman for her intelligence. What he dislikes is her competitiveness and argumentativeness. No normal man wants to come home to a debate or to be challenged by his wife, or anyone else, every time he opens his mouth. Discussion is one thing; argument is something else, and a steady diet of that can sour any marriage."

We discussed her problem over a period of months. From time to time we "role played" various situations. Among other things she began to try to develop a sense of humor and actually learned to tell jokes at the office. I gave her one or two each week, which she tried out on her fellow workers.

Eventually this serious, depressed, argumentative woman became a rather delightful person, and our sessions ended after she reported, with great satisfaction, that she had begun to have some dates and that one man in particular was showing considerable interest in her.

A common complaint of many wives is that their husbands show little or no affection except when they are interested in sexual relations. In order to feel loved and cherished a woman needs to have love expressed frequently in many ways, verbally and otherwise. Tenderness should be a part of it.

A wife who never receives affection without sex relations can become rejecting, a natural response to feeling rejected by her husband.

One undemonstrative husband expressed his love for his wife in the only way of which he was capable. He was adept at building things, and the house was full of evidences of his handiwork. He built, repaired, tinkered, but his wife complained, "He never tells me he loves me." Of course, in his own way he was demonstrating the fact that he loved her. Ideally he could have tried to learn how to be more physically and verbally demonstrative, and she could have tried to accept the fact that he might never be able to verbalize his feelings. An undemonstrative wife, reared in a home where little physical affection was displayed, tried to express her love for her husband by being a good housekeeper and cook. Her husband, who was much more demonstrative, understandably wanted his wife to be more affectionate. He came to accept the fact that it was difficult for his wife to express affection in the way he desired, and she made a determined effort to become more responsive. It is essential in a satisfactory marriage relationship to try to give love in a manner that is understood and needed by the other.

In a group session in which a minister and his wife participated, I saw the power of the small group to elicit unexpected responses from various members. During the course of the first session the minister's wife said, "I feel frustrated in one aspect of my marriage. My husband and I met in college, and we married before he entered the seminary. He took the usual course prescribed for ministers, and I studied virtually the same courses he did. We graduated at the same time, each with the same degree. I had intended to become a Christian education director. Then the children started coming, and I've been taking care of them for the past fourteen years, while he has been engaged in the very activities for which I was as well prepared as he was. I feel cheated because I have never had a chance to use my education. When am I going to be able to be a person in my own right and have a career, as I had planned?" She displayed considerable frustration and a certain amount of pent-up hostility as she concluded. Members of their church were present, and I wondered how her husband would react. Without any trace of embarrassment or defensiveness, he expressed understanding and concern. The essence of his response was that he understood how she felt, but that motherhood and a career often proved to be incompatible goals, at least when children are small. He expressed the hope and belief that she could find total fulfillment when the children required less of her time. She could see this intellectually but did not feel it emotionally.

The problem of trying to fulfill such conflicting needs is not easy for many women. There is a strong emotional and biological need in most women to find fulfillment in having children. But in our culture, where many careers are open to women as well as equal educational opportunities, some women find the two drives incompatible and are frustrated in finding a solution.

I recall a woman who resolved this dilemma. She was graduated from medical school, became a pediatrician, and then married. She had five children and virtually supported the entire family. She did an excellent job of combining motherhood and a career, as do many women, though understandably the task is not easy.

In the case of the minister's wife, I sensed that there was something unsaid. Her husband had become prominent in denominational affairs and traveled to board meetings and conventions a great deal. She was left at home with the children, and though it was not expressed, I sensed that she felt that he was having a great old time flying around the country, eating in the best restaurants, staying in the finest hotels, while she felt trapped at home with the children in what was, to her, the unrewarding task of routine housework. There was implicit in her complaint and the circumstances considerable envy of her husband's freedom and his attainments. She seemed to be saying, "He is widely known and respected and highly successful, while I am 'just a housewife.'"

Routine housework and caring for children can prove rather prosaic and dreary compared to the interesting and varied activities in which some men engage. At least it can seem so to a mother who has grown weary of laundry, household chores, cleaning, and the constant demands of small children. Whether her complaint is valid or otherwise, her feelings are quite understandable. A wife and mother who feels trapped in such a situation can remind herself that in the very prime of life she will, under normal circumstances, be freed of the responsibilities of children, and at the very time when her husband may be bearing greater responsibility, she is more free than ever before to do some of the things she has always wanted to do.

A wife once told me that she felt more secure when she was operating "under an umbrella."

She said, "At home my husband is the umbrella. He gives me lots of freedom, but I am always trying to get out from under the umbrella, and the farther out I get, the more anxious I become, but I never have sense enough to get back under, until he chases me back. I'm always angry when he does, and I cry, but I'm so happy! At work my boss is the umbrella, and he knows when I am out of focus. When that happens he takes over. He then becomes very directive, and gently but firmly starts giving orders. I'm always relieved when he does this, because when I am at the end of my rope emotionally I never have enough sense to know what to do."

She was expressing a feeling shared by many women. "I want a man to lean on," one wife expressed it.

I asked, "How is he supposed to know when you want complete autonomy and when you want him to be in charge?"

Without the slightest trace of irony she replied, "He's supposed to be able to tell." It was the most natural thing in the world to expect her husband to be able to fathom her variable moods from day to day, or for that matter from hour to hour, and alter his course of action to suit her moods. A thoughtful and perceptive husband can do this, unless, of course, her "down" happens to correspond with one of his "downs." At that point both are looking to the other for emotional support and understanding. Both are asking and neither is able to give.

Frigidity in the female and impotence in the male are psychological in origin in the majority of instances. Impotence can stem from a variety of causes such as strong guilt feelings, a generalized sense of inadequacy, or a long-held belief in the sinfulness of sex imprinted upon the personality in childhood. A passive male married to a controlling wife sometimes experiences an intensification of his sense of masculine inadequacy. A sensitive or passive husband, if criticized or rejected, may respond unconsciously by becoming partially or totally impotent. He may become withdrawn, or if he has considerable capacity for aggression, may become tyrannical and abusive in an effort to compensate for his feelings of inadequacy.

A sense of masculinity involves a man's concept of himself as a competent person, able to hold his own in a competitive world or in an argument with his wife. If he is berated and made to feel less than a man, or experiences a deep sense of failure and defeat, the result may be impotence. Women often mistakenly assume that the outwardly aggressive male feels as competent as he pretends. Overly aggressive men often feel inwardly unsure of themselves and overcompensate by assuming an outer pose of dominance or aggressiveness. Such a man may be inordinately sensitive to criticism and ashamed to admit that he has been hurt. If he has strong doubts about his capabilities, his unconscious mechanism may respond by rendering him impotent, or partially so.

From thirty-seven to forty percent of women are believed by most authorities to experience frigidity in some degree. There are many causes. Some have been molested in childhood, and a surprisingly large number of women have totally repressed the memory. Others were improperly instructed in childhood about human sexuality and came to feel that sex is somehow dirty or sinful. The brief wedding ceremony has no power to counteract the warnings of anxious, well-meaning parents. If human sexuality is shrouded in mystery for a child, associated with evil, or made to seem vulgar, in adult life such a person may become emotionally incapable of responding normally. My own estimate is that less than one parent in ten is capable of imparting the emotional, physical, and spiritual aspects of sex to children. Besides, it is not only what is taught, but what is "caught" by the child from parents and other adults early in life. "Feeling tones" are being constantly picked up by children, who often learn more from a tone of voice or a pained silence or embarrassment than from what is taught directly.

Frigidity in the female and impotence in the male are seldom resolved by reading books, though often one can gain considerable insight into probable causes and the type of treatment that may be necessary. There are many such books on the subject, but usually long-term therapy is indicated. One should have no hesitancy about seeking professional help. The problem is a common one, and can often be resolved if one is determined to seek an answer through therapy.

There are hundreds of books dealing with the sexual aspect of marriage, but one important fact needs to be stressed at this point: sex means something different for men and for women. Most women need to feel loved and cherished for sexual relations to be acceptable or desired. A man needs to have sexual relations in order to feel loved. A husband who has been argumentative or thoughtless or inconsiderate cannot expect his wife to be sexually responsive. Her sexual response involves the totality of her nature, and if there is some unresolved conflict she may be totally incapable of giving herself fully.

Incompatible needs are a part of every marriage. A happily married couple reported that they had resolved one area of their incompatibility with a happy compromise. She hated camping, which he loved. She liked the opera, which he detested. As an expression of his concern for her happiness he agreed to attend the opera with her, and she, in turn, went camping with him. Had either given in with poor grace, the results would not have been satisfactory. It was a compromise in which each sought to make the other happy. They sensed, quite rightly, that love is far more than an emotion: it is an action. They were acting in love. They proved themselves to be emotionally mature in arriving at this solution.

Serious arguments which disturb a couple's relationship are usually symptomatic of some deeper problem. The surface issue is seldom the real difficulty. However, it is sometimes necessary to start by eradicating the symptom before it is possible to work on the real problem.

In a family counseling situation involving a father, mother, and two teen-age children, I discovered that the peace of the home was being seriously disturbed by constant bickering. Fierce arguments often erupted, becoming so severe that the wife announced flatly that she was leaving unless things got better.

In the initial session I proposed a threefold rule for them to abide by. First, no arguments. Second, there would be no effort to control each other. Third, they must give up any attempt to change each other.

One of the children quite perceptively said: "The arguments are only a symptom of some deeper problems. If we stop arguing and just withdraw, the real problem will remain unsolved."

I said, "You are quite right. However, it is going to take a fairly long time to get to the root of the problem. This is not really so much of a family problem as a series of personality problems. While we are working to uncover the basic difficulties, I just want you to 'disengage.'" Then I went on to explain to them that when nations are involved in war, there are usually three essential steps to bringing about peace. First, there must be a cease-fire. Second, there is an armistice, which is a cessation of hostilities and a declaration of an intention to work out the terms of the peace treaty. Third, there is the somewhat complex problem of gathering around the peace table and finding a basis upon which there can be a permanent peaceful settlement of the conflict. Something like that must often—though not always—be done in bringing about peace in the home. There is the disengagement, a refusal to spend psychic energy in bickering and argument; if this can be achieved, there is more possibility of discovering the basic cause of the conflict.

One couple with whom I worked had argued heatedly about trifles for years. In counseling, it became apparent that the difficulty stemmed from their in-ability to communicate. They had been sending coded messages but never communicating their true feelings. The wife felt that her husband had slighted her mother and that he spent too much time hunting and fishing, but she had never been able to state these as basic problems. In his case, we discovered, he resented the amount of time she spent with her mother and felt she had never really cut the cord with either parent. When they were encouraged to "disengage" and stop arguing about trifles, they were free to discuss the basic issues. With some help they were able to resolve these problems and achieve a workable marriage.

13   LOVE

> . . . As boundless as the sea
> My love as deep; the more I give thee
> The more I have, for both are infinite.
> —*Juliet,* in Shakespeare's *Romeo and Juliet*

Someone tells of a wealthy husband, considerably older than his wife, who asked her if she would still love him if he lost all his money. She assured him that she would.

"Would you love me if I became an invalid?" he asked.

"Yes, of course."

"But would you still love me if I became blind and deaf?"

"Yes," she said, "I'd still love you."

"But what if I lost all my money, was a blind and deaf invalid, and lost my mind?"

"Don't be ridiculous!" she said. "Who could love an old, penniless, blind, deaf imbecile! But I'd take care of you."

The story, probably apocryphal, illustrates two basic factors: the need which everyone feels for unconditional love, and the innate practicality of the female. Everyone, consciously or unconsciously, is seeking unconditional love, despite the fact that no one is capable of giving unconditional love constantly. The desire is perhaps a holdover from the time when the infant does receive unconditional love. He is loved because he is his mother's child. He need not do anything to merit love. His needs are all met and he has no responsibility to do anything whatever other than to be just what he is, a helpless infant.

The infant always resident within us goes on wanting some of this unconditional love and acceptance. The reasonably mature adult learns in time that he must give love as well as receive it. Marriage is a reciprocal arrangement in which, ideally, we each seek to meet the needs of the other. If we meet the needs of the marriage partner in order that our needs shall be met, a kind of barter takes place: I'll do this for you if you'll do that for me. One who loves in a mature sense seeks to meet the needs of another, not in a manipulative sense, but simply because loving expresses itself in a concern for the welfare of the other.

There are three basic, elemental needs, holdovers from childhood, which all of us experience.

1. We want, consciously or unconsciously, to have all of our needs met.
2. We want to control or change those about us so that they will meet these needs.
3. We all yearn for unconditional love.

These three basic inner drives are almost universal. A marriage can be successful to the extent that both husband and wife mature emotionally and spiritually to the point where these early childhood longings are replaced by more mature concepts. Ideally one must achieve sufficient emotional maturity to be able to change these to read:

1. Instead of demanding that all of my needs be met, I will seek to meet the valid needs of my marriage partner.
2. Rather than trying to change others, I will recognize that I cannot change anyone else. I can change only myself, and when I change, others tend—in time—to change in relation to me.
3. Instead of expecting unconditional love, I will face the fact that no one can give this kind of

limitless love consistently. I will give love rather than demanding or expecting it, believing that love begets love.

Carl and Barbara provide a case in point. She grew up in a family which was demonstrative, verbal, and often explosive. There was a kind of emotional volatility in their home. No one suppressed any feelings. This kind of home atmosphere can create an unconscious need for a home environment which has somewhat more emotional stability.

Consequently she married Carl. His home background had been quite different from hers. No one ever shouted. There was little arguing. Life moved along at a rather serene pace. Understandably, Carl's calm, unemotional nature responded to Barbara's volatile, spontaneous, sometimes explosive personality. It was no accident that they found each other.

But after some years of living together they found that their emotional differences were so great as to cause serious problems. Carl was hopelessly out of touch with his feelings. He was not even aware of the times when he was angry. Anger showed in his eyes or voice, but he would steadfastly insist that he felt no hostility. Barbara, in an effort to reach him at a feeling level found herself "pushing all of his buttons," as she expressed it. Her tactics varied from screaming rages to physical and emotional symptoms in an unconscious effort to blast him loose from his infuriatingly calm, logical approach to every situation. For his part, Carl was sick of her emotional outbursts and finally told her that unless she got control of herself he wanted a divorce.

In an unconscious effort to find their counterparts, each had sought out an emotional opposite. She needed his emotional stability, but because he was out of touch with his feelings, he could not understand or communicate with her. He needed a wife more in touch with her feelings than he was, but could not endure her emotional outbursts.

When they consulted me about their shaky marriage, each told of the indignities which they had suffered. There was the natural human tendency to have me discover who was right and who was wrong.

After a number of counseling sessions, I gave them both some psychological inventories, which resulted in a kind of emotional X-ray. When her test results revealed that she had as many emotional problems as he, she refused to continue with the counseling sessions. He returned for one more session and reported that she had issued a final ultimatum. She demanded he go alone to see a psychiatrist for extensive counseling, or she would move out and file for divorce.

Here was an impasse. Both threatened divorce in an effort to force the other to effect changes. However, he was the more mature of the two. He recognized that both had emotional problems which needed to be resolved. He felt that he still loved his wife, but I could detect in his wife nothing resembling love—only a ruthless demand that he conform to her expectations. I held out little hope for their marriage.

Our English word "love" is a hopelessly inadequate one with which to convey all of the semantic connotations which we demand of it. We say, "I just love this dessert"; "Do you promise to love, honor, and cherish?"; "Come on, prove your love, just this once"; "I love to travel"; "And Jonathan loved David"; "So, faith, hope, and love abide, these three; but the greatest of these is love."

The various facets of love which we are considering in this chapter include romantic love, that wonderful and glorious emotion which engulfs and possesses two persons who have "fallen in love"; married love, which lacks the luster and passion of the initial experience, but which involves companionship, mutual caring for one another, consideration, and fondness; and the *agape* of the New Testament—Christian love.

Romantic love is a powerful emotion. The vast majority of songs, books, plays, and operas have to do with this overwhelming passion. I have been performing marriage ceremonies for more than forty years, and I do not recall a single instance in which a wedding had to be postponed because of the illness of either the bride or groom. Nor, for that matter, do I recall an instance when, despite frantic wedding preparations and attendant fatigue and anxiety, any bride or groom ever showed up with a head cold. Even, when as occasionally happens, there was discord or dissension between various members of the family, and sometimes a genuine crisis, the euphoria produced by the state of "being in love" seemed sufficient to guarantee that the couple could remain immune to infection even during the flu epidemics. There is, I believe, ample evidence that being deeply in love is conducive to good health. The entire organism is buoyed up, exhilarated.

A bride of thirty-eight, never previously married, stuttered terribly. I had never heard her utter a sentence without the greatest difficulty. However, at the wedding rehearsal when I suggested that we forego or simplify the repetition of the marriage vows, she emphatically insisted upon going through the entire ceremony without any deletions. To my surprise, she managed to repeat the vows without the slightest difficulty.

Romantic love is such an exciting and overwhelming experience that it is usually somewhat of a disappointment to discover that the initial glow tends to wear off in the first weeks or months of marriage. One idealistic young husband told me that it was the greatest tragedy of his life to discover that his marriage settled down after a few months to such realities as budgets, disagreements, and frustration. He wanted to know whether this was normal, or whether they had failed at some point in being unable to keep the romantic fires burning as brightly as they had initially.

A romantic love which would continue undiminished through the years would be most extraordinary. The initial glow of romance causes us to reveal our best side to the other. We show our ideal selves, not so much in an effort to deceive, but because romantic love stimulates us to *be* our better selves. In addition, we perceive the loved person through a kind of idealized haze and are blinded to faults which an objective person perceives all too clearly. It is this phenomenon which gives rise to the ancient adage, "Love is blind." The rational, reasoning part of the self tends to be short-circuited.

Love of this kind is based on a dissatisfaction with ourselves, a desperate attempt to escape from one's limited self in search of an ideal self. In loving, one imagines he has found this ideal self in the beloved.

Usually the early glow gives way, in time, to a growing sense of companionship, mutuality, a striving toward a common goal, deepening understanding and respect for each other. Many couples spend the first five, ten, or twenty years working out a satisfying relationship: giving and forgiving, growing, maturing, learning to accept anger as not incompatible with love.

Love is a supreme effort to escape from the prison of our aloneness, to seek completeness for our incompleteness, to trade our isolation for companionship. We need expect no perfect marriages, since there are no perfect people. Nor can we even hope for an ideal marriage, since none of us is an ideal person. We cannot demand that another person gratify all of our needs, for no one person can ever be expected to satisfy all of our variable needs.

One's ability to give and receive love depends upon whether he was loved as a child, and the manner in which he was loved. Quite often a child is given love, but in a manner he is incapable of accepting. Consequently he may be showered with affection but feel quite unloved and alienated. Dr. William Menninger points out that we learn how to love only when we were loved in infancy. Parents may shower a child with evidence of their love but at the same time set standards which he is unable to meet. As a consequence the child may go through life feeling a sense of all-pervasive guilt.

Someone in a semi-facetious vein has delineated the ages of woman as the following:

> In her infancy she needs love and care.
> In her childhood she wants fun.
> In her twenties she wants romance.
> In her thirties she wants admiration.
> In her forties she wants sympathy.
> In her fifties she wants cash.

A woman usually needs to be needed more than a man. It appears to be one of her spiritual and emotional necessities. If she does not feel needed, she feels deprived, unloved, alienated from herself and others. She must be needed in order to be fulfilled. A woman likes to be *told* that she is loved, admired, needed. While a man has the same basic need to be loved and admired, often for different reasons, he may be embarrassed to express it verbally. A woman needs more constant reassurance that she is loved, chiefly because of her somewhat greater insecurity and more fluid emotional nature.

Freud thought that happiness is found in the fulfillment of our childhood wishes, which is one reason that money alone does not bring happiness, since the possession of money was not one of our basic childhood wishes. Theodore Reik, a disciple of Freud, modifies the assertion by saying that happiness ensues when the wishes of our childhood *seem* to come true. For most humans, happiness is a fleeting or momentary emotion. Usually we must be satisfied with contentment, that half-sister of happiness; the achieving of an enduring contentment is no little accomplishment.

A woman said to me once, "Everyone knows that the way to a man's heart is through his stomach, so

I go to great pains to prepare the best possible meals for my husband."

I said, "Your actions are commendable, but your basic assumption is rubbish. The way to a man's heart is not through his alimentary canal. A man's basic need is for love and affection. A woman's fundamental need is for security."

She said, "I think it's just the other way around. Men work hard in order to be economically secure, while women are the ones so desperately in need of love."

"Wrong again," I said. "Consult your emotions, not your book of aphorisms or your intellect. Your basic need as a woman includes love, but this involves a whole spectrum of needs. Security for a woman means to feel loved, to find fulfillment in her husband, children, home, and to have economic security so she can enjoy them without anxiety. She wants to be taken care of and cherished while she fulfills a basic emotional and biological need, which is to bear and rear children. To achieve this she requires the security of her husband's love."

A typical male, on the other hand, is not emotionally insecure in the same way. He works, not basically to be financially secure, but because he is a doer, an achiever, a creator of things and circumstances. The financial rewards are symbols of his success in achieving his goal. The male functions better in reaching his goal if he has the emotional support and affection of his wife. A woman would bite her tongue rather than admit that security is her fundamental need, while a man will usually go to any lengths rather than admit that love and affection are his basic needs.

The need for love is universal. No one ever receives enough love, but men and women differ in the reasons for wanting to be loved. Women basically want to be loved for what they are, men for what they can do. This is readily perceived in children at least by the

243

age of six. A little girl will want to be admired because she is pretty, a boy for what he can achieve. Whether this is an innate characteristic or the result of environmental conditioning is not known, but I strongly suspect that it is an inborn characteristic.

There are several kinds of persons who appear to be incapable of loving deeply:

1. The self-satisfied and thoroughly self-sufficient person may love, but not deeply. Such an individual does not "need to be needed" as much as others. Consequently he is rendered, by his very self-sufficiency, incapable of giving and receiving love at a deep level.

2. Those who dislike themselves, having no proper self-love, feel unworthy of love. Persons of this type have a weak self-image, feel unworthy, and cannot readily believe that anyone could love them. We can give and receive love only to the degree that we love ourselves adequately. To love properly, one needs some self-esteem. When we dislike ourselves we project our self-contempt onto others in the form of criticism.

Dolores had a rejecting, critical, unloving mother, and a hostile, drunken father. There were also three older brothers who terrorized her. She fled from this hostile environment at an early age and tried to make her way alone in the world. Having never been given love and acceptance, she had a very poor self-image. Though she was physically attractive, dressed well, and presented an initial appearance of poise, she lived in a state of perpetual fear. She managed to secure a job and finally married a fine young man. He tried to help her by pointing out her faults. She took his attempts with inward hostility, but felt incapable of defending herself. After a few short months of marriage she was sent to a mental institution .

Upon her release, she was sent to me for extensive counseling. I found her almost paralyzed with fear. She feared both men and women and could not accept love, tenderness, or any other manifestation of concern. Her early life had rendered her suspicious and hostile. Her self-image was so weak that she found it impossible to believe that anyone could genuinely care about her, yet she longed with all of her being to be loved and cared for.

Fortunately, few of us are so badly damaged in childhood, and possess enough ego strength or self-worth to enable us to learn how to give and receive love.

3. Then there are those who are so thoroughly absorbed in their work, who are so completely dedicated to some project or goal, as to rule out any capacity to relate to another with deep affection. History is replete with accounts of such individuals. Quite often they are gifted persons who are inwardly so insecure that they passionately pursue fame, wealth, or adulation as substitutes for love. They seem to be saying, "I am, in myself, unworthy of being loved, but I will win the world's adulation on such a grand scale that the love of any one person will be insignificant by comparison." Some such persons are incapable of close personal relationships, but can accept medals, fame, wealth, degrees, or other impersonal evidences of approval and success.

The emotions, by themselves, have no "sense." The feelings, unguided by rational thought, can sometimes lead us astray. I once knew a highly intelligent young man, the son of well-integrated, loving parents, who made a tragic mistake in his marriage. I was aghast at the magnitude of his error. His young wife was physically unattractive, caustic and hostile, critical beyond belief. I observed how, on numerous occasions, she insulted him and his parents in the presence of guests. She seemed utterly incapable of observing any of the basic fundamentals of decent human behavior.

As I studied her I suddenly became aware of a slight physical resemblance to the young man's mother, whom he adored. It became obvious that he had been unconsciously attracted to the young woman because she looked a little like his mother, though she was at best only a kind of caricature of the charming and delightful mother. Love, unaided by the intellect, is indeed blind.

Few husbands and wives manage to maintain in marriage the same affectionate consideration for each other which they showed during courtship. The daily round of irritating circumstances can wear patience thin. Minor differences can flare into futile and exasperating arguments, or worse, can cause wounds which are difficult to heal.

Many wives are surprised to discover that their husbands are far more sensitive than they had imagined. A husband related an incident which illustrates this. He and his wife were starting on a lengthy trip. He commented on the fact that he had a sore throat, which persisted for several days. He referred to it a number of times, until she finally exploded, "You're always moaning about something! It doesn't help any to be constantly complaining about it."

He said to me later, "I realized that I was, like many men, a groaner when I didn't feel well, and decided to give up the childish habit." Sometime later he was seriously ill. "My wife asked me each morning how I felt, and I told her I was feeling much better, though obviously I was still weak and shaky. Finally she said, 'Oh, don't try to be a big strong, silent martyr. If you're sick, admit it. There's no sense in pretending you're feeling fine when you aren't.'"

The husband said of this exchange, "I decided, rather childishly perhaps, that I'd keep all of my feelings to myself thereafter. If I were dying she'd have to find it out from someone else. I've never felt any need to alter this attitude."

A wife asked, "When is a wife supposed to talk to her husband about family problems? If I bring up something at breakfast he'll say, 'Must you ruin my day by bringing up things like that?'

"In the evening when he comes home from work if I mention any family matter, he says, 'Let me read my paper first.'

"After dinner if I start to talk to him he'll usually respond with something like, 'Please let my meal digest before you start.' I don't dare disturb him when he's watching television, and if I bring up the subject before we go to bed, he'll ask, 'How do you expect me to get a decent night's sleep with that sort of thing on my mind?' Our children get the same treatment. How do you go about talking to a man like that?"

This type of situation brings us to the inescapable fact that love, to endure, must be thought of as more than a feeling or tender emotion. It is also an *action*. One must not only expect to be treated with love and consideration, but to act with consideration as well. One must not only *feel* love, but *act* in love. In his beautiful chapter on love, in the first letter to the Corinthians the Apostle Paul writes: "Love is patient and kind; love is not jealous or boastful; it is not arrogant or rude. Love does not insist on its own way; it is not irritable or resentful; it does not rejoice at wrong, but rejoices in the right. Love bears all things . . ." (v. 4-7).

Not only is it impossible for one to give unconditional love all the time, but it is even difficult to be consistent in our expressions of love. Few of us feel like being tender, thoughtful, considerate, or helpful day in and day out. When the physical, mental, and emotional selves are all in harmony with each other and with the outside world, one may reveal the utmost in consideration for another. But when we are out of focus emotionally, or rushed or exasperated, another side of our nature may manifest itself.

A husband related an experience which illustrates this. "I had been working long hours, six and seven days a week, for months. I was really holding down two jobs, and one morning my thoughtful wife said,

'Honey.' you've been working too hard. Let me bring you breakfast in bed.' I demurred, but finally consented. As she served breakfast she said, 'Now any time you want breakfast in bed, just let me know. Anytime, understand? Just let me know.'

"A few weeks later," he said, "I was feeling pretty well dragged out. I sat up in bed wondering if I was going to make it. I finally managed to do something I find quite difficult. I am fiercely independent and find it hard to ask or permit people to do things for me. But remembering her fervent offer of some weeks before, I said, 'Dear, how about breakfast in bed this morning? I'm really bushed.'

"My wife said, with some irritation, 'Nothing doing. I'm tired too.'

"That did it," he related. "I had been booby-trapped again. I have seldom asked her to do anything for me since. I'm not interested even when she volunteers. If she insists, I may accept the gesture because I feel I owe it to her to let her feel needed, but I'd rather she didn't bother. I suppose I'd prefer to have my old, total independence than to be even partially dependent on someone who blows hot and cold."

Men and women are both sensitive, but about different things. Men often are irritated that women can be so easily upset about things which, to a male, seem insignificant. Women are equally puzzled over the seeming overreaction of their husbands to issues which would never disturb a woman.

A man is generally sensitive in the area of his capacity to earn a living and to succeed in his work. If he is compared to other husbands to his disadvantage, he feels emasculated. Any criticism of his performance or achievement which touches on some vulnerable point can affect him deeply. He may either explode in a rage, and attack, or he may become defensive and mildly hostile, or retreat into silence. Each individual man has his own sensitive areas, and a wise wife will make it her business not to push those particular "red buttons."

Women have their own areas of sensitivity which are usually quite different from those of the male. Criticism of her houskeeping, cooking, appearance, her performance as mother, or any depreciation of her femininity can leave a woman crushed. Anything which strikes at her self-image is devastating.

An insensitive husband may walk into his home after a hard day's work and ask, "Good grief, what have you been doing all day?" The house may look cluttered, especially if there are children. Even if she has been washing, ironing, shopping, driving the children thither and yon, doing a bit of gardening, running errands, and planning a dinner party for the next day, there may be no visible signs of activity to validate her frenzied and hectic day. She may be physically and emotionally drained by the incessant demands of children, telephone, and doorbell, but to her husband it may appear that she has been watching television all day. On the other hand, a husband who puts in a full day at his job may well have some grounds for complaint if his wife, with only a small house or apartment and possibly a child or two, fails to keep up with her work. "My wife has a small house to take care of," said a husband, "and it's usually a mess. We have one child who never has any clean clothes to wear. Ironing is stacked up all over the house. She watches television hours every day and complains of being tired at night. So far as I'm concerned she isn't earning her keep."

In one of our small sharing groups a man told us that his wife and just filed suit for divorce. It was his first night with the group.

"She's been after me for years to do something about our marriage," he said. "I guess I was too preoccupied with earning a living to heed the warning signals. Now she's moved out."

"I grew up in poverty," he went on, "and I've kept

my nose to the grindstone ever since I was a kid. I have put in long hours on the job ever since we were married. I guess she felt neglected; in fact, she often complained that we never went anywhere together, but I only half heard her. My whole concern was to keep the business going. I went broke twice, and that didn't add to my self-esteem. My wife wanted all the niceties of life, and I kept on working to provide these for her, but I neglected her as a person. I thought she wanted to be well taken care of financially, but she wanted some of me. I didn't get her signals. Now I suppose it's too late."

After she divorced him he left his highly competitive business venture and took an eight-hour-a-day job. "Perhaps," he said, "she'd have been satisfied with less money and more husband. Maybe it was not so much her demands on me financially, as my own neurotic expectations which were self-imposed demands."

Many a woman, in her heart, wishes her husband would pay less attention to his car and more to her. It is difficult for some women to admit that they are jealous of their husband's work or hobbies. On a conscious level a wife is proud of her husband's success and realizes that he must devote the major portion of his time and energy to his job, but at the same time she would like for him to cherish her as the center of his devotion and interest.

A wife may be caught in conflicting needs, wanting the luxuries or necessities which her husband's diligence can provide, but at a feeling level she may resent the fact that he brings work home from the office or seems more devoted to his job than to her. She gets a tired husband at the end of the day, just when she both wants and needs some emotional support and conversation.

She cannot have it both ways—a hard-working husband providing for her financial needs, and a gay, relaxed communicative Latin lover ready to take her out on the town. Nor, for that matter, can he have it both ways. He cannot ignore his wife's needs and expect her to be affectionate and responsive.

They are caught, now, in the situation which confronts most married couples: they have incompatible needs. She has conflicting needs within herself, as does he; the needs of one are incompatible with the needs of the other. The answer lies initially in a willingness to learn the art of communication. Arguments, charges and countercharges, accusations and recriminations not only will not solve the problem, they make matters worse and leave scars which are difficult to heal.

Very often both marriage partners are sending "coded messages," difficult to decode, or one will explode over some trifle which bears no relationship to the real and more basic problem.

A marriage relationship may not erupt into angry arguments, but may settle into a dull, almost meaningless routine. T. S. Eliot describes such a marriage:

> They do not repine;
> Are content with the morning that separates
> And the evening that brings together
> For casual talks before the fire
> Two people who know they do not understand each
>   other,
> Breeding children whom they do not understand
> And who will never understand them.

To avoid a stalemate in which both husband and wife settle for a dull half-marriage with nothing to communicate about except the weather, the neighbors, or the minutiae of life, couples need to learn the art of communication. Often this can be achieved only with the aid of a competent marriage counselor or with the help of a sharing group. Strangely enough, in a competently led group, many couples learn for the first time how to communicate at a deep level more easily than in the privacy of their own home. There is a certain anonymity about such a group. The relaxed atmosphere, the honesty, the support of the group, all provide a setting in which it is possible to see more clearly the fundamental problem.

Actually there are few marital problems. There are chiefly personal problems which are compounded by marriage. In a group, or with a competent third person, charges and countercharges eventually give way to an inner search for one's own emotional barriers.

We can seldom understand the basic problem in an impaired marriage unless we can understand the two persons involved. This is made the more difficult because no one fully understands himself. Men are admonished not to try to understand women, but to empathize with them, feel with them. Yet most women would die rather than have their innermost motives revealed to a man. They want to be understood, but do not wish to have their intimate feelings exposed.

On the other hand, men wish to be understood, but are usually reluctant to "go probing around on the inside," as one husband said. Most men have made a big investment of time and psychic energy in hiding their inner feelings, and they feel threatened at the thought of having someone discovering what they are like at a feeling level. They prefer to operate on an intellectual level and reject introspection or anything to do with emotions.

But until we are honest enough to look within and discover what we are really like, and learn to communicate true feelings, there is little hope of improving the marriage.

If the truth were known, most of us are somewhat reluctant to admit the degree to which we want to be loved and understood. It is almost as though to admit this would be a confession of weakness, a blow to our self-esteem. We surround ourselves with various layers of insulation. We pretend a self-confidence we do not feel, or over-compensate in some way that is perfectly obvious to everyone but ourselves.

The need to love and be loved varies enormously

with individuals, of course. At one end of the scale is the neurotic personality caught in a paradox: such a person is incapable of loving, but desperately needs to be loved. At the other end is the self-reliant individual who needs affection, but cannot accept it. The neurotic personality needs endless quantities of love and reassurance. In fact, reassurance is the chief aspect of love that such a person requires. However, these are "bottomless pits" which can never be filled. No amount of love is ever enough. The neurotic person will push, prod, manipulate, threaten, or become ill in an effort to secure the monumental quantity of love which he requires. There is no end.

Such persons are usually masochistic in some degree; that is, they have an inner self-punishing mechanism. Their unconscious goal is victory through defeat. They will *unconsciously* go to any lengths to achieve their goal. Unable to accept love normally, they may become physically or emotionally ill, or alcoholic. Some are accident-prone, an unconscious effort to secure attention, first cousin to love. Others are disaster-prone. Inwardly feeling unworthy of love, they settle for attention, or as a last resort, pity. This type of person can seldom achieve a satisfactory marriage relationship without intensive therapy.

In a group session involving about ten persons I said, in a facetious vein, "Maybe the trouble is that men are playing around, and women are playing for keeps." One young divorcée erupted with instant hostility and wanted to argue the point. I asked, "Why are you so hostile?"

She thought a moment, then laughed: "Because I know it's true."

The core of truth in my statement lies in the fact that marriage usually—though not always—means more to a woman than to a man. A man's basic drive is usually to fulfill himself through achieving some goal in the outer world. A woman's basic drive is to fulfill herself through achieving a successful marriage, with all of its implications: children, security, and inner contentment. For a typical male, marriage and the home may be of great importance, but because his work takes him into the outer world of facts, things, and events, the home tends to become a refuge rather than a primary goal.

For this reason the woman is the keeper of the home, and she must assume the primary responsibility for initiating changes and improvements. This is because she is usually more intuitive, more in touch with her emotions, better equipped emotionally to deal with such things as personal relationships. Most of the persons who seek counselors for any reason are women, not because they are emotionally less stable, but because they are more realistic. Often, though not always, when a wife is able to effect some changes in her attitudes and personality, even a reluctant husband will agree to undertake some form of therapy or marriage counseling. When she demonstrates to him by her improved performance that she is deriving some benefit from counseling or group therapy, he will often be more open to the suggestion that they seek help together.

Love, far from being just an emotion, is a whole set of responses. It can involve, in a typical marriage, any or all of the following actions:

1. *Listening.* What the marriage partner has to say may not seem important to you, but it is important to the one relating it. Love implies caring enough to listen attentively. Usually, if a problem is being discussed, there is no need to offer solutions. Just listening with interest is an act of love. If one is tired or bored, it is not always easy. But love goes the second mile and listens; at that moment, listening is an act of love.

2. *Thoughtfulness and consideration.* To love means to be concerned for the welfare of another. "Give and it shall be given unto you," said Jesus. If you have needs which are unmet, instead of making

demands or accusations, try to meet the needs of your marriage partner. Love begets love; resentment begets hostility; rejection begets rejection.

Many men are not as thoughtful as they might be concerning things which are important to their wives. Wedding anniversaries, birthdays, and special occasions need attention. I was aware of this fact, but bungled it badly early in my marriage, to my consternation. I had put in my date book a reminder to purchase a birthday gift for my wife. But fearful that I might forget, I asked my secretary to put it on her calendar and remind me a day or so in advance. My wife happened to be in the outer office one day, and as it would have to be, she happened to glance at my secretary's open desk reminder, on which was written: "Remind Dr. O to get birthday gift for wife." Understandably my wife reacted with some indignation later. "If you can't remember by yourself, you can forget it." She was right.

3. *Compromise.* Since any two persons have incompatible goals, it is obvious that in the intimate relationship of marriage there will have to be a lifetime of cheerful compromises. If one wants to spend a vacation camping, and the other prefers visiting relatives, it doesn't mean that either is unreasonable. You can visit relatives one summer and go camping the following year, or spend half the vacation with relatives and the other half camping. Any compromise must be made with no thought of "giving in." Only the immature or infantile expect to have all of their needs met all of the time. If we can achieve our goals half the time in the marriage relationship, that isn't too bad. And, one's displeasure over visiting relatives should not be taken out on the relatives or in futile recriminations later. Similarly, one who hates camping must not make the experience miserable for the other by constant complaints.

4. *Avoidance of attack and accusation.* When we are attacked or criticized, we instinctively defend our-

selves, or counterattack. This is a poor basis for communication. However, we each have a perfect right —in fact, a duty—to let the other know how we feel about matters that are important to us. Instead of the accusation, which puts the other immediately in the wrong, one can begin by saying, "When you do that it makes me feel angry." One's anger may be infantile or reasonable, as the case may be. We are responsible for our own reaction, but the feeling is valid, and we have a right to express it. We are not making any demand that the other shall change, just communicating our feelings.

Instead of saying, "I have no intention of spending my vacation visiting your neurotic relatives, and it's selfish of you to expect me to do so," one might better phrase it, "Visiting relatives, either yours or mine, is not my idea of how to spend a restful vacation; but perhaps we can work out some kind of a compromise so we will both be satisfied."

"You never take me anyplace!" is likely to produce a defensive reaction. Abandoning the martyr-stance or the accusatory tone, one might better say, "Honey, we've both been knocking ourselves out lately. How about dinner out this week or next?" Perhaps more important than the actual wording is the feeling that accompanies it. Abandon the judgmental, critical, attacking method, and use a loving approach. If you don't feel loved, expressing this fact with hostility is not likely to make you more lovable.

5. *Meeting valid needs.* Instead of insisting that your needs be met, try to meet all of the valid needs of the other. We are all selfish to some degree. Love is unselfish and seeks to discover and satisfy the needs of others. Often, because humans are egocentric, neither husband nor wife goes to the trouble to discover the basic needs of the other. Displaying a fourth of the tender solicitude shown during courtship would go a long way toward creating a happier marriage. Instead of brooding silently or talking angrily about

one's unmet needs, a far better solution would be to sit down for an hour-long discussion concerning needs.

A husband might well ask his wife, "Will you tell me the ways in which I could make you happier?"

She, in turn, could appropriately say, "I'll make out a list, but I'd feel better about it if you'd make out a list of the ways in which I could make you happier." A discussion based on their lists can be the starting point for a new relationship.

6. *Forgiveness.* Learn to forgive and refuse to dig up the past. "To err is human, to forgive is divine." We tap our inner divinity when we can forgive. No one says it is easy to forgive hurts, but it is the price we must pay for inner peace and for a harmonious relationship. Again it needs to be emphasized that love is not just a feeling, but also an action; to forgive is a loving act. A husband confessed his infidelity to his wife in my presence. At first she could not forgive or accept him back. Eventually, however, she forgave him and they established a better marriage than ever, due in part to a year or two in a sharing group. Her ability to forgive rendered her a more mature person.

A husband said, "My wife has been playing around for some years. She is secretive and furtive. It shows in her personality and actions. She isn't nearly as good an actress as she thinks. I don't know whether I have forgiven her or not, because she has never admitted anything. How do you forgive someone who admits no wrongdoing?" They have what appears outwardly to be a good marriage. Both do all of the appropriate things. She, however, is not forgiven because she has confessed nothing; he feels guilty over his inability to accept her fully. "I go through all the motions of being a good husband," he said. "I'm 'faking' it, and don't feel too good about it. Something dropped out of our marriage so far as I'm concerned."

7. *Avoidance of competition.* Make sure you are not competing with each other. Everyone knows of

instances in which a wife has little or nothing to say in a group, but who, when her husband is not present, opens up and becomes a real person in her own right. The converse is also common, with a wife doing all the talking for both.

Sometimes this can be attributed to the fact that one or the other is naturally timid, but when a capable and otherwise responsive person permits the marriage partner to take over the conversation and answer for both of them, there is a power struggle going on.

I recall a dinner party during which a highly successful man of great ability was constantly interrupted by his wife. She corrected him on minor details and challenged most of his quiet observations. He eventually subsided and permitted her to carry on her loud-voiced monologue.

Just as often an overly aggressive husband is determined to dominate his wife in public and at home. I recall a thoroughly competent man with a deep sense of insecurity who made every effort to ridicule his wife in public. One sensed that he was expressing the buried hostility he could not express at home.

The power struggle goes on in millions of homes. Each has a point to prove or a position to defend or some subtle punishment to mete out. A mature and lasting love has in it elements of deep concern for others. It does not seek to control or to change another person. It is not defensive or easily upset. It looks for ways to meet the needs of others.

Love is gentle, but not weak. One who loves deeply also loves himself properly and respects himself, mingling elements of both humility and strength.

One who is capable of loving fully is also capable of accepting love, feeling worthy of love. Loving God and truth, one loves himself and others in equal amounts. Love is the ultimate in living and expresses itself best by giving, without thought of return. Love is, in the final analysis, the ultimate in human growth and maturity.

LEADER'S GUIDE

by Nancy Becker

Contents

Introduction

In an age when happily married couples are becoming the exception rather than the rule, Christian couples have a great opportunity to exemplify God's love in marriage and family relationships. Our increasingly complicated society places strains on even good marriages. Hence, Christians, too, need to learn and strive to better their relationships.

Dr. Osborne strikes a needed note—one partner cannot completely fulfill the other's needs, nor can he expect the other to fulfill all his basic elemental needs. Couples must realistically understand themselves and give up remaking a partner to fit a preconceived image. Much truth from psychology is used in this book. As a teacher and class member, your responsibility is to think critically and assess this truth in the light of Scripture. Much of the Bible study is inductive, which means that the real digging will be done by class members.

Many short statements quoted from the text are included as agree-disagree discussion questions. To be fair to the author, please use the entire context of the statements in your group thinking. Space does not permit the quoting of complete ideas.

Because of the nature of this study, it will be best to limit the composition of the class to couples only. Then each partner will be able to understand principles given in the context of the class session.

This course is difficult, but then so is the task of keeping a marriage exciting, productive, and a lighthouse of God's love to a love-starved society.

—*Nancy Becker*

Marriage Can Be Frustrating—and Wonderful

Set Goals for the Session:
1. Students will look at examples of biblical marriages.
2. Class members will recognize the impossible expectations with which most couples enter marriage.
3. Spouses will write letters to their mates telling what first attracted them to each other.

Prepare for the Session:
1. Read carefully Chapter 1 in the text, pp. 9-27. This chapter overviews the entire book and sets the stage.
2. Study the Scripture passages on Bible marriages. Look over the DISCOVER section and choose the ones you wish to emphasize in this session.
3. During this lesson the class will look at the good points and the frustrations experienced in the marriage relationship; three types of marital situations which must be recognized and analyzed before a couple can improve a marriage; and three laws to guide marriage (universal laws of mind and spirit). It is important to take time to do the last exercise, a positive look at what attracted a couple to each other.
4. The quotations at the beginning of each chapter would make attractive posters, overhead transparencies, or board mottoes.

5. Put on an overhead or flip chart the three kinds of marital situations: impossible, personal, situational. These will help guide your discussion.

6. Another overhead, flip chart, or poster with the three universal laws of mind and spirit (p. 24) could be posted for the duration of the course as a reminder of the main thesis of the author.

7. Bring paper, extra pencils, and lists of the Scripture passages for group study.

Presentation:

FOCUS

Pass out paper and have class members reply to the following: "The qualities of an ideal marriage partner are . . ." As a class, make a composit list on the board of the ideal wife and the ideal husband. Refer to Dr. Osborne's descriptions of what women and men wish from each other. (pp. 11-14)

DISCOVER

1. Is it significant that Scripture records no perfect marriages? The only perfect picture of marriage is that spiritual union of Christ and the church. Nevertheless, biblical portrayals of married couples give examples to either follow or avoid. Divide the class into groups, assign each group one or two Bible couples to study, and describe the marriage. The following questions would be helpful in doing so. What does each spouse expect from the other? What are the problems and/or good traits shown? Where does one find manipulation, faulty communication, unconditional love, trust, jealousy, improper priorities? Before class list the Scripture references on paper for each group.

a. Adam and Eve (Gen. 2:18-25; 3:1-24)
b. Abraham and Sarah (Gen. 12:4-5, 10-20; 16:1-9; 18:11-15; 20:1-18; 21:1-13; 23:1-2; 1 Peter 3:5-6)
c. Isaac and Rebekah (Gen. 24:67; 25:20-34; 26:7-12, 34-35; 27:1-46)
d. Moses and Zipporah (Exod. 2:21; 4:20-26; 12:1)

e. Ahab and Jezebel (1 Kings 12:25; 16:31; 18:4; 19:1-2; 21:4-16)

f. Joseph and Mary (Matt. 1:18-25; 2:13-15, 19-23; Luke 2:4-7, 41-51)

g. Aquila and Priscilla (Acts 18:2-3, 18, 26; Rom. 16:3; 1 Cor. 16:19; 2 Tim. 4:19)

Other couples of interest are Hosea and Gomer (unfaithfulness and unconditional love; Hos. 1-3), Zachariah and Elizabeth (Luke 1), Jacob and Leah and Rachel (jealousy; Gen. 29-30; 35), Boaz and Ruth (Ruth 2-4). Have the groups report and summarize their findings. Then discuss which marriages are closest to the ideal and why.

2. Discussion Questions:

a. Why is it that all married couples are, to some degree, incompatible? (pp. 16-17).

b. What does the statement mean, "Women are insatiable, men are obtuse"? (pp. 15-16; 56-60).

c. When, if ever, does one give up on a marriage? What neurotic needs destroy a marriage?

3. *Family Circle* magazine, July 26, 1977, printed a report by Ann Landers, "If You Had It to Do All Over Again, Would You Marry the Same Person?" Of mailed in replies, 52% voted "No," 48% said "Yes." Ann Landers states that only one out of 25 marriages could be considered "very good." About half of all marriages are unhappy. How do you think this compares to Christian marriage statistics?

4. List on the board or flip chart the three basic kinds of marital situations (pp. 24-26). Explain each kind and the importance of taking inventory of one's own marriage to improve it. Since no one is a perfect person, there can be no ideal marriage. One can always improve. Call attention to the law of mind and spirit in three parts, p. 24.

RESPOND

Pass out clean sheets of paper to each person and give time for each to write a letter to his or her spouse, a "love letter" if you will, telling that person what specifically attracted him or her to the other. Have each person keep it and give it to the spouse first thing on Monday morning.

Assignment:

1. Read chapter 2, pp. 28-47, "Male and Female Differences."

2. For leader: assign two men and two women to prepare the FOCUS role play for next week.

Male and Female Differences

Set Goals for the Session:

1. Each class member should list basic male-female differences and understand how these affect the marriage relationship.

2. Each person should give thanks to God for the sexual role in which he has been created and for God's wisdom in assigning male-female roles.

3. Each spouse will try to become more understanding and tolerant of the opposite sex's behavior.

Prepare for the Session:

1. Read carefully chapter 2 in the text, pp. 28-47. It would be very useful to list every male-female difference Dr. Osborne mentions in the chapter.

2. Study the Scripture passages Genesis 2:18 and Ephesians 5:21-29. Consult a commentary or two on the Ephesians passage for background and helpful explanations of a difficult passage.

3. Prepare cardboard signs for the role play if you decide to use it. Assign two class members to prepare for this role play.

4. Before class secure the help of two men and two women to create the short role plays that begin the session.

5. Have paper for the groups to list sexual differences and either overhead transparencies, flip chart, or chalkboard space to record their findings.

Presentation:

FOCUS

Have the two men and two women prepared present their role plays. The men will be discussing the impossibility of understanding their wives, the two women their husbands. The women could be sitting under the hairdryer in a beauty salon, watching their children on a park bench, or at a coffee break at work. The men could be golfing, bowling, or on a business lunch. Keep these role plays short, humorous, and attention getting.

DISCOVER

1. After the role plays stressing the differences between the sexes, have the class members consider why God created such different parts of a whole. Use Genesis 2:18 to discuss the purpose of male-female differences.

2. Have the class separate into groups of the same sex and make lists of female and male characteristics. Women would work on female, men on male behavior, using the text (pp. 28-47). Allow plenty of time for this. When the groups are finished, list them on the board or overhead and discuss the differences. Does the class agree with Dr. Osborne's analysis?

3. Prepare six cardboard signs with string attached so that they can be worn around the neck with FATHER (parent), SON (child), HUSBAND (adult), MOTHER (parent), DAUGHTER (child), WIFE (adult) printed in large letters. Have two class members volunteer to prepare a role play using the incidents on pp. 39-40 as starters. Each "husband" and "wife" should change signs during the role play to show the appropriate ego state each is portraying. After the role play, discuss the three ego states within all of us (parent, child, adult) and within our spouses. How does one deal with these in oneself and spouse? (See text, pp. 40-41.) Someone might be

interested in reading *I'm OK, You're OK* by Thomas A. Harris, which deals with these in detail.

4. Ephesians 5:21-29. The Apostle Paul takes into special account male-female differences in his application to each sex in his text, "and be subject to one another in the fear of Christ" (v. 21). To the male who naturally is the doer, the creator, the activist, Paul says, "Love your wife." Learn to submit your doing temperament to feelings; learn to love. Paul exhorts the female, who naturally is the be-er, the one who lives on a feeling level, to "obey," to become a doer as well as a be-er. Each side must submit to the basic incompatibilities and different needs of the other. Have the class read this passage and discuss it in the light of male-female differences.

RESPOND

1. Spend time in silent prayer during which each person can thank God for the sexual role God has given him or her and for help in understanding and dealing creatively with the differences in one's spouse.

Assignment:
Read chapter 3, pp. 48-71, "Women's Needs and Problems."

Women's Needs and Problems

Set Goals for the Session:

1. Each class member should recognize and understand the basic needs of women.

2. The group will study Proverbs 31 to see the biblical ideal of a woman.

3. Each husband should resolve to validate his wife's feelings and to try this technique in a specific situation this week.

Prepare for the Session:

1. Read carefully chapter 3, pp. 48-71. Discuss this chapter with your spouse before teaching it to get his or her reaction.

2. Study the traits of an ideal woman in Proverbs 31. Also study passages which show how Christ dealt with his own feelings of anger. (See Mark 3:5; John 2:13-22; etc.)

3. Bring paper for group work.

Presentation:

FOCUS

Divide the men and women into separate groups, three to a group. Have the men list what men desire in a woman and have the women list what needs women most desire met. How do these lists compare with Dr. Osborne's portrayal of woman's deepest longings? (pp. 50-55)

DISCOVER

1. As a class, study Proverbs 31:10-31 and list the qualities and activities of a virtuous woman. Does this picture agree with the stereotyped ideal woman of our culture?

2. Discussion Questions:

a. Read the list of feminine traits listed on p. 52. Are these accurate?

b. What happens if a woman's needs are not met? What are the ways of dealing with them if her husband refuses to meet these needs?

c. Genesis 2:18 calls woman a helper. What does this say to women who seek dominance in the home or job? What is the difference between equality and dominance? (See pp. 55-56.) What has happened to women in a society where her role has become confused? Should she stay home or have a career or both? Why is Matthew 6:33 so important for a woman in today's confusing society?

d. Read the three paragraphs on pp. 64-65 beginning "In marriage we are seeking to fulfill . . ." Do you agree or disagree with this analysis? Why?

e. What is the difference between repression and suppression of one's angry feelings? What are some creative ways of dealing with anger? You might wish to consult various Scripture passages on Jesus and anger. How did He deal with anger—suppression and/or repression? What can we learn from the way Jesus dealt with these feelings?

f. Dr. Osborne repeatedly stresses the need for marriage preparation of at least one or two years' duration. What can the church do to help prospective marriage couples? What kind of preparation for marriage do you think is necessary? (See p. 62.)

g. Why is it unreasonable to expect marriage problems to be solved in less time than they developed? How does one convince a troubled couple to give their marriage four years or more to solve a problem?

h. If one's personality is formed by the age of five or six and behavior patterns are already molded, what is one's responsibility for his actions? What can the church do to help parents of young children? What sort of nursery program should a church have in the light of this important first five years of a person's life?

3. Role Play:

Have two people portray an upset woman trying to get through to her husband who is avidly watching a ballgame on television. She should resort to the reactions listed on pp. 70-71 when he fails to respond. Do the same situation again, only this time have the man validate the feelings of the woman. Discuss the different approaches.

RESPOND

1. Have class members think back to the last time either one was upset and their reactions to the other. Would they do it differently now? Challenge them to use the technique of validating feelings this week.

2. Spend time in prayer for the parents of young children in your church, for those considering marriage, for women seeking to find security and a comfortable role in today's church and society, and for each spouse that the other will be sensitive to and seek to meet the needs of their mate.

Assignment:

1. Read chapter 4, pp. 72-93. Observe couples in restaurants, walking down the street, etc., to see if married couples really do not talk to each other.

2. Leader: during this week collect all the cartoons and jokes you can find that deal with the "war between the sexes." "Blondie" is a good place to start.

The Human Male

Set Goals for the Session:

1. Each class member will be able to recognize and understand the special needs of men.

2. Each spouse will seek to better understand the other and give unconditional love in a tangible way this week.

Prepare for the Session:

1. Study carefully chapter 4, pp. 72-93. List for yourself in summary form the specific male characteristics and needs mentioned in the chapter.

2. Study Luke 6:38 and 1 Corinthians 13:5, 8.

3. If you had no time for the role play on feeling validation last week, plan to include it in this session.

4. Decide which approach you wish to use (see Focus) and gather the necessary materials, either cartoons or pictures of men to post around the room.

5. Write on board, transparency, or chart the reactions of men to manipulation (pp. 90-91).

6. Have cards or small slips of paper for the response exercise.

Presentation:

Focus

1. Post cartoons and jokes around the room portraying the "war between the sexes." Check to see (if possible)

how many authors are male or female. Why are so many written by men? An interesting sidelight would be to check MS magazine or the newspaper for jokes from the women's liberation movement. Are these comparable to male jokes on the "war between the sexes?" For starters, see p. 72 and p. 87.

2. Another approach might be to get magazine pictures of men: "he-men" with bulging muscles, harried executive types, hen-pecked husbands, sportsmen, young and old men. Post these on a bulletin board or pass them around. What do these say about the American stereotype of the male?

3. Check back for the observations of class members during the week of couples on the street, in cars, restaurants. Is it valid to say that married people do not speak to each other? Are married people all "talked-out"?

DISCOVER

This lesson lends itself well to discussion. Lead your class in a summary of the contents of the chapter and such questions as would be of special interest to your own situation. Small groups could also discuss one or two of the sections.

1. List reasons for the non-communicative husband (pp. 72-73).

2. What has the strong, silent, totally competent image of the male done to the self-image of the ordinary man? Why does Dr. Osborne say that the statement, "He's such a good boy," is a dangerous fallacy of our culture (p. 82)? Discuss this philosophy of child-rearing in comparison to the one which stresses the happiness, not the goodness, of children. Is this a biblical approach? How has the stereotyped image of a strong, able man caused many problems for the man in his forties? List the problems of the middle-aged man.

3. Are the cartoon portrayals of bossy, dominant women and hen-pecked, stupid husbands an accurate picture of male-female relationships in our society? If not, why are there so many? Can one call U.S. society matriarchal? What about the so-called "feminization" of men

in our culture (pp. 82-84)?

4. List vulnerable areas of males and females in which no spouse should criticize the other (pp. 84-85).

5. Summarize the traits of men that are mentioned on pp. 86-91, and the complications that women tend to add, such as mothering their husbands, trying to change their husbands, faulty communications, etc.

6. Have the male reactions to manipulation listed on the board or flip chart (pp. 90-91) and have class members give examples or dramatize each.

7. What is the answer to the statement, "No one ever receives enough love"? Why is society so preoccupied with love in all its forms? Read Luke 6:38; 1 Corinthians 13:5, 8 as the challenge God gives to all of us.

RESPOND

Pass out cards or slips of paper and have each class member silently consider and write down one living thing he will do this week for his or her spouse. These should be placed in one's Bible as a reminder during the week.

Assignment:

Study chapter 5, "Conflicts that Mar Marriages," pp. 94-115.

Conflicts That Mar Marriages

Set Goals for the Session:

1. Class members will look at some common conflicts of marriage and ways of creatively solving them.

2. Marriage partners will seek to fulfill the needs of their spouse more than their own desires.

3. Class members will learn some communication skills that will better enable them to solve marital conflicts.

Prepare for the Session:

1. Read carefully chapter 5, "Conflicts that Mar Marriages," pp. 94-115. List for yourself the different kinds of conflicts mentioned and the principles Dr. Osborne recommends in solving them.

2. Prepare group assignments for the role play situations.

3. Study Scripture: Philippians 2:13; Luke 6:38.

Presentation:

Focus

Read the incident about the six-year-old's comments on Cinderella, p. 94. Are getting married and living happily ever after synonymous?

This chapter lends itself well to role play and discussion of how to deal with specific situations that cause conflicts in marriage. Drama allows people to put themselves in someone else's skin, protects their own feelings of not wanting to be too personal and enables them to see solutions more objectively. It is important to discuss both the "right" and "wrong" ways of dealing with conflict. Allow plenty of time for both planning, giving, and discussing each situation. You should choose the situations most meaningful to your own group.

1. Role plays:

a. Based on her father's ability to take care of a house, a wife has a preconceived picture of her husband fixing sticking screen doors, leaking plumbing, and building little projects. However, her husband is not handy with tools and finds even the simplest chore frustrating (see pp. 94-96).

b. A husband feels that his wife should stay at home during the day and keep the house spotless, prepare good meals from scratch, and in general, run a well-ordered home. The wife, however, finds the house too confining and wants to have a career (see pp. 96-98).

c. A wife has had a horrible day at home. When her tired husband comes in the door from work, he senses something has gone badly wrong. The wife, however, denies any need for help and support but really wishes for it (see pp. 102-3).

d. A wife is a lark—up at 6 a.m., in bed at 10:30. Husband is an owl, preferring to watch the late show on television and get up just in time to get to work, and later on weekends (see pp. 106-7).

e. A young wife finds herself with two small children crowded into a much smaller, poorer house than she has dreamed of, a husband who is gone 10-11 hours a day at work and travel time. Her husband comes home exhausted every night, her four-month-old has colic. All her expectations of a blissful marriage are dashed to pieces.

2. Lead a discussion on how to solve conflicts. Include these and other points:

a. One's basic attitude must be that of Philippians 2:13. "How can I meet the needs of my partner?" and not "How can my needs be met?" Also Luke 6:38.

b. The challenge of the 30's and 40's is to meet one's internal emotional needs.

c. One can raise the level of one's ability to tolerate frustration by seeking physical and emotional well-being and by gaining new spiritual resources. What are some specific ways one can go about improving his level of tolerance?

d. Avoid all criticism.

e. Learn to communicate. Your class might wish to work on specific communication skills, such as sharing feelings. "When you _____ (do so and so), I feel _____."

f. Validate feelings.

g. Seek help. What about fellowship groups?

h. Is the marriage commitment "Till death do us part" a goal or a command? Is divorce ever necessary?

RESPOND

Have a time of prayer when each couple present may join hands and pray silently about problem areas in their own marriages and for the mind of Christ in solving them.

Assignment:

1. Read chapter 6, "Incompatibility in Marriage," pp. 116-34.

2. Leader: secure divorce statistics for your area, both state and city, if possible. Is the rate climbing? Ask your pastor for help in also checking the number of families with either divorced children or parents in your church.

Incompatibility in Marriage

Set Goals for the Session:

1. Class members will look at reasons for the breakup of marriages.

2. The group will look at biblical teaching on guilt and forgiveness applied to the marriage relationship and at Christ's teaching on divorce.

3. Each couple will have a chance to evaluate their own marriage.

Prepare for the Session:

1. Study carefully chapter 6, pp. 116-34.

2. Study the Scriptures: Proverbs 3:6; Matthew 5:31-32; 19:4-9; Mark 10:2-12; Luke 7:47; John 8:11; 17:17; Ephesians 4:32.

3. Many commentators differ on Christ's teaching on divorce and remarriage. Consult several in your preparation. This subject is a whole new course, but should be looked at briefly in connection with incompatibility in marriage. The main point at hand is how to deal redemptively with those already caught in the dilemma of divorce and to slow the rush to the divorce courts.

4. Have the divorce rate figures you have found for your particular area ready for presentation.

Presentation:

FOCUS

Have class members estimate divorce rates in your area. Give the figures you located this week. Why is the rate so high? What is happening to the marriage/divorce rate in evangelical churches? In your own church?

DISCOVER

1. Have class members read aloud the Scripture passages on divorce: Matthew 5:31-32; 19:4-9; Mark 10:2-12. Is this teaching the ideal or a command or both? What does this Scripture say to today's accepted forms of "serial monogamy"? What would you say to the person who says that he believes God wants him to get a divorce? Why must one sincerely accept Proverbs 3:6 and John 17:17 before one can know God's will in regard to divorce and remarriage?

2. Discussion Questions:

a. What is the most common reason for breakup of marriage according to Dr. Osborne, p. 119? Do you agree? Why?

b. Why do married people have affairs (pp. 116-17; 123-25; 129-31)? React to this statement: "In fifty percent of marriages, either the husband or wife commits adultery at least once" (p. 121). Is this realistic?

c. Why is the divorce of older couples who stay together for the sake of the children and then call it quits becoming more common?

d. What are alternatives for wives of alcoholics or unsaved husbands? How would you counsel a wife who has an alcoholic husband and three young children?

e. How does one treat a divorced person? John 8:11; Luke 7:47.

f. How does one deal with feelings of guilt (especially over a divorce, an infidelity, a sex sin) and experience the forgiveness of God and self? How about the hurt spouse? Ephesians 4:32.

3. Agree/Disagree Statements:

a. "Virtually any marriage can be radically improved if

both husband and wife are determined to work at it" (p. 131).

b. "There are obviously instances in which divorce is the only solution to an intolerable situation" (p. 128). Is there ever a situation where Christians *must* divorce?

c. "We make no significant change in personality except as the result of stress or suffering" (p. 133).

RESPOND

1. Have members rate their marriage on a scale of one to ten. Is it a third or fourth rate marriage?

2. Pray for troubled couples in your acquaintance and for sensitivity to help them conquer their incompatibilities.

3. Plan to include a divorced person in a social event with your family soon.

Assignment:

Read chapter 7, pp. 135-56, "Almost Any Marriage Can Be Improved."

Almost Any Marriage
Can Be Improved

Set Goals for the Session:

1. Group members will review some basic principles for improving marriage.

2. Each couple will be challenged with a goal for their marriage: seeking emotional and spiritual maturity.

3. Ephesians 4:15, "speaking the truth in love," will be the trait for special concentration this week.

Prepare for the Session:

1. Read thoroughly chapter 7, pp. 135-56. In this chapter Dr. Osborne reviews his basic assumptions for improving a marriage. This will be a good time to emphasize one or more aspects that you have had little time to discuss or ones that especially interest the group.

2. Study the following Scriptures: Luke 6:38; Genesis 3:12-13; Ephesians 4:15.

Presentation:

FOCUS

Work out the following hypothetical situation: A young woman is considering marriage to a man who everyone else says is immature. He lives for his car, drives recklessly, drinks too much, and runs with a "wild bunch." The girl, in her starry-eyed infatuation, says she can change her boyfriend. He has promised to settle down when he gets married. Include Dr. Osborne's insight that marriage intensifies neurotic tendencies (p. 135).

DISCOVER

1. Spend time to review the basic assumptions underlying the achieving of spiritual and emotional maturity (pp. 139-43). Use the board and include the following:

a. No one person can satisfy all of another's needs. Humans are basically selfish. Only when one applies the principle of Luke 6:38 will one's own needs be met.

b. One must seek to meet the needs of the other. Include in the discussion at this point:

"A woman has much more to gain from a good marriage and more to lose from a bad one" (p. 142).

"A wife has the primary responsibility for the 'climate' in the home" (p. 142).

"Don't expect too much of the persons around you, whether they be in-laws, children, or marriage partner" (p. 143).

"If the wife most often must take the initiative in improving the marriage, the husband bears an equal responsibility in responding to change in his wife's altered approach" (pp. 144-45).

2. Discuss several problem areas of concern to your group.

a. Determining spheres of influence

b. In-law and relative relationships

c. Communication

Blame and attack. For the classic biblical example, see Genesis 3:12-13.

Coded messages. Have four volunteers read pp. 151-53 assuming the roles of wife and husband sending coded messages. Have one woman read what the wife says out loud and another read what she really means, and likewise for the husband.

How does one "speak the truth in love"? (Eph. 4:15). What is meant by the statement, "To be loving is more important than to be honest, yet to be loving involves facing, at times, the fact that one must speak honestly" (p. 154). When should one keep one's opinions to himself and when should they be expressed?

Work out a role play showing a very tactless woman correcting her husband's behavior at a party and another with her "speaking the truth in love." Discuss what was different and how to go about telling someone else how you feel without destroying their self-image.

RESPOND

1. Give time for couples to discuss privately (or if facilities will not allow) to write down for discussion later, an area of their marriage that they feel needs improvement.

2. Challenge class members to try the "speaking the truth in love" approach in a definite situation this week.

Assignment:
1. Read chapter 6, pp. 157-70, "Ten Commandments for Wives".

Ten Commandments for Wives

Set Goals for the Session:

1. Group members will consider Dr. Osborne's ten commandments for wives and compare them with their own ideas.

2. Each couple will pick one area of special concentration for the next week.

3. Members will seek special strength from God for patience in the day-to-day life of marriage.

Prepare for the Session:

1. Read carefully chapter 8, pp. 157-70. List the ten commandments for wives either on a flip chart, transparency, or the board for easy reference in class.

2. Think about the implications of Ephesians 5:21 and 1 Corinthians 13:4, 7, 8.

3. Provide paper for the group activity.

Presentation:

FOCUS

Divide the group into smaller groups of three or four. Each group will write a letter of advice to their own daughter who is contemplating marriage. What are the most important things she should know? After the groups have had time to formulate their letter, have them report to the entire group.

DISCOVER

Compare the group's advice to Dr. Osborne's list of ten commandments for wives. Hand out to each class member a copy of these for easy reference or ask them to turn to pp. 157-58, if each has access to a text. Discuss these ten commandments using the following questions as springboards and amplification of the ten principles. The numbers of the questions correspond to the numbers of the commandments as listed by Dr. Osborne.

1. If no one ever receives enough love, what is his primary responsibility if he wishes to be loved? Why is Luke 6:38 so important here? How is it true that "love never fails" (1 Cor. 13:8)?

2. Why should one give up dreams of a "perfect" marriage?

3. How does one discover one's husband's needs and try to meet them?

4. What about the relationship to in-laws? Is the statement, "Never criticize your husband's relatives," too strong?

5. Develop a short skit depicting a tired but happy husband coming home from work. He is late, but his boss has praised him. The contract he has worked so hard on will bring him a promotion. The wife has spent a good part of the day preparing a special dinner which is partially ruined by the husband's lateness. Have the skit members portray a wife applying the fifth commandment.

6. What are the signs in a wife of over-possessiveness of her husband?

7. How does a couple resolve the basic incompatibility of a tired husband in need of quiet coming home from work to a wife in need of adult conversation and getting out of the house?

8. Why is criticism a futile attempt to change your husband?

9. How can parents of daughters keep them from the princess syndrome and yet give them an honest, healthy

sense of self-esteem?

10. What does Dr. Osborne mean when he states that patience with a husband does not mean loss of personal choice? When (if ever) should a woman not obey her husband?

RESPOND

1. Have each wife present consider the ten commandments for wives and choose one as the one most needing concentrated effort for next week. Each husband should choose the one he desires most in his wife. At home sometime this week, couples should discuss these. Do both sense a need in the same areas? What can be done about them?

2. Spend time in silent prayer for needed patience.

Assignment:

Read chapter 9, "Ten Commandments for Husbands," pp. 171-84 for next week.

Ten Commandments for Husbands

Set Goals for the Session:

1. Class members will look at ten principles for understanding and dealing sensitively with wives.

2. Husbands will choose one area of need in their relationships with their wives for work on in the coming week.

Prepare for the Session:

1. Read carefully the ten commandments for husbands, chapter 9, pp. 171-84. Unless each class member has access to a text, you will need to type a copy of the ten commandments for husbands so that each group member may have it for easy reference during the discussion.

2. This session is mainly a group discussion on the ten principles. Give thought to which ones you should stress and which discussion questions would apply to your own group.

3. Have paper ready for the group activity which is letter writing.

Presentation:

Focus

Have groups draft a letter of advice to a son who is

getting married. What would you as a parent feel is most important to tell him about women in general?

DISCOVER

The following questions for discussion are numbered corresponding to Osborne's ten commandments, p. 171.

1. Why must one not equate strength with quietness or gentleness with passivity? What do you think of this statement, "A woman wants to be 'taken,' and taken care of" (see p. 171). What is the difference between being in charge and being domineering?

2. What are some reasons for woman's basic insecurities? Why does a woman wish to hear "I love you" so often? How do you feel about the statement, "It is never hypocritical to do the appropriate thing" (p. 174)?

3. Why is the statement, "Let the final decision rest with the one who is best qualified," (p. 175) a simplistic answer? How does this commandment square with the exhortation for the husband to be the head of his wife and for the wife to obey her husband? How can husbands of working wives share more of the home responsibilities? Would you agree generally that a man's job is the expression of his personality and that a woman's home is an extension of hers (pp. 175-76)? Is this a cultural, taught difference or a basic personality trait of male and female? What if a woman is better talented and equipped to earn a living? What is the scriptural base for man earning and woman nesting? You might check Genesis 2:18-25 or other Scripture passages.

4. List the six things that will happen to a wife if her husband criticizes her (pp. 176-77). Many people cling to the idea of "constructive criticism." Dr. Osborne feels almost all criticism is destructive (p. 177). What are better methods of achieving results?

5. What are some ways a husband can meet his wife's need for little remembrances and tokens of affection (especially on a very tight budget)?

6. How can one reconcile the differing tastes and needs of two marriage partners? (For example, differing tastes in museums, music, sports, recreation, social life, type of

vacation.) Why is it unhealthy to ignore these differences?

7. How does simply listening to a wife reinforce her sense of security?

8. How does a man recognize the validity of a woman's mood swings? Why is "Snap out of it" poor advice? What is the fallacy in taking a wife's moods personally?

9. Why should a husband not feel threatened if his wife is continually nagging to improve their marriage?

10. How does one discover a wife's special needs? What amount of family sacrifice should be made to meet a woman's needs? Is it fair to expect a woman to put her husband through school and then later have her husband refuse to put her through, if that is her special need?

RESPOND

1. Give time for each husband to consider the ten commandments for husbands and choose one as the most needing work for next week. Each wife should choose the area in which she feels her husband should improve. Sometime at home next week, couples should discuss these. Do both sense a need in the same areas? What can be done about it?

2. Spend time in prayer for understanding of one's spouse and strength of character to seek the good of the other.

Assignment:

Read chapter 10, "Eight Types of Neurotic Husbands," pp. 185-99, for next week.

Eight Types of Neurotic Husbands

Set Goals for the Session:

1. Each class member will look at and recognize eight symptoms of neurotic behavior in men.

2. Each husband will evaluate himself in the light of these behavioral patterns.

3. Each person will thank God for his or her past experiences and not use them as an excuse or blame them for immature behavior.

Prepare for the Session:

1. Read carefully chapter 10, pp. 185-99 and familiarize yourself with the eight types of behavior mentioned.

2. Part of the session will be an inductive application of Scripture and the ten commandments for wives discussed in previous lessons. In your own preparation, list Scriptures and principles that apply to each of the eight behavioral patterns.

3. This and the next session center on some symptoms of underlying personality disorders which require professional help for remedying. It is important that the main concern of the session not be in describing in detail the neurotic symptoms but in positively dealing with them to bring improvement. Handwringing over one's past and

inadequacies brings no solution.

4. Because of the similarity of format of this and the next session, you may run the two together and spend more time on one or more of the neurotic behaviors of special interest to your group. Role plays are fun, but the crucial point is feedback. Do not neglect this discussion time afterward. Here is where insights of both negative and positive ways of dealing with each behavior jell. You may have to skip one or two of the types of behavior in order to teach thoroughly those in which your group is interested.

5. Have ready for easy reference the ten commandments for husbands and wives.

Presentation:

FOCUS

If possible, find a cartoon depicting a person blaming his predicament on not being allowed to throw his oatmeal off his highchair in babyhood or on faulty toilet training. Any cartoon of a person blaming or excusing his behavior on past experiences will work. Ask, "Is a person justified in blaming his past if he has had no parental love and affection, an underprivileged, poverty-ridden home, a domineering mother, or no chance to get ahead?" Psychologists have delved into the past experiences of persons to seek causes of neurotic behavior. How should one deal with such knowledge? (Keep this discussion short. It will be easy to preach "sermons" here, see text, p. 194.)

DISCOVER

Depending on the size of your group, divide into groups of three or four and have each group work out a role play depicting one type of neurotic behavior. After a group has had time to prepare and present their play, spend class time discussing ways of dealing with each kind of behavior. What Scripture would apply? What principles studied in weeks before would be helpful? Refer back to the ten commandments for wives and husbands (pp.

157-58, 171). It will be more beneficial to spend enough time to discuss thoroughly a few that apply than to try to cover all eight.

1. The explosive, argumentative, domineering husband, pp. 185-88
2. The compulsive husband, pp. 188-89
3. The uncommunicative husband, pp. 190-91
4. The child husband, pp. 191-92
5. The hypochondriac husband, pp. 192-93
6. The passive, silent passive, or retreating husband, pp. 193-94
7. The playboy husband, pp. 194
8. The neurotic tightwad, pp. 194-95

The section at the end of the chapter, pp. 195-99, should be studied and discussed carefully in connection with these role plays.

RESPOND

Refer back to the cartoon or discussion held at the beginning of the session. If one sees symptoms of neurotic behavior in oneself, his responsibility is not to condemn either himself or others but to take definite steps in solving his problems. Have time for male group members to evaluate themselves on a scale of one to five for each of the eight neurotic behavioral patterns. Is there one or more areas in need of solution? Spend time in prayer thanking God for the circumstances He has allowed each one to experience in the past, good and bad, and ask for grace to build upon them creatively and not use them to excuse faults and sinful habits.

Assignment:
Read chapter 11, pp. 200-214, "Eight Types of Neurotic Wives."

Eight Types of Neurotic Wives

Set Goals for the Session:
1. Each class member will be able to recognize and understand eight types of neurotic behavior in women.
2. Each wife will evaluate herself in the light of these behavioral patterns.
3. Each couple will strive to contribute to the relationship rather than insist on one spouse's being right or wrong.

Prepare for the Session:
1. Read thoroughly chapter 11, pp. 200-214, and be sure you know the eight kinds of behavior mentioned.
2. As in the last session, class members will apply Scripture and Dr. Osborne's principles to each type of behavior. Specific Scriptures mentioned in the chapter for you to study are: Exodus 20:9; Matthew 22:37-39; 1 Corinthians 13:5, 8; Ephesians 4:15, James 5:16. Place these Scripture passages on an overhead or on the board before class for easy reference during the discussion.
3. Evaluate for yourself the most effective discussion from last session's role plays. Change the format so that you take advantage of this evaluation for the most effective use of class time.

Presentation:

FOCUS

Explain that during this session members will look at neurotic behavior of wives in much the same way as the last session dealt with men. You will probably need little time for introduction of the role play method used as it will be familiar to the group.

DISCOVER

Divide the members into small groups to create short role plays that picture in concrete situations the eight types of neurotic behavior in wives. As in the last session, spend time in discussion after each presentation, listing ways of dealing with such behavior, using Scripture and the ten commandments for wives and husbands.

1. The overly dominant wife, pp. 200-201
2. The narcissistic woman, pp. 201-3, Matthew 22:37-39
3. The adult-infantile wife, pp. 204-6, James 5:16
4. The masculine-protest wife, pp. 206-7
5. The martyr wife, pp. 207-8
6. The passive-aggressive wife, pp. 208-10, Ephesians 4:15
7. The jealous-possessive wife, pp. 210-12
8. The depressed wife, pp. 212-13, Exodus 20:9

How does the statement, "the relationship is more important than whether one person is right or to blame" work out in one of the above concrete situations?

RESPOND

1. Dr. Osborne recommends professional help for several of these neurotic behavior patterns. What if one cannot afford or has no access to such help? In what way can one say that God can solve one's emotional illnesses? Must a Christian be ashamed to admit a need for psychiatric help?

2. A Kansas church makes possible a periodic "mother's day out" by providing free supervised child care so that mother can go shopping or just be alone.

Could your church take over such a project for mothers who cannot afford the babysitting fees?

3. Have the women evaluate themselves on a scale of one to five on each of the eight behaviors studied. Again, the course of action after recognition of need is more important than blame or excuse.

4. Pray for sensitivity to the needs of others and for creative ways to help each other be all that God meant us to be.

Assignment:

Read chapter 12, pp. 215-35, "Incompatibility and Paradoxes in Marriage."

Incompatibility and Paradoxes in Marriage

Set Goals for the Session:

1. Group members will analyze ways of coping with incompatibilities in marriage.

2. Couples will challenge themselves to work on keeping their marriages vital and alive by first, taking inventory of the progress in their own relationship, and second, planning how to improve on it.

Prepare for the Session:

1. Study chapter 12, pp. 215-35. This deals with seemingly dead marriages and methods to revive them.

2. Study the Scriptures: Philippians 3:12-16; 1 John 3:18 and others that stress love as an action.

3. Depending on your class situation, you may decide to spend more time on one or another aspect of this chapter; for instance, sexual difficulties and education, premarital counseling of prospective marrieds. In any case, the "Jeremiah" chart is a most useful tool for couples to take stock of their relationship, so allow plenty of time for completion of this exercise. Furnish clean paper.

Presentation:

Focus

Read or dramatize the incident beginning on the first

full paragraph, p. 221, "There is on record . . .," the story of the woman who wished to make life as miserable as possible for her husband. Explain that in this session, the class will discuss ways to keep good marriages alive and how to revive dead relationships.

DISCOVER

1. Be careful whom you marry. "An ounce of prevention. . . ."

a. How can one determine before marriage who is a poor marriage risk? How important are differences in family background, relatives, money, personality problems, incompatible needs?

b. How would you counsel a Christian girl who feels she loves a non-Christian man?

c. What kind of premarital education would be practical and helpful?

2. For most of us, the choice of mate has been made. Using the principles Dr. Osborne outlines in this chapter, how would you advise a couple who say, "We no longer feel anything for each other. Our love is dead." List class contributions on the board or divide into groups to consider this question.

a. In connection with this discussion, have someone read 1 John 3:18, stressing that love is action, not only emotion. How does this apply to a dead marriage?

b. How is the statement that it is "easier to act your way into new thinking than to think your way into new cting" (p. 222) true? How does this apply to a marriage?

it hypocritical to act loving when you do not feel loving?

Mention the power of praise and simple compli-
's.

Communication is crucial.

enderness is a deep need.

Discussion Questions:

a. One wife feels that in marriage you "give up your freedom and take the consequences." In the Christian view of marriage, how would you reply?

b. Discuss Dr. Osborne's theories on why women live longer (pp. 220-21). How can a wife unwittingly kill her husband prematurely? What can she do to help him face increased responsibility?

c. Dr. Osborne estimates that less than one parent in ten is "capable of imparting the emotional, physical, and spiritual aspects of sex to children" (p. 232). How can the church help (or should it)? What resources are available to parents? (If this is of special interest to your group, check out the publications of Concordia, Family Concern.) Have the class discuss the state's taking over the sexual education of children in the public schools.

d. How can a person deal with his unrealistic needs (see p. 223) and those of one's spouse?

e. How do you feel about William Glasser's theory that all emotional illness stems from the failure to feel loved? (pp. 222-23)

f. "We have a vested interest in not knowing ourselves at a deep level" (p. 226). Why? How does this complicate the marriage relationship?

4. Discuss the steps of problem solving:

a. Cease-fire

b. Armistice

c. Negotiating peaceful settlement

Why is each step necessary?

RESPOND

Allow at least 15 minutes for class members to make a "Jeremiah" chart of their marriage, recording the ups and downs of their own relationship. Pass out clean paper for every person. Beginning at the left side of the paper, each person should divide the paper into the number of years they have been married. A horizontal line across the middle of the sheet is the baseline, the "normal," neither extra good nor bad, above the line, above average, below the line, difficult times. Chart the "ups" and "downs" of your own marriage relationship in terms of this baseline. To help jog memories, have each person list highlights of their marriage—birth of children, special events— alongside the year divisions. After everyone has had time to complete his chart, allow couples time to discuss and compare their charts with each other. Do both perceive their marriage in the same way? Afterwards, allow time for general discussion. What caused relationships to deteriorate, to improve? What was the effect of moves, losses of job or family member, new additions to the family?

In closing, ask someone to read Philippians 3:12-16 as a challenge to married couples. Encourage couples to spend time this week to consider what areas of their relationship could be improved.

Assignment:

For next week, read chapter 13, pp. 236-58. Also, encourage couples to read 1 Corinthians 13 every day and be ready to share what this has meant to them next week.

Love

Set Goals for the Session:
1. Group members will consider the nuances of the word "love" and the difference Christian love makes in a marriage.
2. Couples will review their progress in light of their new knowledge and practice in improving their marriages in the last thirteen sessions.
3. The class will be challenged to build on progress made.

Prepare for the Session:
1. Group members will give their reactions to reading 1 Corinthians 13 every day during the last week. Be sure that you as the teacher have also done this.
2. Read chapter 13, pp. 236-58.
3. Prepare the poster or board drawing of examples of the many meanings of "love." Use brightly colored pens to make an eyecatching display.
4. List the 7 love responses (pp. 254-58) on the board or overhead before class. Make either a flip chart or transparency of the three unrealistic elemental needs and on the other side, the mature response (see pp. 237-38.)
5. Provide paper for the group study of 1 Corinthians 13.

Presentation:

Focus

On the board or with brightly colored pens on a poster in graffitti style, list the following and others if you can think of them:

America: Love it or leave it.

I just love pecan pie!

Torrid love

Do you promise to love, honor, and cherish?

Come on, prove your love, just this once . . .

And Jonathan loved David.

So, faith, hope, and love abide, these three; but the greatest of these is love.

Discover

1. After getting initial class reaction to the varied meanings of "love," mention the three kinds of love—romantic love, married love, and Christian love. Read or have someone in the group read T. S. Eliot's description of a dull marriage, p. 251, as an example of what can happen to married love.

2. Discuss the principles Dr. Osborne gives to keep married love from turning sour.

a. Persons who appear incapable of loving deeply: the self-satisfied, those who dislike themselves, those totally dedicated to their work or some other goal (pp. 244-46).

b. The three basic elemental needs and the mature responses to them. Use the flip chart or transparency that you have prepared here. (See pp. 237-38.)

c. Areas of sensitivity in the male and the female (pp. 248-49) which mates must respect.

d. The thesis that marriage compounds personal problems and that few true *marital* problems exist (p. 252).

e. How is it true that marriage usually means more to a woman than to a man? (p. 253)

f. List the seven love responses on the board or overhead (pp. 254-58).